Teach Yourself VISUALLY™ Photoshop® CS

by Mike Wooldridge

Visual™

From

maranGraphics®

&

Wiley Publishing, Inc.

Teach Yourself VISUALLY™ Photoshop® CS

Published by
Wiley Publishing, Inc.
111 River Street
Hoboken, NJ 07030

Published simultaneously in Canada
Copyright © 2004 by Wiley Publishing, Inc., Indianapolis, Indiana
Certain designs and illustrations Copyright © 1992-2004 maranGraphics, Inc., used with maranGraphics' permission.

maranGraphics, Inc.
5755 Coopers Avenue
Mississauga, Ontario, Canada
L4Z 1R9

Library of Congress Control Number: 2003114617

ISBN: 0-7645-4181-1

Manufactured in the United States of America

10 9 8 7 6 5 4 3 2

Trademark Acknowledgments

Wiley, the Wiley Publishing logo, Visual, the Visual logo, Teach Yourself VISUALLY, Read Less - Learn More and related trade dress are trademarks or registered trademarks of John Wiley & Sons, Inc. and/or its affiliates. The maranGraphics logo is a trademark or registered trademark of maranGraphics, Inc. Photoshop is a registered trademark of Adobe Systems, Inc. All other trademarks are the property of their respective owners. Wiley Publishing, Inc. and maranGraphics, Inc. are not associated with any product or vendor mentioned in this book.

Important Numbers

For U.S. corporate orders, please call maranGraphics at 800-469-6616 or fax 905-890-9434.

For general information on our other products and services or to obtain technical support please contact our Customer Care Department within the U.S. at 800-762-2974, outside the U.S. at 317-572-3993 or fax 317-572-4002.

Permissions

maranGraphics:
Certain text and illustrations by maranGraphics, Inc., used with maranGraphics' permission.

Wiley Publishing, Inc.

U.S. Corporate Sales	U.S. Trade Sales
Contact maranGraphics at (800) 469-6616 or Fax (905) 890-9434.	Contact Wiley at (800) 762-2974 or fax (317) 572-4002.

Some comments from our readers...

"I have to praise you and your company on the fine products you turn out. I have twelve of the *Teach Yourself VISUALLY* and *Simplified* books in my house. They were instrumental in helping me pass a difficult computer course. Thank you for creating books that are easy to follow."

— *Gordon Justin (Brielle, NJ)*

"I commend your efforts and your success. I teach in an outreach program for the Dr. Eugene Clark Library in Lockhart, TX. Your *Teach Yourself VISUALLY* books are incredible, and I use them in my computer classes. All my students love them!"

— *Michele Schalin (Lockhart, TX)*

"Like a lot of other people, I understand things best when I see them visually. Your books really make learning easy and life more fun."

— *John T. Frey (Cadillac, MI)*

"I have quite a few of your Visual books and have been very pleased with all of them. I love the way the lessons are presented!"

— *Mary Jane Newman (Yorba Linda, CA)*

"I write to extend my thanks and appreciation for your books. They are clear, easy to follow, and straight to the point. Keep up the good work!"

— *Seward Kollie (Dakar, Senegal)*

"I am an avid fan of your Visual books. If I need to learn anything, I just buy one of your books and learn the topic in no time. Wonders! I have even trained my friends to give me Visual books as gifts."

— *Illona Bergstrom (Aventura, FL)*

"Thank you for making it so clear. I appreciate it. I will buy many more Visual books."

— *J.P. Sangdong (North York, Ontario, Canada)*

"I was introduced to maranGraphics about four years ago and YOU ARE THE GREATEST THING THAT EVER HAPPENED TO INTRODUCTORY COMPUTER BOOKS!"

— *Glenn Nettleton (Huntsville, AL)*

"Compliments to the chef!! Your books are extraordinary! Or, simply put, extra-ordinary, meaning way above the rest! THANK YOU THANK YOU THANK YOU! for creating these."

— *Christine J. Manfrin (Castle Rock, CO)*

"I just purchased my third Visual book (my first two are dog-eared now!) and, once again, your product has surpassed my expectations. The expertise, thought, and effort that go into each book are obvious, and I sincerely appreciate your efforts. Keep up the wonderful work!"

— *Tracey Moore (Memphis, TN)*

"Thank you, thank you, thank you...for making it so easy for me to break into this high-tech world. I now own four of your books. I recommend them to anyone who is a beginner like myself. Now...if you could just do one for programming VCR's, it would make my day!"

— *Gay O'Donnell (Calgary, Alberta, Canada)*

"You're marvelous! I am greatly in your debt."

— *Patrick Baird (Lacey, WA)*

maranGraphics is a family-run business located near Toronto, Canada.

At **maranGraphics**, we believe in producing great computer books — one book at a time.

maranGraphics has been producing high-technology products for over 25 years, which enables us to offer the computer book community a unique communication process.

Our computer books use an integrated communication process, which is very different from the approach used in other computer books. Each spread is, in essence, a flow chart — the text and screen shots are totally incorporated into the layout of the spread.

Introductory text and helpful tips complete the learning experience.

maranGraphics' approach encourages the left and right sides of the brain to work together — resulting in faster orientation and greater memory retention.

Above all, we are very proud of the handcrafted nature of our books. Our carefully-chosen writers are experts in their fields, and spend countless hours researching and organizing the content for each topic. Our artists rebuild every screen shot to provide the best

clarity possible, making our screen shots the most precise and easiest to read in the industry. We strive for perfection, and believe that the time spent handcrafting each element results in the best computer books money can buy.

Thank you for purchasing this book. We hope you enjoy it!

Sincerely,

Robert Maran
President
maranGraphics
Rob@maran.com
www.maran.com

ABOUT THE AUTHOR

Mike Wooldridge is a Web developer in the San Francisco Bay area. He has authored several other VISUAL books, including *Teach Yourself VISUALLY Photoshop Elements 2, Photoshop Elements 2: Top 100 Simplified Tips & Tricks*, and *Master VISUALLY Dreamweaver MX and Flash MX*.

AUTHOR'S ACKNOWLEDGMENTS

Many thanks to project editor Sarah Hellert for her top-notch editing and guidance. Also, thanks to technical editor Dennis R. Cohen and acquisitions editor Jody Lefevere.

To my wife Linda. I couldn't have
done it without you.

TABLE OF CONTENTS

Chapter 1

GETTING STARTED

Work with Images 4
Understanding Photoshop 6
Start Photoshop on a PC 8
Start Photoshop on a Mac 9
The Photoshop Workspace 10
Find Images for Your Projects 11
Set Preferences 12
Get Help 14
Open an Image 16
Browse for an Image 18
Create a New Image 20
Exit Photoshop 21

Chapter 2

UNDERSTANDING PHOTOSHOP BASICS

Magnify with the Zoom Tool 24
Adjust Views 26
Change Screen Modes 28
View Rulers and Guides 30
View a Grid 32
Using Shortcuts to Select Tools 33
Undo Commands 34
Revert an Image 35

Chapter 3

CHANGING THE SIZE OF AN IMAGE

Change the On-Screen Size of an Image 38
Change the Print Size of an Image 40
Change the Resolution of an Image 42
Crop an Image 44
Crop and Straighten Photos 46
Trim an Image 47
Change the Canvas Size of an Image 48

Chapter 4

MAKING SELECTIONS

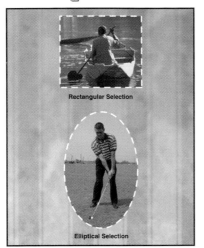

Rectangular Selection

Elliptical Selection

Select with the Marquee Tools 52

Select with the Lasso Tool 54

Select with the Magnetic Lasso Tool 56

Select with the Magic Wand Tool 58

Select with the Color Range Command 60

Select All the Pixels in an Image 62

Move a Selection Border 63

Add to or Subtract from Your Selection 64

Expand or Contract Selections 66

Invert a Selection .68

Grow a Selection .69

Create Slices 70

Chapter 5

MANIPULATING SELECTIONS

Move a Selection .74

Copy and Paste a Selection 76

Delete a Selection .78

Rotate a Selection .79

Scale a Selection .80

Skew or Distort a Selection 82

Feather the Border of a Selection 84

Extract an Object .86

Chapter 6

SPECIFYING COLOR MODES

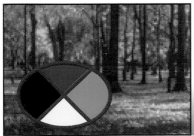

Work in RGB Mode 90

Convert a Color Image to Grayscale 92

Create a Duotone .94

Create a Bitmap Image 96

TABLE OF CONTENTS

Chapter 7

PAINTING AND DRAWING WITH COLOR

Select the Foreground and Background Colors . . .100

Select a Web-Safe Color 102

Select a Color with the Eyedropper Tool 103

Select a Color with the Swatches Palette 104

Add a Color to the Swatches Palette 105

Using the Paintbrush Tool 106

Change Brush Styles 108

Create a Custom Brush 110

Using the Pencil Tool 112

Apply a Gradient 114

Using the Paint Bucket Tool 116

Fill a Selection 118

Stroke a Selection .120

Using the Clone Stamp 122

Using the Pattern Stamp 124

Using the Healing Brush 126

Using the Patch Tool 128

Using the History Brush 130

Using the Eraser 132

Replace a Color 134

Chapter 8

ADJUSTING COLORS

Change Brightness and Contrast 138

Using the Dodge and Burn Tools 140

Using the Blur and Sharpen Tools 142

Adjust Levels 144

Adjust Hue and Saturation 146

Using the Sponge Tool 148

Adjust Color Balance 150

Using the Variations Command 152

Match Colors Between Images 154

Correct Shadows and Highlights 156

Chapter 9

WORKING WITH LAYERS

What Are Layers? 160

Create and Add to a Layer 162

Hide a Layer 164

Move a Layer 165

Duplicate a Layer 166

Delete a Layer 167

Reorder Layers 168

Change the Opacity of a Layer 170

Merge and Flatten Layers 172

Rename a Layer 174

Transform a Layer 175

Create a Solid Fill Layer 176

Create a Gradient Fill Layer 178

Create a Pattern Fill Layer 180

Create an Adjustment Layer 182

Edit an Adjustment Layer 184

Link Layers 186

Blend Layers 188

Chapter 10

APPLYING LAYER EFFECTS

Apply a Drop Shadow 192

Apply an Outer Glow 194

Apply Beveling and Embossing 196

Apply Multiple Effects to a Layer 198

Edit a Layer Effect 200

Apply a Style 202

TABLE OF CONTENTS

Chapter 11

APPLYING FILTERS

Turn an Image Into a Painting 206

Blur an Image .208

Sharpen an Image 210

Distort an Image 212

Add Noise to an Image 214

Turn an Image Into Shapes 216

Turn an Image Into a Charcoal Sketch 218

Apply Glowing Edges to an Image 220

Add Texture to an Image 222

Offset an Image 224

Using the Liquify Filter 226

Apply Multiple Filters 228

Generate a Pattern 230

Chapter 12

DRAWING SHAPES

Draw a Shape 234

Draw a Custom Shape 236

Draw a Straight Line 238

Draw a Shape with the Pen 240

Edit a Shape 242

Chapter 13

ADDING AND MANIPULATING TYPE

Add Type to an Image 246

Add Type in a Bounding Box 248

Change the Formatting of Type 250

Change the Color of Type 252

Apply a Filter to Type 254

Apply an Effect to Type 256

Warp Type 258

Chapter 14

AUTOMATING YOUR WORK

Record an Action .262

Play an Action 264

Batch Process by Using an Action 266

Create a Contact Sheet 268

Create a Picture Package 270

Create a Web Photo Gallery 272

Create a Panoramic Image 274

Chapter 15

SAVING IMAGES

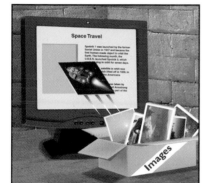

Save in the Photoshop Format 280

Save an Image for Use in Another Application . . .282

Save a JPEG for the Web 284

Save a GIF for the Web 286

Save a GIF with Transparency 288

Save a GIF with Web-Safe Colors 290

Compare File Sizes 292

Add Descriptive and Copyright Information 294

Save a Sliced Image 296

Chapter 16

PRINTING IMAGES

Print on a PC 300

Print on a Macintosh 302

Preview a Printout .304

HOW TO USE THIS BOOK

Teach Yourself VISUALLY Photoshop CS contains straightforward sections, which you can use to learn the basics of shooting, editing, and storing your digital video. This book is designed to help a reader receive quick access to any area of question. You can simply look up a subject within the Table of Contents or Index and go immediately to the section of concern. A *section* is a set of self-contained units that walks you through a computer operation step-by-step. That is, with rare exception, all the information you need regarding an area of interest is contained within a section.

The Organization Of Each Chapter

Teach Yourself VISUALLY Photoshop CS has 16 chapters. Chapter 1 introduces you to the program, while Chapter 2 shows you how to set up the program to fit your needs. Chapter 3 teaches you how to change the size of your images. Chapters 4 and 5 show you how to select specific areas of your images and also manipulate the selected areas. Chapter 6 teaches you how to specify and use different color modes. Chapter 7 shows you how to paint and draw with different tools. Chapter 8 explains how to adjust and optimize colors in your images. Chapter 9 introduces you to layers and shows you how to use them, while Chapter 10 teaches you how to apply effects to those layers. Chapter 11 explains how to add interesting effects to your images with filters. Chapter 12 shows you how to draw and edit shapes in your images. Chapter 13 explains how to add type to your images and also edit that type. Chapter 14 explains how to automate your image-editing work. Chapter 15 shows you how to save your images for print and for the Web. Chapter 16 teaches you how to print out your finished work in Photoshop.

Who This Book is For

This book is highly recommended for the visual learner who wants to learn the basics of Photoshop CS, and who may or may not have prior experience with a computer.

What You Need to Use This Book

To perform the tasks in this book, you need a computer installed with one of the following:

- Photoshop® CS for Windows®
- Photoshop® CS for Macintosh®

Windows Requirements

- Intel® Pentium® class III or 4 processor
- Microsoft® Windows® 2000 with Service Pack 3, or Windows® XP
- 192MB of RAM (256MB recommended)
- 280MB of available hard disk space
- Color monitor with 16-bit or greater video card
- 1024x768 or greater monitor resolution
- CD-ROM drive

Mac Requirements

- Mac OS® 10.2.4 or later
- PowerPCR processor (G3, G4, or G5)
- 192MB of RAM (256MB recommended)
- 320MB of available hard disk space
- Color monitor with 16-bit or greater video card
- 1024x768 or greater monitor resolution
- CD-ROM drive

Conventions When Using the Mouse

This book uses the following conventions to describe the actions you perform when using the mouse:

Click

Press and release the left mouse button. You use a click to select an item on the screen.

Double-click

Quickly press and release the left mouse button twice. You double-click to open a document or start a program.

Right-click (Control +click)

Press and release the right mouse button (Control +click). A shortcut menu, a list of commands specifically related to the selected item, appears.

Click and Drag, and Release the Mouse

Position the mouse pointer over an item on the screen and then press and hold down the left mouse button. Still holding down the button, move the mouse to where you want to place the item and then release the button. Click and dragging makes it easy to move an item to a new location.

The Conventions in This Book

A number of typographic and layout styles have been used throughout *Teach Yourself VISUALLY Photoshop CS* to distinguish different types of information.

Bold

Indicates text, or text buttons, that you must click in a menu or dialog box to complete a task.

Italics

Indicates a new term being introduced.

Numbered Steps

Indicate that you must perform these steps in order to successful perform the task.

Bulleted Steps

Give you alternative methods, explain various options, or present what a program will do in response to the numbered steps.

Notes

Give you additional information to help you complete a task. The purpose of a note, which appears in italics, is three-fold: It can explain special conditions that may occur during the course of the task, warn you of potentially dangerous situations, or refer you to tasks in the same, or a different chapter. References to tasks within the chapter are indicated by the phrase "*See the section...*" followed by the name of the section. References to other chapters are indicated by "*See Chapter...*" followed by the chapter number.

Icons

Icons in the steps indicate a button that you must click to perform a section.

Operating System Differences

Although most of the examples in this book show you how to perform steps using a PC, you can perform the same steps on a Mac.

If a keyboard key or menu option differs between PC and Mac, this book lists the PC convention first, followed by the Mac convention in parentheses. For example:

1 Click **Select**.

2 Click **All**.

■ You can also press Ctrl + A (⌘+ A) to select all the pixels in an image.

CHAPTER 1

Getting Started

Are you interested in creating, modifying, combining, and optimizing digital images on your computer? This chapter introduces you to Adobe Photoshop, a popular software application for working with digital images.

Work with Images 4

Understanding Photoshop 6

Start Photoshop on a PC 8

Start Photoshop on a Mac...................9

The Photoshop Workspace 10

Find Images for Your Projects..............11

Set Preferences...............................12

Get Help 14

Open an Image 16

Browse for an Image 18

Create a New Image 20

Exit Photoshop 21

WORK WITH IMAGES

Photoshop lets you create, modify, combine, and optimize digital images. You can then save the images to print out or use online.

Manipulate Photos

As its name suggests, Photoshop excels at editing digital photographs. You can use the program to make subtle changes, such as to adjust the color in a digital photo or scanned print, or you can use its elaborate filters to make your snapshots look like abstract art. See Chapter 8 for more about adjusting color and Chapter 11 for more about filters.

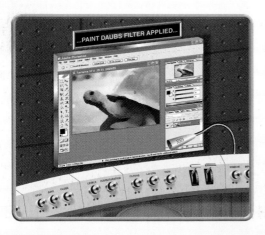

Paint Pictures

Photoshop's painting features make it a formidable illustration tool as well as a photo editor. You can apply colors or patterns to your images with a variety of brush styles. See Chapter 7 for more about applying color. In addition, you can use the program's typographic tools to integrate stylized letters and words into your images. See Chapter 13 for more about type.

Create a Digital Collage

You can combine different image elements in Photoshop. Your compositions can include photos, scanned art, text, and anything else you can save on your computer as a digital image. By placing elements in Photoshop onto separate layers, you can move, transform, and customize them independently of one another. See Chapter 9 for more about layers.

Access and Organize Your Photos

Photoshop's File Browser interface offers an easy-to-use tool to access and preview images that are stored on your computer. See the section "Browse for an Image" in this chapter. Photoshop also offers useful ways to keep your images organized after you have edited them. You can archive your images on contact sheets or display them in a Web photo gallery. See Chapter 14 for details.

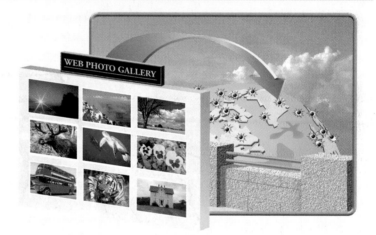

Put Your Images to Work

After you edit your work, you can utilize your images in a variety of ways. Photoshop lets you print your images, save them in a format suitable for placement on a Web page, or prepare them for use in a page-layout program. See Chapter 16 for more about printing. See Chapter 15 for more about saving images for the Web.

UNDERSTANDING PHOTOSHOP

Photoshop's tools let you move, color, stylize, and add text to your images. You can optimize photographs, or turn them into interesting works of art.

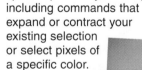

Understanding Pixels

Digital images in Photoshop consist of tiny, solid-color squares called pixels. Photoshop works its magic by rearranging and recoloring these squares. If you zoom in close, you can see the pixels that make up your image. For more about the Zoom tool, see Chapter 2.

Choose Your Pixels

To edit specific pixels in your image, you first must select them by using one of Photoshop's selection tools. See Chapter 4 for more about the selection tools. Photoshop also has a number of commands that help you select specific parts of your image, including commands that expand or contract your existing selection or select pixels of a specific color.

Paint

After selecting your pixels, you can apply color to them by using Photoshop's paintbrush, airbrush, and pencil tools. You can also fill your selections with solid or semitransparent colors, patterns, or pixels copied from another part of your image. Painting is covered in Chapter 7.

Adjust Color

You can brighten, darken, and change the hue of colors in parts of your image with Photoshop's Dodge, Burn, and similar tools. Other commands display interactive dialog boxes that let you make wholesale color adjustments, letting you precisely correct overly dark or light digital photographs. See Chapter 8 for details.

Apply Effects and Filters

Photoshop's effects let you easily add drop shadows, frame borders, and other styles to your images. You can also perform complex color manipulations or distortions by using filters. Filters can make your image look like an impressionist painting, apply sharpening or blurring, or distort your image in various ways. Chapters 10 and 11 cover effects and filters.

Add Type

Photoshop's type tools enable you to easily apply titles and labels to your images. You can combine these tools with the program's special effects commands to create warped, 3D, or wildly colored type. You can find out more about type in Chapter 12.

You can start
Photoshop on a PC
and begin creating
and editing digital
images.

START PHOTOSHOP ON A PC

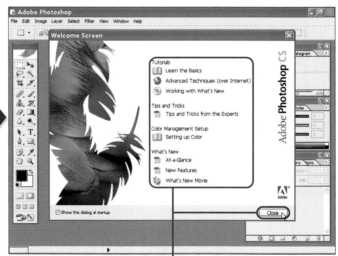

1 Click **Start**.

2 Click **All Programs**.

3 Click **Adobe Photoshop CS**.

Note: Your path to the Photoshop program may be different, depending on how you installed your software.

■ Photoshop starts.

■ A Welcome Screen window appears.

■ You can click an icon to learn more about Photoshop.

4 Click **Close** to close the window and begin working with Photoshop.

You can start Photoshop
on a Macintosh and
begin creating and
editing digital images.

START PHOTOSHOP ON A MAC

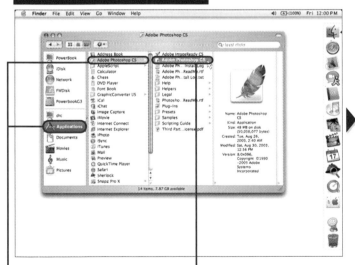

1 Click **Applications**.

2 Click the Adobe
Photoshop CS folder ( ).

3 Double-click the Adobe
Photoshop CS icon ( ).

*Note: The exact location of the
Adobe Photoshop icon may be
different, depending on how you
installed your software.*

■ Photoshop starts.

■ A Welcome Screen
window opens.

■ You can click an icon to
learn more about
Photoshop.

4 Click **Close** to close the
window and begin working
with Photoshop.

THE PHOTOSHOP WORKSPACE

You can use a combination of tools, menu commands, and palette-based features to open and edit your digital images in Photoshop.

Menu Bar
Displays the menus that contain most of Photoshop's commands.

Options Bar
Displays controls that let you customize the selected tool in the toolbox.

Palettes
Are small, free-floating windows that give you access to common commands and resources.

Image Window
Contains each image you open in Photoshop.

Toolbox
Displays a variety of icons, each one representing an image-editing tool. You click and drag inside your image to apply most of the tools.

Status Bar
Displays information about the size of the current image and the selected tool. On a Mac, the Status Bar appears at the bottom of each document window.

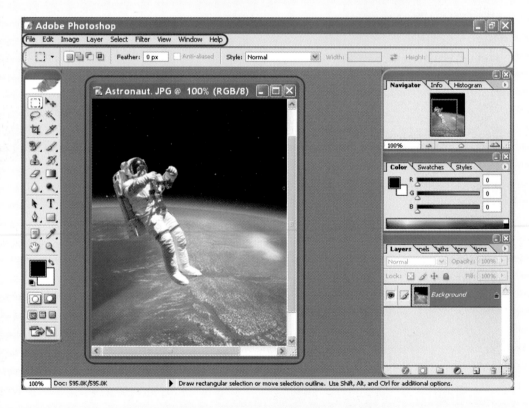

FIND IMAGES FOR YOUR PROJECTS

You can get raw material for using Photoshop from a variety of sources.

Start from Scratch

You can create your Photoshop image from scratch by opening a blank canvas in the image window. Then you can apply color and patterns with Photoshop's painting tools or cut and paste parts of other images to create a composite. See the section "Create a New Image" in this chapter for more about opening a blank canvas.

Digital Photos

Digital cameras are a great way to get digital images onto your computer. Most digital cameras save their images in JPEG or TIFF format, both of which you can open and edit in Photoshop. The program's color adjustment tools are great for correcting color and exposure flaws in digital camera images.

Scanned Photos and Art

A scanner gives you an inexpensive way to convert existing paper-based content into digital form. You can scan photos and art into your computer, retouch and stylize them in Photoshop, and then output them to a color printer.

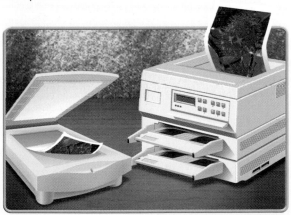

Clip Art

If you want a wide variety of image content to work with, consider buying a clip art collection. Such collections usually include illustrations, photos, and decorative icons that you can use in imaging projects. Most software stores sell clip art; you can also buy downloadable clip art online.

SET PREFERENCES

Photoshop's Preferences dialog boxes let you change default settings and customize how the program looks.

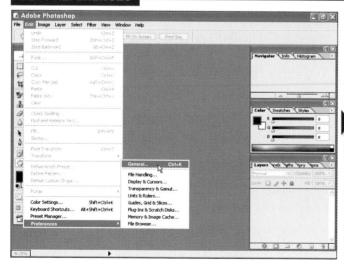

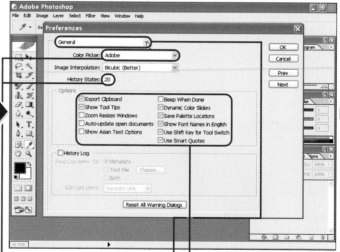

■ 1 Access the Preferences menu.

■ In Windows, click **Edit**, **Preferences**, and then **General**.

■ In Mac OS X, click **Photoshop**, **Preferences**, and then **General**.

■ The Preferences dialog box appears and displays General options.

■ 2 Click here to determine which dialog box appears when you select a color.

■ 3 Type the number of states to store in the History palette.

Note: See Chapter 2 for more about the History palette.

■ 4 Click the interface options you want to use (☐ changes to ☑).

■ 5 Click ☑ (🔹) and select **Display & Cursors**.

12

What type of measurement units should I use in Photoshop?

Typically, you should use the units most applicable to the type of output you intend to use. Pixel units are useful for Web imaging because monitor dimensions are measured in pixels. Inches, centimeters, or picas are useful for print because those are standards for working on paper.

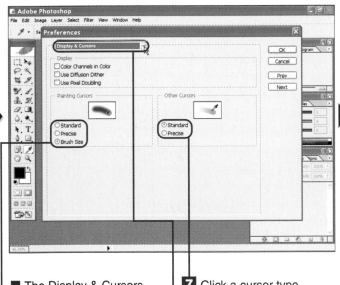

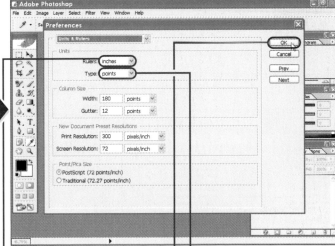

■ The Display & Cursors Preferences options appear.

6 Click a cursor type to use for the painting tools — the paintbrush, eraser, and others (○ changes to ◉).

7 Click a cursor type to use for the other tools (○ changes to ◉).

8 Click ▾ (▾) and select **Units & Rulers**.

■ The Units & Rulers Preferences options appear.

9 Click here to select the units for the window rulers. These units become the default units selected when you resize an image.

10 Click here to select the default units for type.

11 Click **OK**.

■ Photoshop sets preferences to your specifications.

GET HELP

Photoshop comes with plenty of electronic documentation that you can access in case you ever need help.

GET HELP

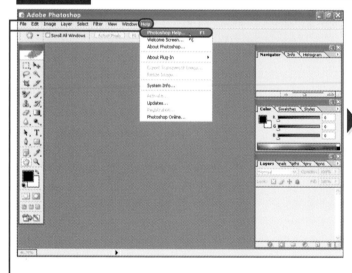

1 Click **Help**.

2 Click **Photoshop Help**.

■ You can also press F1 (⌘ + /) to access Photoshop Help.

■ Photoshop opens your default Web browser and displays the Help interface.

3 Click **Search** to search for information about a particular topic.

**How can I find details about my
Photoshop software?**

Click **Help** and then **System Info**.
A window opens displaying
information about your Photoshop
software, including where it is
installed and what plug-ins
you have available. It also
lists basic information about
your computer's operating
system and memory.

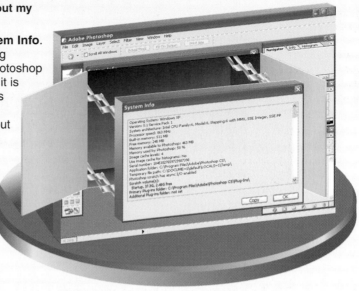

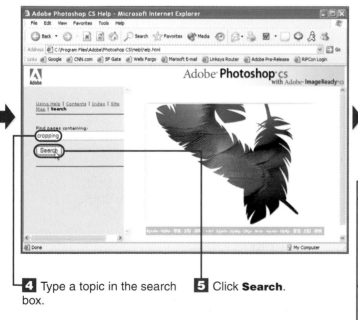

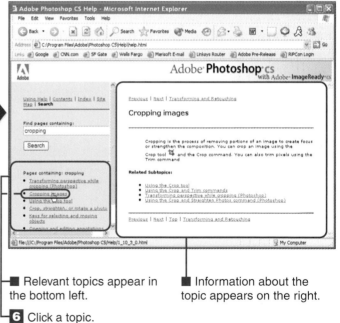

4 Type a topic in the search
box.

5 Click **Search**.

■ Relevant topics appear in
the bottom left.

6 Click a topic.

■ Information about the
topic appears on the right.

OPEN AN IMAGE

You can open an existing image file in Photoshop to modify it, or use it in a project.

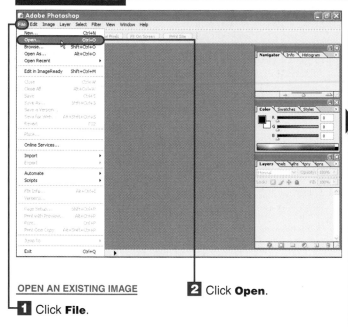

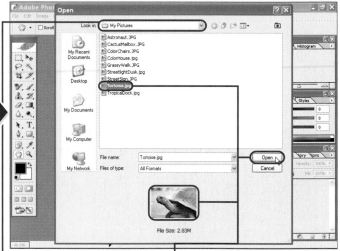

OPEN AN EXISTING IMAGE

1 Click **File**.

2 Click **Open**.

■ The Open dialog box appears.

3 Click here to browse to the folder that contains the image you want to open.

4 Click the image you want to open.

■ A preview of the image appears.

5 Click Open.

TEACH YOURSELF

How do I open an existing image in Mac OS X?

Mac OS X Jaguar (10.2) and Panther (10.3) have their own Open dialog boxes, extended with the additional Photoshop-specific controls. In either case, you start by navigating to the image you want to open. Then, you can double-click the image's name or icon to open the image, or you can click the image's name or icon and then click **Open** or press **Return**.

Mac OS X Jaguar

You can navigate to recently used and favorite folders using the From ⊡, or to any folder by using the File Browser in the center of the dialog box.

Mac OS X Panther

You can navigate to frequently used and favorite folders using the Sidebar, or navigate to any folder using the File Browser to the right of the Sidebar.

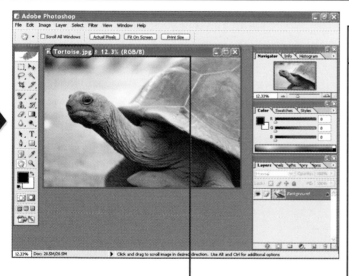

■ Photoshop opens the image in a new window.

■ The filename appears in the title bar.

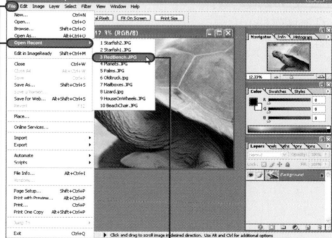

OPEN RECENTLY ACCESSED IMAGES

1 Click **File**.

2 Click **Open Recent**.

■ A list of recently opened files appears.

3 Click the image's filename.

■ Photoshop opens the image in a new window.

BROWSE FOR AN IMAGE

You can open an existing image file by using Photoshop's File Browser. Browsing offers a user-friendly way to find and open your images.

BROWSE FOR AN IMAGE

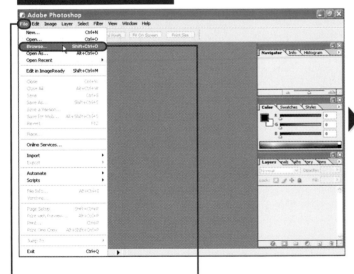

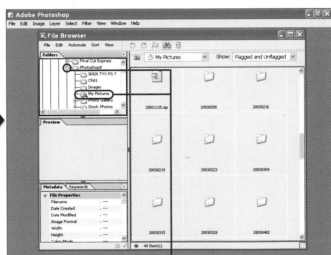

1 Click **File**.

2 Click **Browse**.

■ The File Browser opens.

3 Press **Tab** to hide the toolbox and palettes.

4 Click ⊞ (▶) to open folders on your computer (in Windows, ⊞ changes to ⊟; on a Mac, ▶ changes to ▼).

5 Click a folder on your computer to browse.

How do I change settings in the File Browser dialog box?

The Preferences settings in Photoshop enable you to customize settings in the File Browser. Click **Edit (Photoshop)**, **Preferences**, and then **File Browser**. You can specify how the browser deals with large image files, how many recently used folders it remembers, and other settings.

Where should I store my images on my computer?

You may find it helpful to keep all of your images in a single folder somewhere central on your computer, such as on your desktop or inside your My Pictures folder (or your Documents or Pictures folder on a Macintosh). You may want to create subfolders named with dates or subjects to further organize the images. Keeping images in one place makes it easy to access them from Photoshop.

■ The folders and files inside the location appear.

6 Click an image.

■ A preview and information about the image appear.

7 Double-click the image file to open it.

■ The image opens.

■ You can also click and drag an image file from the File Browser to the work area to open it.

■ You can press **Tab** to show the toolbox and palettes.

CREATE A NEW IMAGE

You can start a
Photoshop project by
creating a blank image.

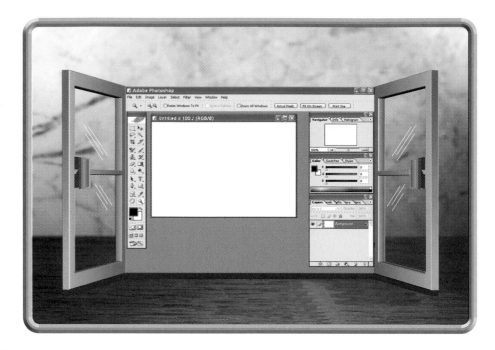

CREATE A NEW IMAGE

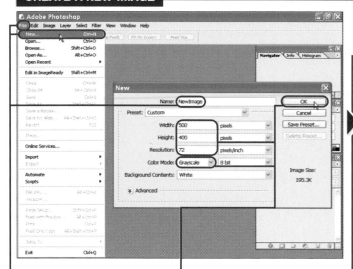

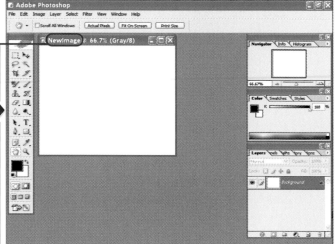

1 Click **File**.

2 Click **New**.

■ The New dialog box
appears.

3 Type a name for the new
image.

4 Type the dimensions and
resolution you want.

5 Click ∨ (⬍) and select a
color mode.

*Note: See Chapter 6 for more about
color modes.*

6 Click **OK**.

■ Photoshop creates a new
image window at the
specified dimensions.

■ The filename appears in
the title bar.

7 Use Photoshop's tools
and commands to create
your image.

*Note: To save your image, see
Chapter 15.*

EXIT PHOTOSHOP

You can exit Photoshop after you finish using the application.

EXIT PHOTOSHOP

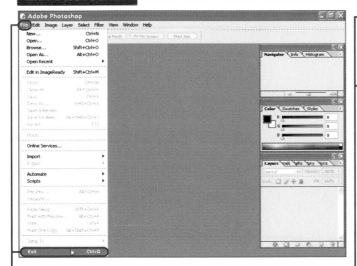

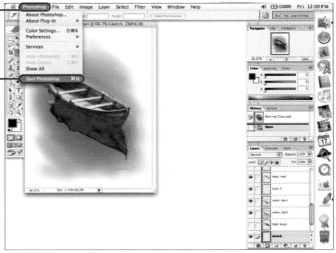

EXIT PHOTOSHOP ON A PC

1 Click **File**.

2 Click **Exit**.

■ Before exiting, Photoshop alerts you to any open images that have unsaved changes so you can save them.

Note: See Chapter 15 to save image files.

EXIT PHOTOSHOP ON A MAC

1 Click **Photoshop**.

2 Click **Quit Photoshop**.

■ Photoshop exits.

■ Before exiting, Photoshop alerts you to any open images that have unsaved changes so you can save them.

Note: See Chapter 15 to save image files.

CHAPTER 2

Understanding Photoshop Basics

Are you ready to start working with images? This chapter shows you how to select tools and fine-tune your workspace.

Magnify with the Zoom Tool 24

Adjust Views 26

Change Screen Modes 28

View Rulers and Guides 30

View a Grid 32

Using Shortcuts to Select Tools 33

Undo Commands 34

Revert an Image..............................35

MAGNIFY WITH THE ZOOM TOOL

You can change the
magnification of an
image with the Zoom
tool. With the Zoom
tool, you can view
small details in an
image or view an
image at full size.

MAGNIFY WITH THE ZOOM TOOL

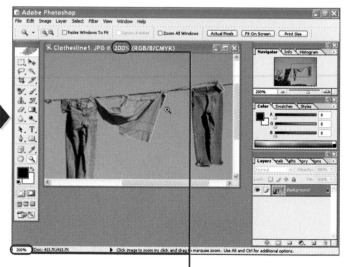

INCREASE MAGNIFICATION

1 Click the Zoom tool (🔍).

■ ⌖ changes to ⌖.

2 Click the image.

■ Photoshop increases the
magnification of the image.

■ The point that you clicked
in the image is centered in
the window.

■ The current magnification
shows in the title bar and
status bar.

■ You can choose an exact
magnification by typing a
percentage value in the
status bar.

24

**How do I quickly return an image
to 100% magnification?**

Double-click  in the
toolbox, click **Actual
Pixels** on the Options
bar, or click **View** and
then **Actual Pixels** from
the menu.

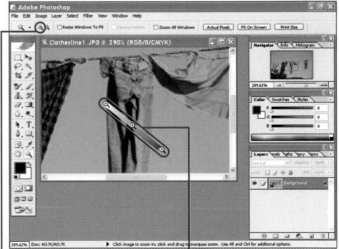

DECREASE MAGNIFICATION

1 Click the Zoom Out
button (🔍).

■ ⬚ changes to 🔍.

2 Click the image.

■ Photoshop decreases the
magnification of the image.

■ The current magnification
shows in the title bar and
status bar.

■ You can also press and
hold **Alt** (**option**) and click
the image to decrease
magnification.

MAGNIFY A DETAIL

1 Click the Zoom In
button (🔍).

2 Click and drag with the
Zoom tool to select the
detail.

■ The object appears
enlarged on-screen.

ADJUST VIEWS

You can move an image within the window by using the Hand tool or scroll bars. The Hand tool helps you navigate to an exact area on the image.

The Hand tool is a more flexible alternative to using the scroll bars because, unlike the scroll bars, the Hand tool enables you to drag the image freely in two dimensions.

ADJUST VIEWS

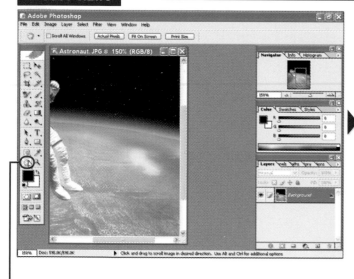

USING THE HAND TOOL

1 Click the Hand tool ( ).

Note: For to produce an effect, the image must extend outside the boundary of the image window.

■ changes to .

2 Click and drag inside the image window.

How can I quickly adjust the image window to see the entire image at its largest possible magnification on-screen?

You have three different ways to magnify the image to its largest possible size: By double-clicking , by clicking the **Fit On Screen** button on the Options bar, or by clicking **View** and then **Fit on Screen** from the menu.

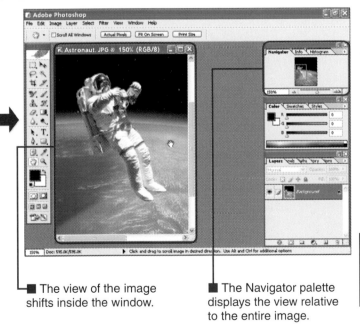

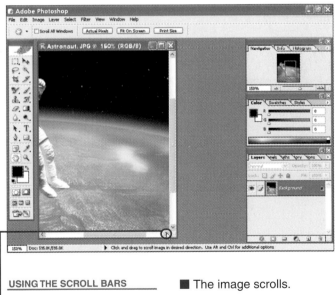

■ The view of the image shifts inside the window.

■ The Navigator palette displays the view relative to the entire image.

USING THE SCROLL BARS

1 Click and hold one of the window's scroll bar buttons.

■ The image scrolls.

CHANGE SCREEN MODES

You can switch the screen mode to change the look of your workspace on-screen.

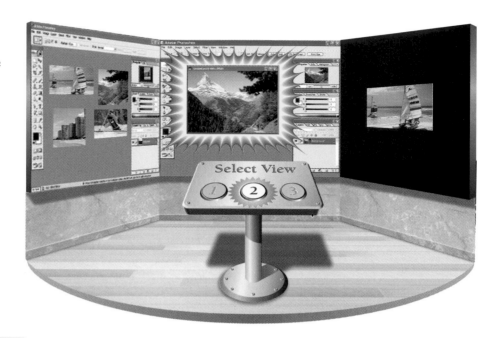

SWITCH TO FULL SCREEN MODE

Note: In the standard screen mode, you can view multiple images at the same time, each in a different window.

1 Click the Full Screen Mode with Menu Bar button ().

■ Photoshop puts the current image window in the center of a blank, full-screen canvas with the menu bar at the top of the screen.

■ On a Macintosh, the status bar is not visible in full screen with menu bar mode.

How do I display the menu bar when in Full Screen mode?

Press Shift + F to toggle the view of the menu bar in full screen mode.

SWITCH TO FULL SCREEN

1 Click the Full Screen Mode button (▣).

■ The image appears full screen without the menu bar. The Options bar, toolbox, and palettes are still present.

■ On a Macintosh, the status bar is not visible in full screen mode.

CLOSE TOOLBOX AND PALETTES

1 Press Tab.

■ Photoshop closes all toolboxes and palettes.

Note: The Tab *feature works in all of Photoshop's screen modes.*

Note: To view the toolbox and palettes, you can press Tab *again.*

VIEW RULERS AND GUIDES

You can turn on rulers and create guides to help accurately place elements in your image.

You can turn on a grid to place objects with even more precision. See the section "View a Grid" for more information.

VIEW RULERS AND GUIDES

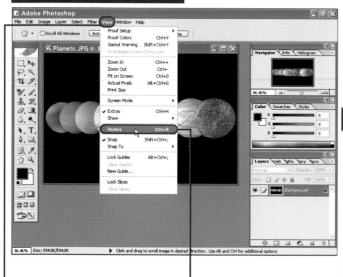

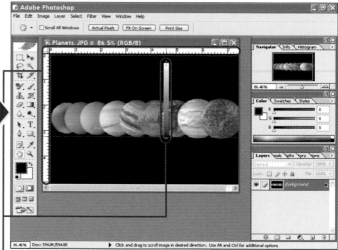

1 Click **View**.

2 Click **Rulers**.

Note: To change the units of the rulers, see the section "Set Preferences" in Chapter 1.

■ Photoshop adds rulers to the top and left sides of the image window.

3 Click one of the rulers and drag the cursor into the window.

■ ⇪ changes to ⇳.

■ Drag the top ruler down to create a horizontal guide. Drag the left ruler to the right to create a vertical guide.

TEACH YOURSELF

How do I make objects in my images "snap to" my guides when I move those objects?

You can make objects in the different layers of your image automatically snap to any nearby guides by clicking **View**, **Snap To**, and then **Guides**. The "snap to" feature can be useful when you are trying to align elements in a row horizontally or in a column vertically. For more about layers, see Chapter 9.

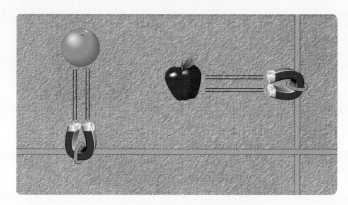

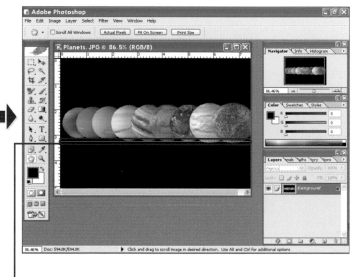

■ A thin colored line called a guide appears.

Note: Guides help you position different elements while you work on your Photoshop project. These lines do not appear in the printed image, or in images that have been saved for the Web.

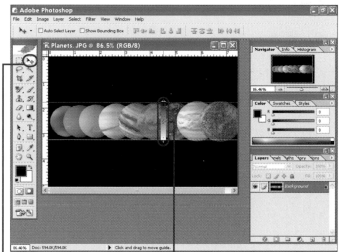

MOVE A GUIDE

1 Click the Move tool (🕂) to adjust the placement of a guide.

■ 🔓 changes to ↕.

2 Place the cursor over a guide and click and drag.

VIEW A GRID

You can turn on a grid that overlays your image. A grid can help you precisely organize objects within your image, especially when you use it with rulers turned on. See the section "View Rulers and Guides" in this chapter for more about rulers.

The grid does not appear when you print your image.

VIEW A GRID

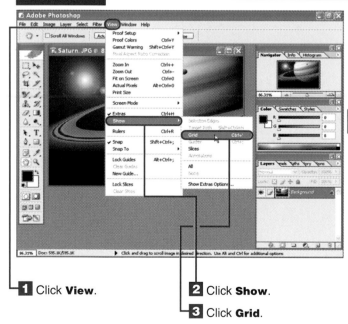

1 Click **View**.

2 Click **Show**.

3 Click **Grid**.

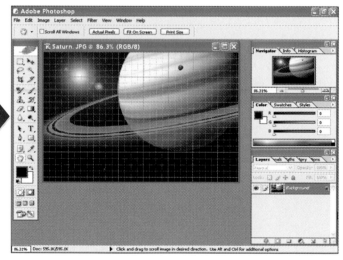

■ A grid appears on top of the image.

■ To adjust the space separating the grid lines, click **Edit**, **Preferences**, and then **Guides, Grid & Slices**.

■ On a Macintosh, click **Photoshop**, **Preferences**, and then **Guides, Grid & Slices**.

■ When you click **View**, **Snap To**, and then **Grid**, objects in an image align with the grid lines when you move the objects close to them.

You can press
letter keys to
select items in
the toolbox.
You may find
this more efficient
than clicking
the tools.

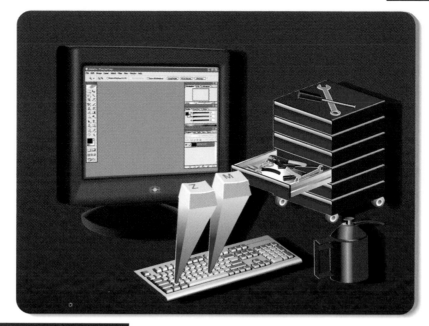

Each tool in the
toolbox has a letter
associated with it.

USING SHORTCUTS TO SELECT TOOLS

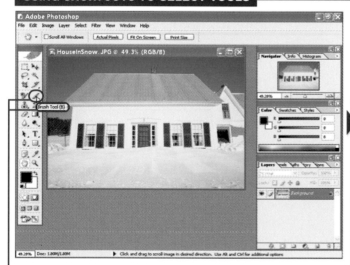

1 Place the cursor ( ) over a tool in the toolbox and hold it there.

■ A small box appears that names the tool and its shortcut key.

2 Press the indicated letter key to select the tool.

■ If a button in the toolbox features more than one tool, you can press the letter repeatedly to cycle through the different tools.

■ Photoshop automatically selects the tool icon in the toolbox, and becomes the new tool.

Note: You can modify the shape of the cursor by adjusting Photoshop's Preferences settings. See the section "Set Preferences" in Chapter 1 for more information.

■ You can use the following shortcut keys for some common Photoshop tools:

Marquee	M	Move	V
Lasso	L	Paintbrush	B
Type	T	Zoom	Z

UNDO COMMANDS

You can undo multiple commands using the History palette. This enables you to correct mistakes or change your mind about elements of your image.

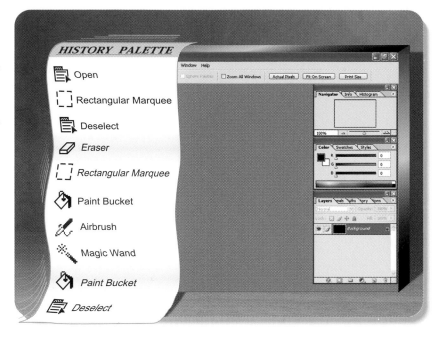

The History palette lists recently executed commands with the most recent command at the bottom.

UNDO COMMANDS

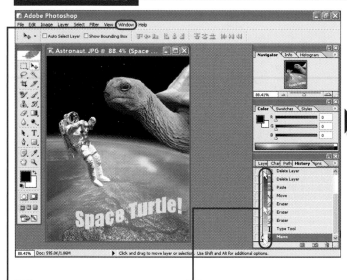

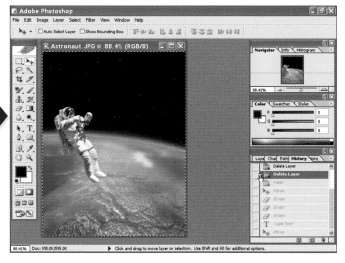

1 Click **Window**.

2 Click **History**.

3 Click and drag the History slider (▷) upward.

■ Alternatively, you can click a previous command in the History palette.

■ Photoshop undoes the previous commands.

■ You can click and drag the slider down to redo the commands.

REVERT AN IMAGE

You can revert an image
to the previously saved
state and start your
image editing again.

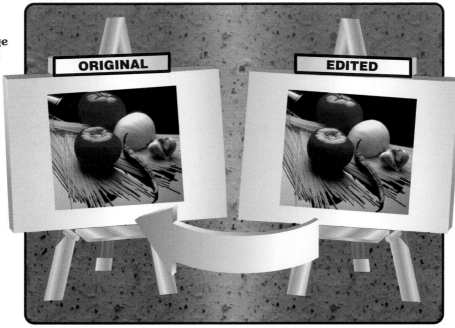

ORIGINAL   EDITED

REVERT AN IMAGE

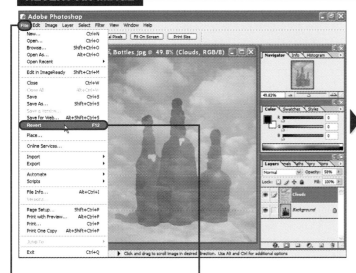

1 Click **File**.

2 Click **Revert**.

■ Photoshop reverts the
image to its previously saved
state.

■ You can click **Edit** and
then **Undo Revert** to return
to the unreverted state.

360 pixels

288 pixels

CHAPTER 3

Changing the Size of an Image

Do you want to change the size of your image? This chapter shows you how to change the on-screen or print size and print resolution as well as how to crop an image.

Change the On-Screen
  Size of an Image 38

Change the Print Size of an Image......40

Change the Resolution of an Image 42

Crop an Image 44

Crop and Straighten Photos...............46

Trim an Image 47

Change the Canvas
  Size of an Image 48

CHANGE THE ON-SCREEN SIZE OF AN IMAGE

You can change the size at which an image displays on your computer monitor so that viewers can see the entire image.

Because you lose less sharpness when you decrease an image's size than when you increase it, consider starting with an image that is too big rather than with one that is too small.

CHANGE THE ON-SCREEN SIZE OF AN IMAGE

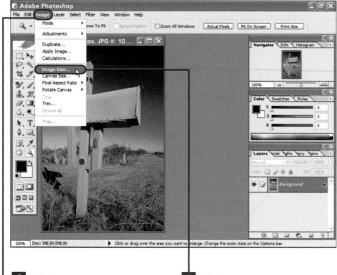

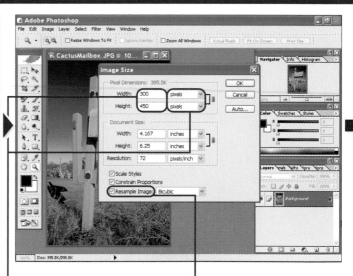

1 Click **Image**.

2 Click **Image Size**.

■ The Image Size dialog box appears, listing the on-screen height and width of the image.

■ To resize by a certain percentage, click ⌄ (⬍) and change the units to **percent**.

3 Make sure **Resample Image** is checked (☐ changes to ☑).

Note: Resampling is the process of increasing or decreasing the number of pixels in an image as its size changes.

What is the difference between an image's on-screen size and its print size?

On-screen size depends only on the number of pixels that make up an image. Print size depends on the number of pixels as well as on the print resolution, which is the density of the pixels on a printed page. Higher resolutions print a smaller image, while lower resolutions print a larger image, given the same on-screen size.

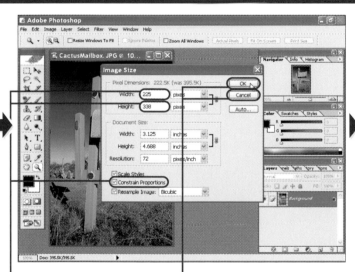

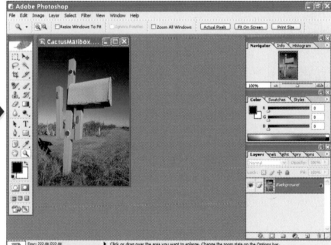

4 Type a size for a dimension.

■ Click **Constrain Proportions** (☐ changes to ☑) to force the other dimension to change proportionally.

5 Click **OK**.

■ You can restore the original dialog box settings by holding down Alt (option) and clicking **Cancel**, which changes to **Reset**.

■ Photoshop resizes the image.

Note: Changing the number of pixels in an image can add blur. To sharpen a resized image, apply the Unsharp Mask filter as covered in Chapter 11.

CHANGE THE PRINT SIZE OF AN IMAGE

You can change the printed size of an image to determine how it appears on paper.

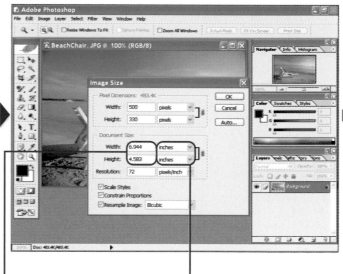

1 Click **Image**.

2 Click **Image Size**.

■ The Image Size dialog box appears, listing the current height and width of the printed image.

■ You can click ∨ ( ) to change the unit of measurement.

40

How do I preview an image's printed size?

Click **File** and then click **Print with Preview**. A dialog box displays how the image will print on the page. Other options let you adjust the size and positioning of the image. See Chapter 16 for more information on printing images.

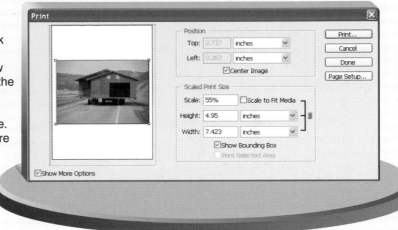

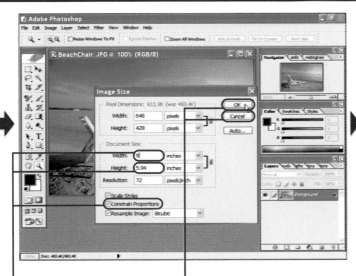

3 Type a size for a dimension.

■ You can click **Constrain Proportions** (☐ changes to ☑) to force the other dimension to change proportionally.

4 Click **OK**.

■ You can restore the original dialog box settings by holding down **Alt** (**option**) and clicking **Cancel**, which changes to **Reset**.

■ Photoshop resizes the image.

Note: Changing the number of pixels in an image can add blur. To sharpen a resized image, apply the Unsharp Mask filter as covered in Chapter 11.

CHANGE THE RESOLUTION OF AN IMAGE

You can change the print resolution of an image to increase or decrease the print quality.

72 dpi

300 dpi

The resolution, combined with the number of pixels in an image, determines the size of a printed image.

The greater the resolution, the better the image looks on the printed page — up to a limit, which varies with the type of printer and paper quality.

CHANGE THE RESOLUTION OF AN IMAGE

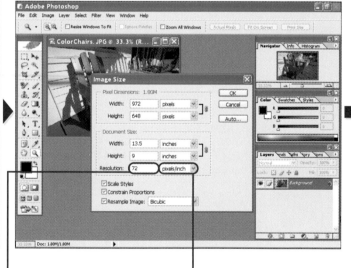

1 Click **Image**.

2 Click **Image Size**.

■ The Image Size dialog box appears, listing the current resolution of the image.

■ You can click ![] (![]) to change the resolution units.

What is the relationship between resolution, on-screen size, and print size?

To determine the printed size of a Photoshop image, you can divide the on-screen size by the resolution. If you have an image with an on-screen width of 480 pixels and a resolution of 120 pixels per inch, the printed width is 4 inches.

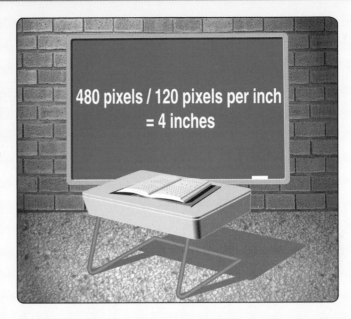

480 pixels / 120 pixels per inch
= 4 inches

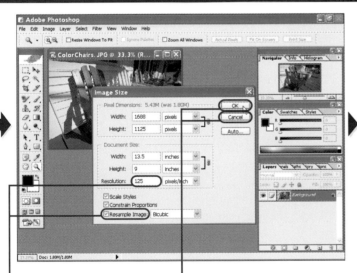

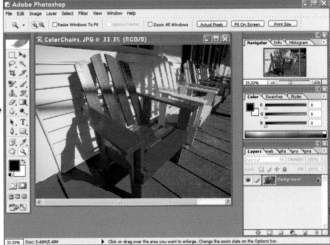

3 Type a new resolution.

■ You can click **Resample Image** (☐ changes to ☑) to adjust the number of pixels in your image and keep the print dimensions fixed.

4 Click **OK**.

■ You can restore the original dialog box settings by holding down Alt (option) and clicking **Cancel**, which changes to **Reset**.

■ Because the change in resolution changes the number of pixels in the image, the on-screen image changes in size while the print size stays the same.

CROP AN IMAGE

You can use the Crop tool to change the size of an image and to remove unneeded space on the top, bottom, and sides.

CROP AN IMAGE

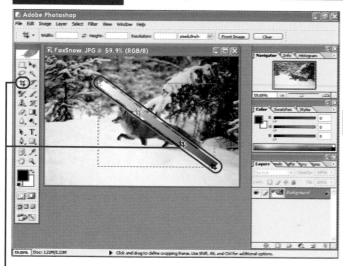

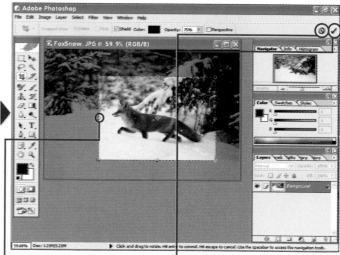

1 Click the Crop tool (🔲).

■ 🔖 changes to 🔲.

2 Click and drag to select the area of the image you want to keep.

■ You can also crop an image by changing its canvas size.

Note: See the section "Change the Canvas Size of an Image" for more information.

3 Click and drag the side and corner handles (☐) to adjust the size of the cropping boundary.

■ You can click and drag inside the cropping boundary to move it without adjusting its size.

4 Click ✓ or press **Enter** (**Return**).

■ To exit the cropping process, you can press **Esc** (⌘ + .) or click 🚫.

How do I increase the area of an image using the Crop tool?

You can enlarge the image window to add extra space around the image. Then, you can apply the Crop tool () so that the cropping boundary extends beyond the borders of the image. When you apply cropping, the image canvas enlarges.

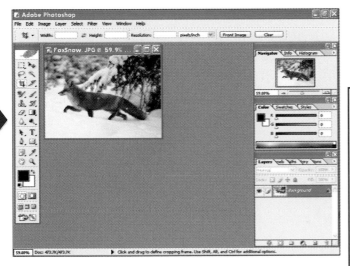

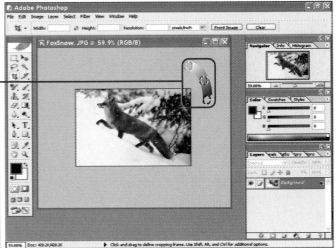

■ Photoshop crops the image, deleting the pixels outside of the cropping boundary.

ROTATE AND CROP

1 Perform steps **1** to **3** on the previous page.

2 Click and drag outside of the boundary lines.

3 Click ✔ or press Enter (Return).

■ Photoshop rotates the image and crops it.

CROP AND STRAIGHTEN PHOTOS

You can automatically crop and straighten one or more photographs in a Photoshop image. After cropping and straightening, Photoshop places each image in its own image window. This feature is useful if you have digitized several images at the same time on a scanner and want to separate them.

CROP AND STRAIGHTEN PHOTOS

1 Click **File**.

2 Click **Automate**.

3 Click **Crop and Straighten Photos**.

■ Photoshop straightens the photos, crops out any blank space, and copies the photos to separate image windows.

Note: To save the newly cropped images, see Chapter 15.

■ The original image remains in its own image window.

TRIM AN IMAGE

You can use the Trim command to automatically remove any blank space surrounding your image. This can be useful for scanned photos, or when you want to minimize the file size of an image.

TRIM AN IMAGE

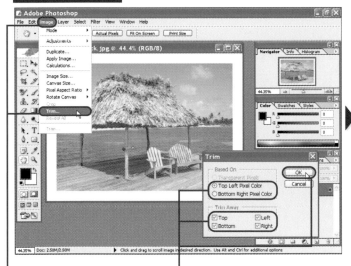

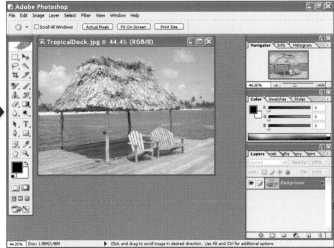

1 Click **Image**.

2 Click **Trim**.

■ The Trim dialog box appears.

3 Click the type of pixels you want to trim away (○ changes to ⦿).

4 Click the areas to trim away (☐ changes to ☑).

5 Click **OK**.

■ Photoshop trims the image.

47

CHANGE THE CANVAS SIZE OF AN IMAGE

You can alter the canvas size of an image in order to change its rectangular shape or to add blank space around its borders.

The *canvas* is the area on which an image sits. Changing the canvas size is one way to crop an image.

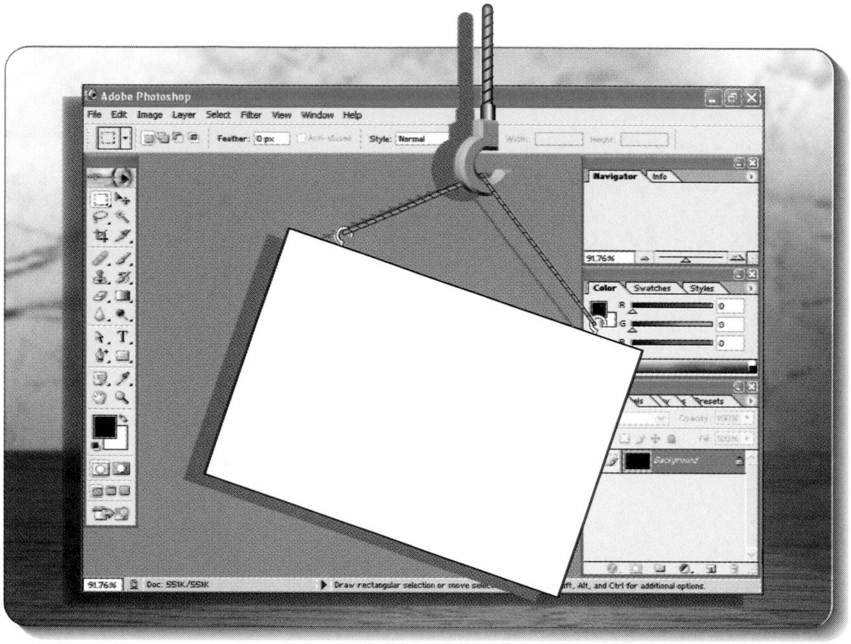

The Crop tool provides an alternative to changing the canvas size. See the section "Crop an Image" for more information.

CHANGE THE CANVAS SIZE OF AN IMAGE

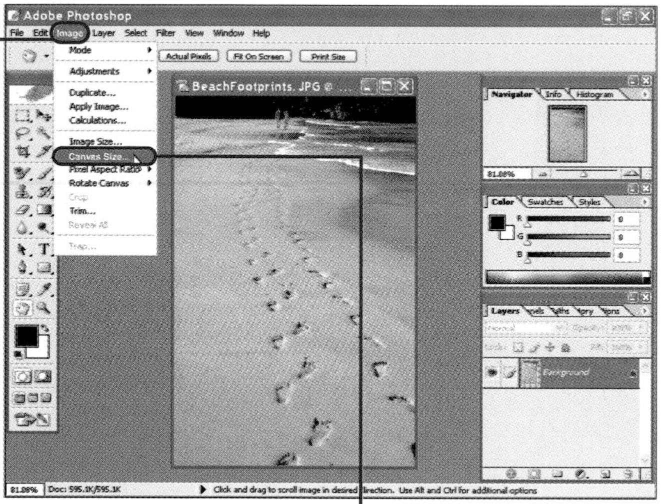

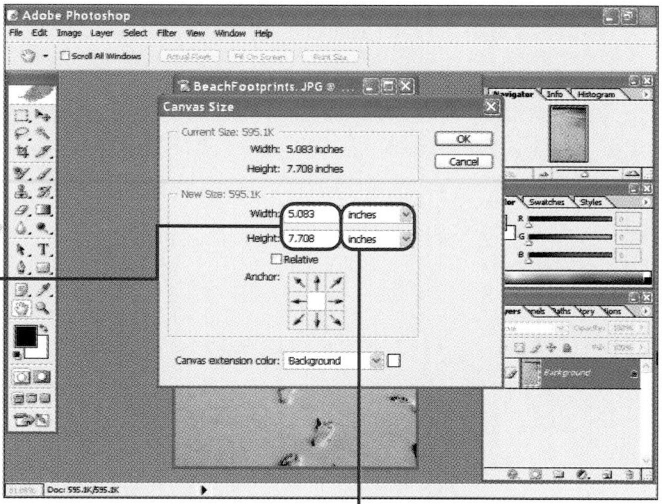

1 Click **Image**.

2 Click **Canvas Size**.

■ The Canvas Size dialog box appears, listing the current dimensions of the canvas.

■ You can click ⌄ (⇕) to change the unit of measurement.

Why would I want to change the canvas size instead of using the Crop tool?

Changing the canvas size can be useful when you want to change the size of an image precisely. You can specify the exact number of pixels that Photoshop adds or subtracts around the border. With the Crop tool ( ), it can be more difficult to make changes with pixel precision.

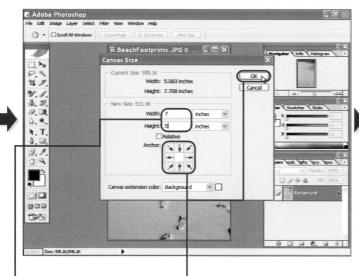

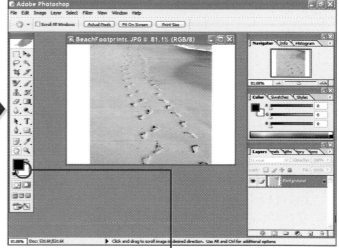

3 Type the new canvas dimensions.

■ You can modify in which directions Photoshop changes the canvas size by clicking an anchor point.

4 Click **OK**.

*Note: If you decrease a dimension, Photoshop displays a dialog box asking whether you want to proceed. Click **Proceed**.*

■ Photoshop changes the image's canvas size.

■ Because the middle anchor point is selected in this example, the canvas size changes equally on opposite sides.

■ Photoshop fills any new canvas space with the background color — in this case, white.

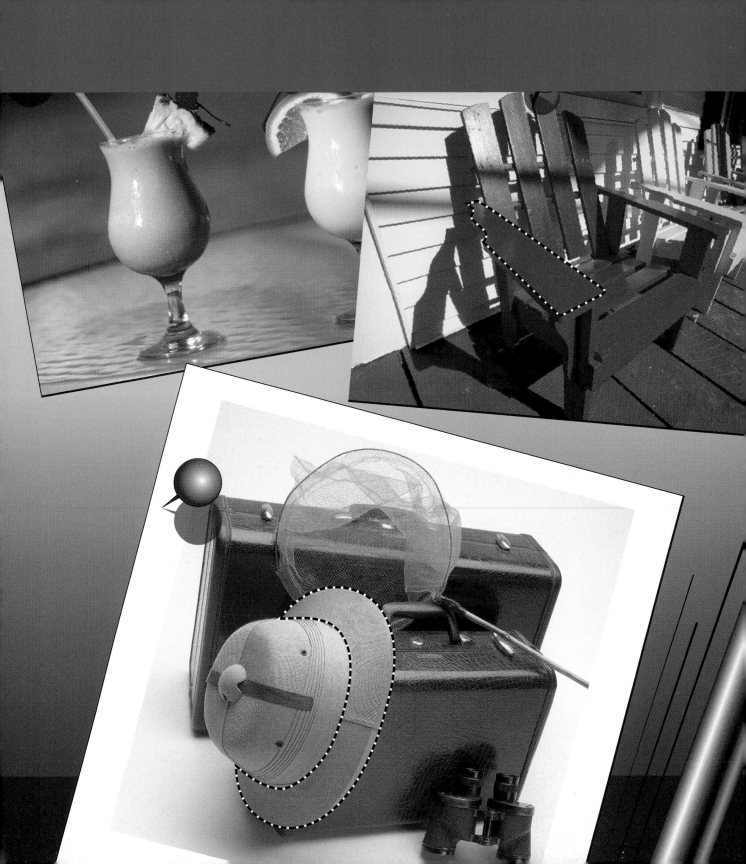

CHAPTER 4

Making Selections

Do you want to move, color, or transform parts of your image independently from the rest of the image? The first step is to make a selection. This chapter shows you how.

Select with the Marquee Tools 52

Select with the Lasso Tool 54

Select with the Magnetic Lasso Tool 56

Select with the Magic Wand Tool........58

Select with the Color
        Range Command 60

Select All the Pixels in an Image 62

Move a Selection Border.....................63

Add to or Subtract
        from Your Selection 64

Expand or Contract Selections 66

Invert a Selection 68

Grow a Selection 69

Create Slices 70

SELECT WITH THE MARQUEE TOOLS

You can select a
rectangular or elliptical
area of your image by
using the Marquee tools.
Then you can move,
delete, or stylize the
selected area using other
Photoshop commands.

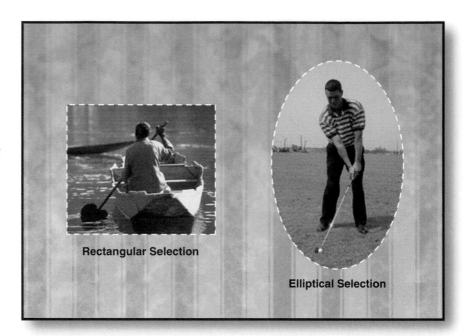

Rectangular Selection

Elliptical Selection

SELECT WITH THE MARQUEE TOOLS

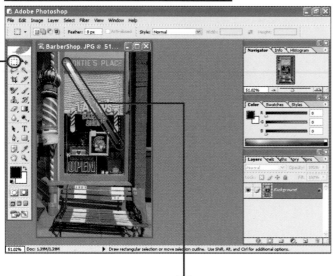

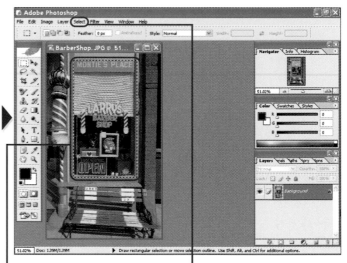

**USING THE RECTANGULAR
MARQUEE TOOL**

1 Click the Rectangular
Marquee tool (▨).

■ ⬚ changes to ＋.

2 Click and drag diagonally
inside the image window.

■ You can hold down Shift
while you click and drag to
create a square selection.

■ Photoshop selects a
rectangular portion of your
image. You can now perform
other commands on the
selection.

■ You can deselect a
selection by clicking **Select**
and then **Deselect**.

52

How do I customize the Marquee tools?

You can customize the Marquee tools (and) by using the text fields and menus in the Options bar. Typing in a Feather value softens your selection edge — which means that Photoshop partially selects pixels near the edge. You can click the Style ▾ to define your Marquee tool as a fixed size or fixed aspect ratio. You can specify the fixed dimensions in the Width and Height boxes.

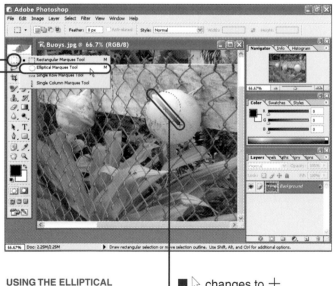

USING THE ELLIPTICAL MARQUEE TOOL

■1 Click and hold the ( ).

■2 From the list that appears, click the Elliptical Marquee tool ( ).

■ ⊾ changes to +.

■3 Click and drag diagonally inside the image window.

■ You can hold down Shift while you click and drag to create a circular selection.

■ Photoshop selects an elliptical portion of your image. You can now perform other commands on the selection.

■ You can deselect a selection by clicking **Select** and then **Deselect**.

SELECT WITH THE LASSO TOOL

You can create oddly shaped selections with the Lasso tools. Then you can move, delete, or stylize the selected area using other Photoshop commands.

You can use the regular Lasso tool to create curved selections. With the Polygonal Lasso tool, you can easily create a selection made up of many straight lines.

SELECT WITH THE LASSO TOOL

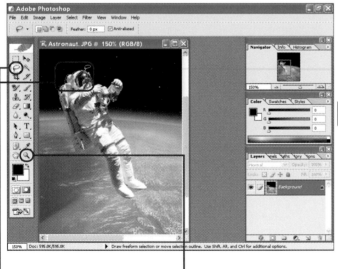

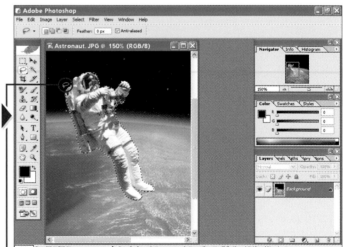

USING THE REGULAR LASSO

1 Click the Lasso tool ( ).

2 Click and drag your cursor ( ) to make a selection.

■ To accurately trace a complicated edge, you can magnify that part of the image with the Zoom tool ( ).

Note: See Chapter 2 for more about the Zoom tool.

3 Drag to the beginning point and release the mouse button.

■ The selection is now complete.

What if my lasso selection is not as precise as I want it to be?

You may find selecting complicated outlines with the Lasso tool (🔾) difficult, even for the steadiest of hands. To fix an imprecise Lasso selection, you can

- Deselect the selection, by clicking **Select** and then **Deselect**, and try again.

- Try to fix your selection. See the section "Add to or Subtract from Your Selection."

- Switch to the Magnetic Lasso tool (🧲). See the section "Select with the Magnetic Lasso Tool."

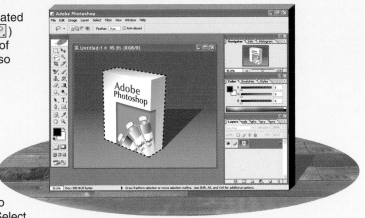

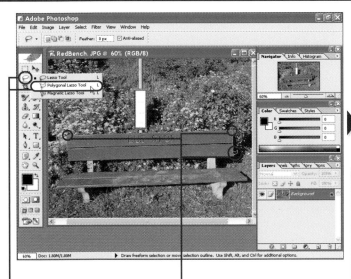

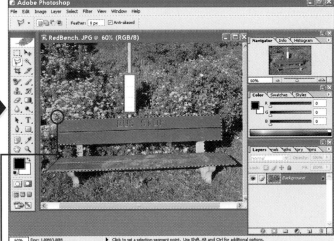

__USING THE POLYGONAL LASSO__

1 Click and hold 🔾.

2 From the list that appears, click the Polygonal Lasso tool (🔾).

- ▷ changes to 🔾.

3 Click multiple times along the border of the area you want to select.

4 To complete the selection, click the starting point.

- You can also double-click anywhere in the image and Photoshop adds a final straight line connected to the starting point.

- The selection is now complete.

- You can achieve a polygonal effect with the regular Lasso tool by pressing **Alt** (**option**) and clicking to make your selection.

55

SELECT WITH THE MAGNETIC LASSO TOOL

You can select elements of your image that have well-defined edges quickly and easily with the Magnetic Lasso tool.

The Magnetic Lasso works best when the element you are trying to select contrasts sharply with its background.

SELECT WITH THE MAGNETIC LASSO TOOL

1 Click and hold ☐.

2 Click the Magnetic Lasso tool (☐) from the list that appears.

3 Click the edge of the object you want to select.

■ This creates a beginning anchor point.

4 Drag your cursor (☐) along the edge of the object.

■ The Magnetic Lasso's path snaps to the edge of the element as you drag.

■ To help guide the lasso, you can click to add anchor points as you go along the path.

How can I adjust the precision of the Magnetic Lasso tool?

You can use the Options bar to adjust the Magnetic Lasso tool's precision:

■ **Width:** The number of nearby pixels the lasso considers when creating a selection. If you magnify the edge you are selecting, you can typically decrease the width.

■ **Edge Contrast:** How much contrast is required for the lasso to consider something an edge. You can decrease the edge contrast to select fuzzier edges.

■ **Frequency:** The frequency of the anchor points. You can increase the frequency for better precision when selecting poorly defined edges.

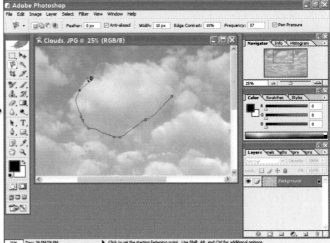

5 Click the beginning anchor point to finish your selection.

■ Alternatively, you can double-click anywhere in the image and Photoshop completes the selection for you.

■ The path is complete.

■ This example shows that the Magnetic Lasso is less useful for selecting areas where you find little contrast between the image and its background.

SELECT WITH THE MAGIC WAND TOOL

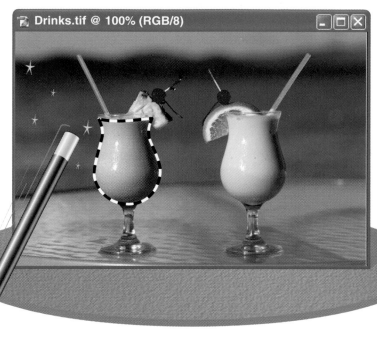

You can select groups of similarly colored pixels with the Magic Wand tool. You may find this useful if you want to remove an object from a background.

You can control how precisely the tool makes the selection by choosing a tolerance value from 0 to 255.

SELECT WITH THE MAGIC WAND TOOL

1 Click the Magic Wand tool ( ).

2 Type a number from 0 to 255 into the Tolerance field.

■ To select a narrow range of colors, type a small number; to select a wide range of colors, type a large number.

3 Click the cursor ( ) in the area you want to select inside the image.

■ Photoshop selects the pixel you clicked, plus any similarly colored pixels near it.

With what type of images does the Magic Wand work best?

The Magic Wand tool ( ) works best with images that have areas of solid color. The Magic Wand tool is less helpful with images that contain subtle shifts in color or color gradients.

4 To add to your selection, press **Shift** and click elsewhere in the image.

■ You can also click the Add to Selection button ( ) in the Options bar.

■ Photoshop adds to your selection.

5 To delete the selected pixels, press **Delete**.

■ Photoshop replaces the pixels with the background color.

■ In this example, Photoshop replaces the pixels with white.

■ If you make the selection in a layer, the deleted selection becomes transparent. See Chapter 9 for more about layers.

SELECT WITH THE COLOR RANGE COMMAND

You can select a set range of colors within an image with the Color Range command. With this command, you can quickly select a region of relatively solid color, such as a sky or a blank wall.

SELECT WITH THE COLOR RANGE COMMAND

1 Click **Select**.

2 Click **Color Range**.

■ The Color Range dialog box appears.

■ ⌖ changes to ✐.

3 Click inside the image window.

■ Photoshop selects all the pixels in the image that are similar to the pixel you clicked. These areas turn white in the Color Range window.

■ The number of pixels that turn white depends on the Fuzziness setting.

How do I limit the area of the image affected by the Color Range command?

Select an area of the image — by using the Marquee, Lasso, or other tool — before clicking **Select** and then **Color Range**.

4 To increase the range of color, click and drag the Fuzziness slider (⬚) to the right.

■ You can decrease the color range by dragging the slider to the left.

■ You can also broaden the selected area by clicking the Add eyedropper (✎) and then clicking other parts of the image.

5 Click **OK** to make a selection in the main image window.

■ Photoshop makes the selection.

■ Sometimes the color range command selects unwanted areas of the image. To eliminate these areas, see the section "Add to or Subtract from Your Selection."

SELECT ALL THE PIXELS IN AN IMAGE

You can select all the pixels in an image by using a single command. This lets you perform a command on the entire image, such as copying it to a different image window.

With the entire image window selected, you can easily delete your image, or copy and paste it into another window.

SELECT ALL THE PIXELS IN AN IMAGE

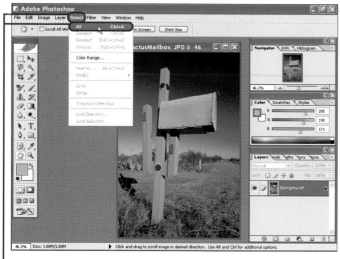

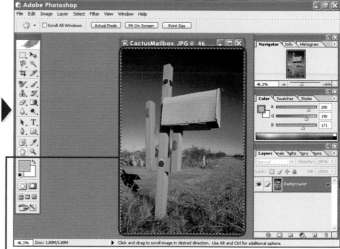

1 Click **Select**.

2 Click **All**.

■ You can also press
Ctrl + **A** (**⌘** + **A**) to select
all the pixels in an image.

■ Photoshop selects the
entire image window.

■ You can delete your image
by pressing **Delete**.

■ To copy your image, press
Ctrl + **C** (**⌘** + **C**).

■ To paste your image,
press **Ctrl** + **V** (**⌘** + **V**).

You can move a selection
border if your original
selection is not in the
intended place.

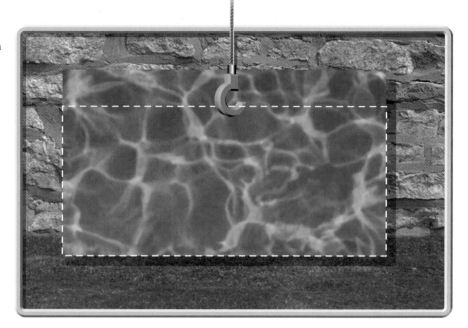

MOVE A SELECTION BORDER

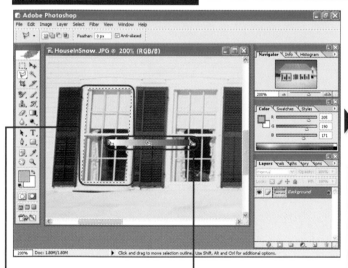

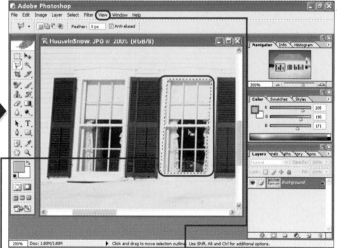

1 Make a selection with
a selection tool (▭, ⊘,
or ✳).

*Note: For more about the various
selection tools, see the previous
sections in this chapter.*

2 Click and drag inside the
selection.

■ ⬚ changes to ▸⬚.

■ The selection border
moves.

■ To move your selection
one pixel at a time, you can
use the arrow keys on your
keyboard.

■ You can hide a selection
by clicking **View** and then
Selection Edges.

ADD TO OR SUBTRACT FROM YOUR SELECTION

You can add to
or subtract from
your selection by
using various
selection tools.

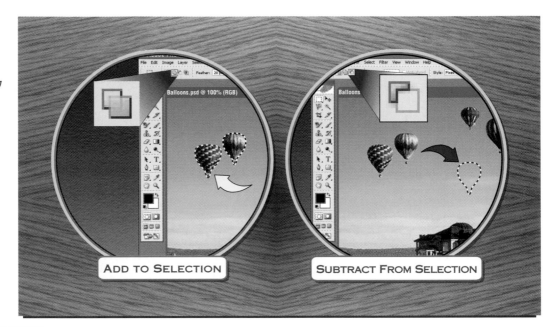

ADD TO SELECTION

SUBTRACT FROM SELECTION

ADD TO A SELECTION

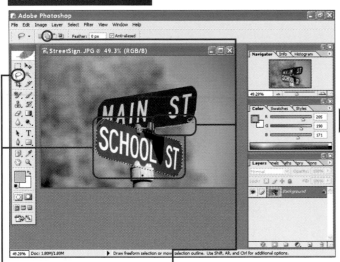

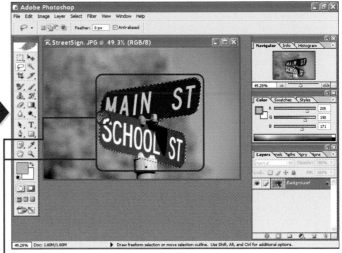

1 Make a selection using
one of Photoshop's selection
tools.

■ The selection in this
example illustrates the use
of the Lasso tool (🔗).

2 Click a selection tool.

*Note: See the previous sections in
this chapter to select the appropriate
tool for your image.*

3 Click the Add to
Selection button (🔳).

4 Select the area you want
to add.

5 Complete the selection
by closing the path.

■ The original selection
enlarges.

■ You can enlarge the
selection further by
repeating steps **2** to **5**.

■ You can also add to a
selection by pressing **Shift**
as you make your selection.

What tools can I use to add to or subtract from a selection?

You can use any of the Marquee, Lasso, or Magic Wand tools (⬚, 🔾, or ✨), discussed in previous sections in this chapter, to add to or subtract from a selection. All three have Add to Selection and Subtract from Selection buttons available in the Options bar when you select them.

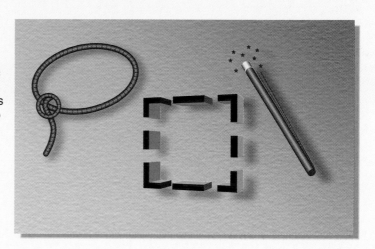

SUBTRACT FROM A SELECTION

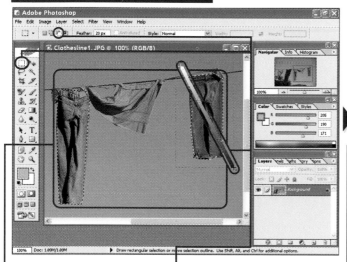

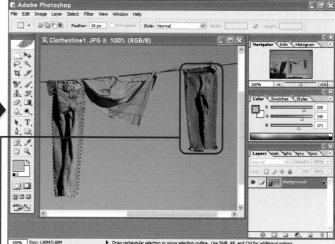

1 Make a selection using one of Photoshop's selection tools.

■ The selection in this example illustrates the use of the Rectangular Marquee tool (⬚).

2 Click a selection tool.

3 Click the Subtract from Selection button (🔾).

4 Select the area you want to subtract.

■ Photoshop deselects, or subtracts, the selected area.

■ You can subtract other parts of the selection by repeating steps **2** to **4**.

■ You can also subtract from a selection by holding down `Alt` (`option`) as you make your selection.

EXPAND OR CONTRACT SELECTIONS

You can expand or contract a selection by a set number of pixels. This lets you easily fine-tune your selections.

You can expand or contract a selection up to 100 pixels at a time.

EXPAND A SELECTION

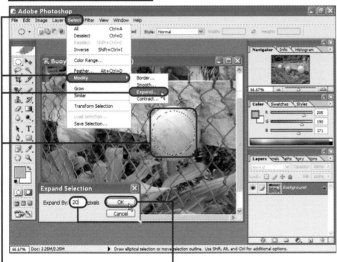

1 Make a selection using one of Photoshop's selection tools.

2 Click **Select**.

3 Click **Modify**.

4 Click **Expand**.

■ The Expand Selection dialog box appears.

5 Type a value in the Expand By field.

6 Click **OK**.

■ Photoshop expands the selection by the specified number of pixels.

■ You can repeat steps **2** to **6** to expand a selection further.

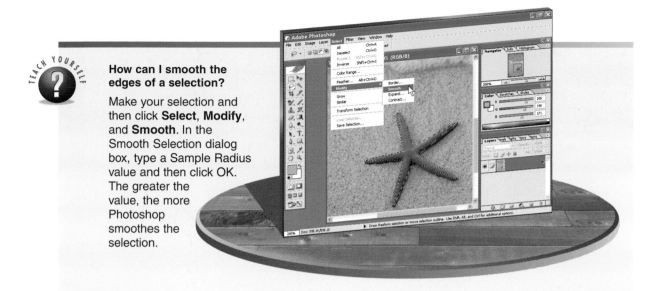

How can I smooth the edges of a selection?

Make your selection and then click **Select**, **Modify**, and **Smooth**. In the Smooth Selection dialog box, type a Sample Radius value and then click OK. The greater the value, the more Photoshop smoothes the selection.

CONTRACT A SELECTION

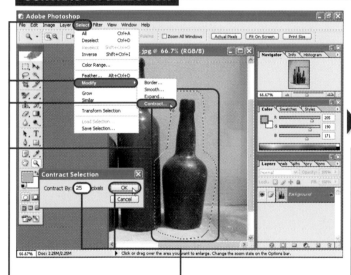

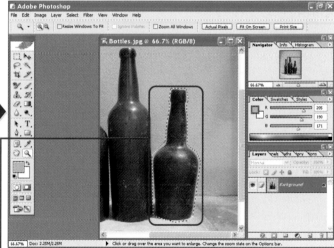

1 Make a selection using one of Photoshop's selection tools.

2 Click **Select**.

3 Click **Modify**.

4 Click **Contract**.

■ The Contract Selection dialog box appears.

5 Type a value in the Contract By field.

6 Click **OK**.

■ Photoshop contracts the selection by the number of pixels specified.

■ You can repeat steps **2** to **6** to contract a selection further.

INVERT A SELECTION

You can invert a selection to deselect what is currently selected and select everything else. This is useful when you want to select a background around an object.

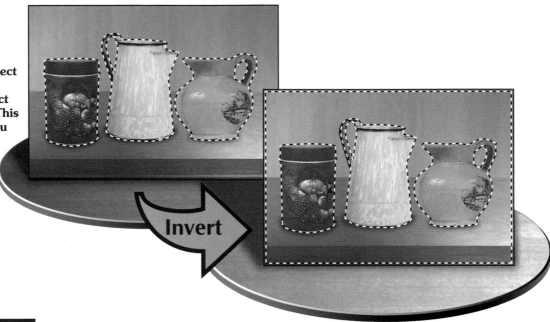

Invert

INVERT A SELECTION

1 Make a selection using one of Photoshop's selection tools.

Note: For more about the various selection tools, see the previous sections in this chapter.

2 Click **Select**.

3 Click **Inverse**.

■ Photoshop inverts the selection.

You can increase the size
of your selection using
the Grow command,
which is useful when you
want to include similarly
colored, neighboring
pixels in your selection.

GROW A SELECTION

1 Make a selection using
one of Photoshop's selection
tools.

*Note: To learn more about the
various selection tools, see the
previous sections in this chapter.*

2 Click **Select**.

3 Click **Grow**.

■ The selection grows to
include similarly colored
pixels contiguous with the
current selection.

■ To include noncontiguous
pixels as well, you can click
Select and then **Similar**.

■ You can change the
number of similarly colored
pixels the Grow command
selects by changing the
Tolerance setting. Click the
Magic Wand tool and type a
new number in the Tolerance
field, Make your selection,
and click **Select** and then
Grow.

CREATE SLICES

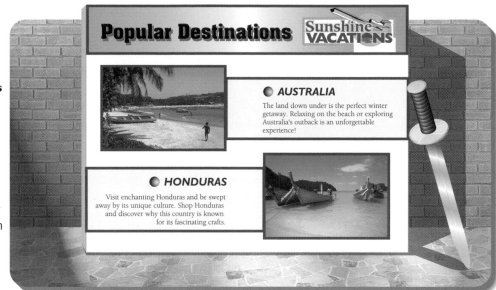

You can divide a large image that you want to display on the Web into smaller rectangular sections called *slices*. The different slices of an image can then be optimized independently of one another for faster download. See Chapter 15 for details.

Slices can also be used to create special Web effects, such as animations and rollovers, in ImageReady. ImageReady is a Web imaging program that comes with Photoshop.

CREATE SLICES

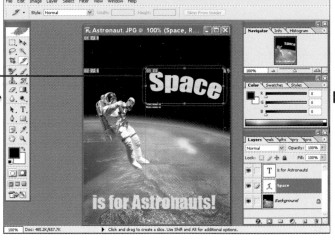

1 Click the Slice tool (▨).

■ ⏳ changes to 🔪.

2 Click and drag inside the image to create a slice.

■ Photoshop creates a slice where you clicked and dragged.

Note: Slices you define are called user-slices.

■ Photoshop fills in the rest of the image with auto-slices.

Note: User-slices remain fixed when you add more slices to your image, whereas auto-slices can change size.

**How do I resize or delete
slices in my image?**

First, select the Slice Select
tool (⬚), which is accessible
by clicking and holding ⬚. To
resize a user-slice, click inside
it and then click and drag a
border handle. To delete a
user-slice, click inside it and
then press `Delete`.

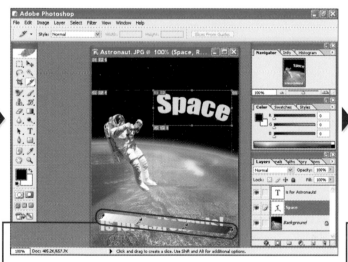

3 Click and drag to define
another slice in your image.

■ Photoshop creates
another slice where you
clicked and dragged.

■ Photoshop creates or
rearranges auto-slices to fill
in the rest of the image.

■ To save the different
slices for the Web, see
Chapter 15.

■ For more about how to
use slices in ImageReady,
see Photoshop's Help
information. See Chapter 1
to access Photoshop Help.

APPLYING DISTORT

PASTING SELECTION IN NEW WINDOW

DELETING SELECTION

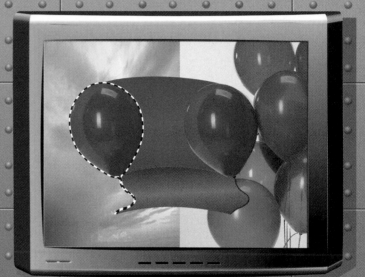

...NOW APPLYING TRANSFORMATION...

MOVE SELECTION

CHAPTER 5

Manipulating Selections

Making a selection defines a specific area of your Photoshop image. This chapter shows you how to move, stretch, erase, and manipulate your selections in a variety of ways.

Move a Selection 74

Copy and Paste a Selection................76

Delete a Selection 78

Rotate a Selection..............................79

Scale a Selection 80

Skew or Distort a Selection 82

Feather the Border of a Selection 84

Extract an Object 86

MOVING SELECTION

ROTATING SELECTION

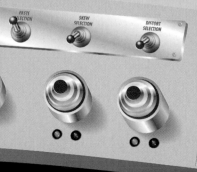

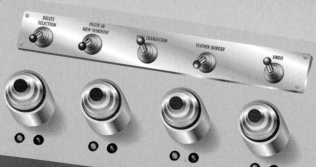

PASTE SELECTION

SKEW SELECTION

DISTORT SELECTION

DELETE SELECTION

PASTE IN NEW WINDOW

FREE TRANSFORM

FEATHER BORDER

UNDO

MOVE A SELECTION

You can move a
selection by using the
Move tool, which lets
you rearrange elements
of your image.

You can place elements of
your image either in the
background or in layers.
For details about layers,
see Chapter 9.

MOVE A SELECTION

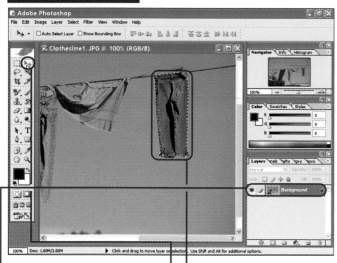

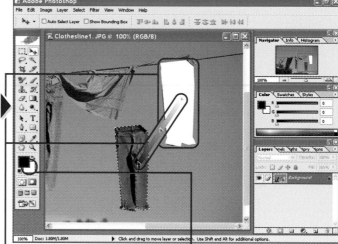

**MOVE A SELECTED OBJECT
IN THE BACKGROUND**

1 Click the Background
layer in the Layers palette.

■ If you start with a newly
scanned image, Photoshop
makes the Background layer
the only layer.

2 Make a selection with a
selection tool.

*Note: See Chapter 4 for more about
the selection tools, and Chapter 9 for
more about layers.*

3 Click the Move tool (⌖).

4 Click inside the selection
and drag.

■ Photoshop fills the original
location of the object with
the current background
color.

■ In this example, white is
the default background color.

How do I move a selection in a straight line?

Hold down the Shift key while you drag with the Move tool (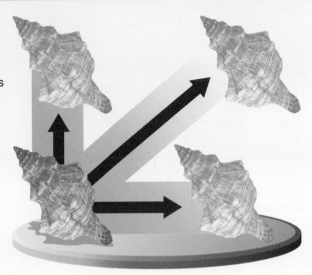). Doing so constrains the movement of your object horizontally, vertically, or diagonally — depending on the direction you drag.

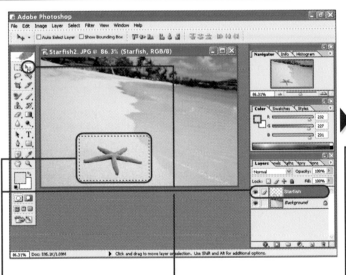

MOVE A SELECTED OBJECT IN A LAYER

1 Click a layer in the Layers palette.

2 Make a selection with a selection tool.

Note: See Chapter 4 for more about the selection tools, and Chapter 9 for more about layers.

3 Click 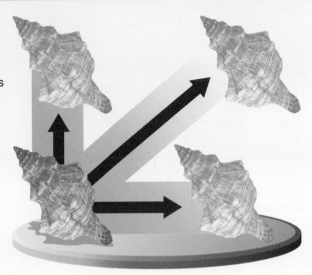.

4 Click inside the selection and drag.

■ Photoshop moves the selection in the layer.

■ Photoshop fills the original location of the object with transparent pixels.

Note: Unlike the background — Photoshop's opaque default layer — layers can include transparent pixels.

COPY AND PASTE A SELECTION

You can copy a selection and make a duplicate of it somewhere else in the image.

COPY AND PASTE A SELECTION

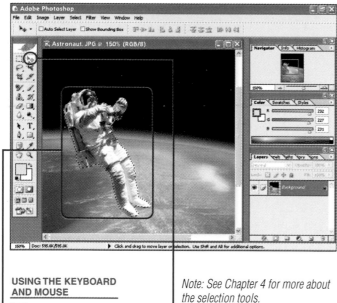

USING THE KEYBOARD AND MOUSE

1 Make a selection with a selection tool.

Note: See Chapter 4 for more about the selection tools.

2 Click ⊕.

3 Press **Alt** (**option**) while you click and drag the object.

4 Release the mouse button to "drop" the selection.

■ Photoshop creates a duplicate of the object, which appears in the new location.

**How can I copy a selection
from one window to another?**

Click  and click and drag
your selection from one window
to another. You can also copy
selections between windows
using the **Copy** and **Paste**
commands in the **Edit** menu.

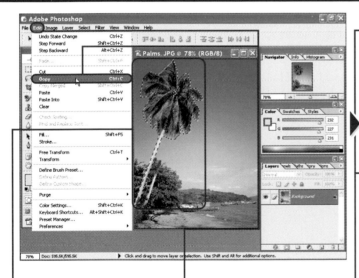

**USING THE COPY AND
PASTE COMMANDS**

1 Make a selection
with a selection tool.

*Note: See Chapter 4 for more about
the selection tools.*

2 Click **Edit**.

3 Click **Copy**.

4 Using a selection tool,
select where you want to
paste the copied element.

■ If you do not select an
area, Photoshop pastes the
copy over the original.

5 Click **Edit**.

6 Click **Paste**.

■ Photoshop pastes
the copy into a new layer,
which you can now move
independently of the original
image.

*Note: See the section "Move a
Selection" for more about moving
your image.*

DELETE A SELECTION

You can delete a
selection to remove
an element from
your image.

1 Make a selection with a
selection tool.

*Note: See Chapter 4 for more about
the selection tools.*

2 Press `Delete`.

■ Photoshop deletes the
selection.

■ If you are working in the
Background layer, the empty
area fills with the background
color — in this example,
white, the default background
color.

■ If you are working
in a layer other than the
Background layer, deleting
an object turns the selected
pixels transparent.

78

You can rotate a
selection to tilt or
turn it upside down
in your image.

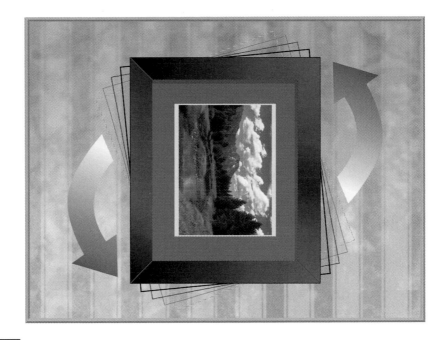

ROTATE A SELECTION

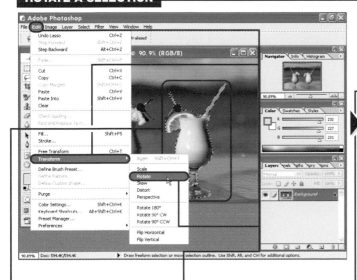

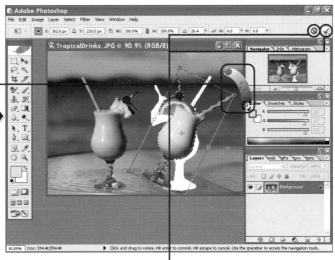

1 Make a selection with a
selection tool.

*Note: See Chapter 4 for more about
the selection tools.*

2 Click **Edit**.

3 Click **Transform**.

4 Click **Rotate**.

■ A *bounding box*, a
rectangular box with handles
on the sides and corners,
surrounds the object.

5 Click and drag to the side
of the object.

■ The object rotates.

6 Click ✔ or press
Enter (**Return**) to apply
the rotation.

■ You can click ⊘ or press
Esc (⌘+.) to cancel.

SCALE A SELECTION

You can scale a selection to make it larger or smaller. By scaling, you can emphasize parts of your image.

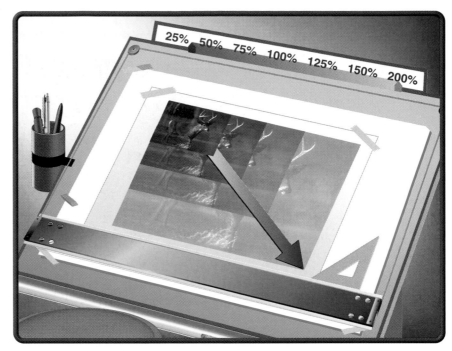

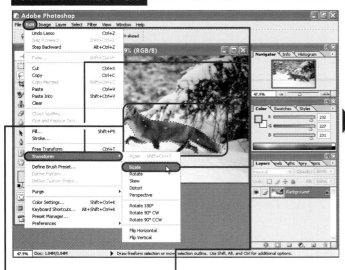

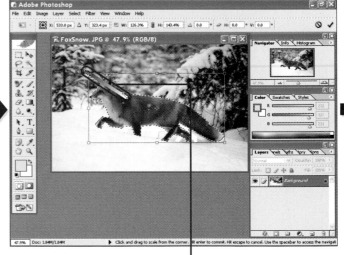

1 Make a selection with a selection tool.

Note: See Chapter 4 for more about the selection tools.

2 Click **Edit**.

3 Click **Transform**.

4 Click **Scale**.

■ A rectangular bounding box with handles on the sides and corners surrounds the object.

5 Click and drag a corner handle to scale both the horizontal and vertical axes.

How do I scale both dimensions proportionally?

Hold down Shift while you scale your selection. The two axes of your selection grow or shrink proportionally. Photoshop does not distort your image.

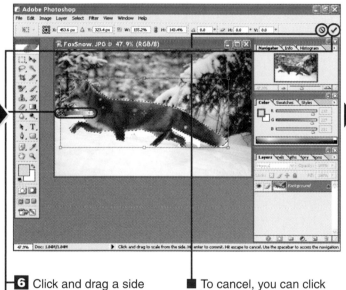

6 Click and drag a side handle to scale one axis at a time.

7 To apply the scaling, click ✓ or press Enter (Return).

■ To cancel, you can click ⊘ or press Esc (⌘+.).

■ Photoshop scales the object to the new dimensions.

SKEW OR DISTORT A SELECTION

You can transform a selection using the Skew or Distort command. This lets you stretch elements in your image into interesting shapes.

1 Make a selection with a selection tool.

Note: See Chapter 4 for more about the selection tools.

2 Click **Edit**.

3 Click **Transform**.

4 Click **Skew**.

■ A rectangular bounding box with handles on the sides and corners surrounds the object.

5 Click and drag a handle to skew the object.

■ Because the Skew command works along a single axis, you can drag either horizontally or vertically.

6 To apply the skewing, click ✓ or press Enter (Return).

■ To cancel, you can click ⊘ or press Esc (⌘+.).

How can I undo my skewing or distortion?

You can click **Edit** and then **Undo** to undo the last handle adjustment you made. This is an alternative to clicking , which cancels the entire Skew or Distort command.

DISTORT A SELECTION

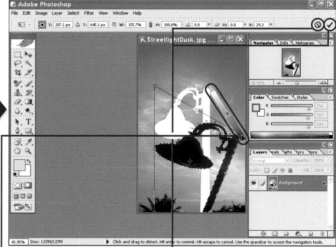

1 Make a selection with a selection tool.

Note: See Chapter 4 for more about the selection tools.

2 Click **Edit**.

3 Click **Transform**.

4 Click **Distort**.

■ A rectangular bounding box with handles on the sides and corners surrounds the object.

5 Click and drag a handle to distort the object.

■ The Distort command works independently of the selection's different axes; you can drag a handle both vertically and horizontally.

6 To apply the distortion, click ✔ or press **Enter** (**Return**).

■ To cancel, you can click ⊘ or press **Esc** (⌘+**.**).

FEATHER THE BORDER OF A SELECTION

You can feather a selection's border to create soft edges.

To soften edges, you must first select an object, feather the selection border, and then delete the part of the image that surrounds your selection.

FEATHER THE BORDER OF A SELECTION

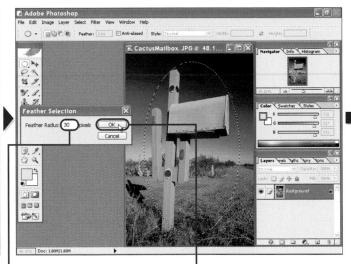

MAKE AND FEATHER THE IMAGE

1 Make a selection with a selection tool.

Note: See Chapter 4 for more about the selection tools.

2 Click **Select**.

3 Click **Feather**.

■ The Feather Selection dialog box appears.

4 Type a pixel value between 0.2 and 250 to determine the softness of the edge. The larger the number, the larger the softened edge.

5 Click **OK**.

What happens if I feather a selection and then apply a command to it?

Photoshop applies the command only partially to pixels near the edge of the selection. For example, if you are removing color from a selection using the Hue/Saturation command, color at the feathered edge of the selection is only partially removed. For more information about the Hue/Saturation command, see Chapter 8.

Is there another way to feather my selection?

When selecting with the Marquee or Lasso tools, you can create a feathered selection by first typing a pixel value greater than 0 in the Feather text field in the Options bar. Your resulting selection will have a feathered edge.

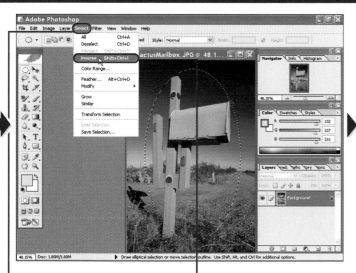

DELETE THE SURROUNDING BACKGROUND

6 Click **Select**.

7 Click **Inverse**.

■ The selection inverts, but remains feathered.

8 Press Delete.

■ You can now see the effect of the feathering.

EXTRACT AN OBJECT

You can remove objects
in an image from their
backgrounds using the
Extract command. This
command can be more
convenient than
removing an object
using the Lasso tool.

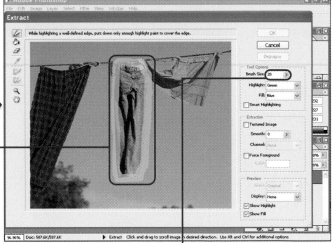

1 Click **Filter**.

2 Click **Extract**.

■ Photoshop displays the
image in the Extract dialog
box.

■ If you make a selection
before you perform the
Extract command, only the
selection is displayed.

3 Click the Edge
Highlighter tool ( ).

4 Highlight the edge of
the object that you want to
extract from the background.

■ The highlighting should
overlay both the object and
the background evenly.

■ You can change the
size of the highlighter. For
defined edges, use a smaller
brush size; for fuzzier edges,
use a larger brush size.

My extraction has rough edges. What can I do?

You can improve a less-than-perfect extraction by clicking **Show** and then **Original** in the Extract dialog box. Click **Show Highlight** and **Show Fill** (☐ changes to ☑). You can then edit your work. Click 🖉 to erase any errant highlighting, and then rehighlight those edges with the highlighter (🖉). Adjusting the value from 0 to 100 in the Smooth box can also help fine-tune the extraction process.

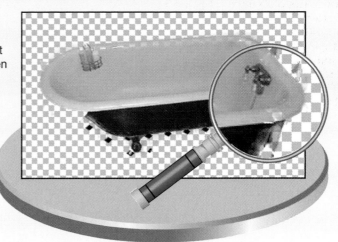

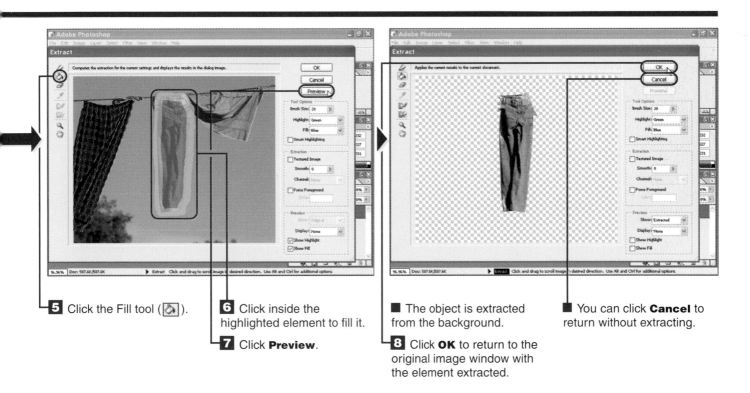

5 Click the Fill tool (🖱).

6 Click inside the highlighted element to fill it.

7 Click **Preview**.

■ The object is extracted from the background.

8 Click **OK** to return to the original image window with the element extracted.

■ You can click **Cancel** to return without extracting.

Specifying Color Modes

Do you want to reduce the number of colors in your image or convert a color image to black and white? This chapter shows you how by specifying different color modes for your images.

Work in RGB Mode 90

Convert a Color Image
   to Grayscale 92

Create a Duotone.............................94

Create a Bitmap Image.....................96

WORK IN RGB MODE

You can work with a color image in RGB mode. RGB is the most common mode for working with color images in Photoshop.

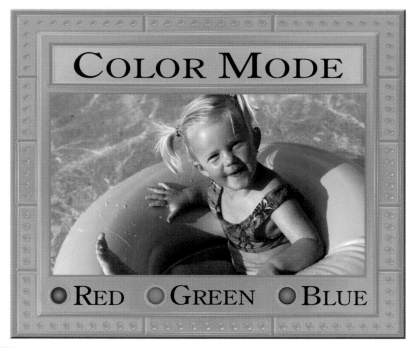

RGB stands for Red, Green, Blue. In RGB mode, the image is stored as a combination of these three primary colors.

WORK IN RGB MODE

1 Click **Image**.

2 Click **Mode**.

3 Click **RGB Color**.

■ *RGB* is displayed in the image's title bar.

■ You can view the different color components of an RGB image with the Channels palette.

4 Click **Window**.

5 Click **Channels**.

■ The Channels palette opens.

6 Click the Red channel.

■ A grayscale version of the image displays the amount of red the image contains. Lighter areas mean lots of red; darker areas mean very little red.

What is CMYK mode?

Photoshop's CMYK mode represents an image's color information as a mix of cyan (C), magenta (M), yellow (Y), and black (K). You can use CMYK mode when your image needs to undergo color separation in preparation for commercial offset printing. To switch to CMYK mode, click **Image**, **Mode**, and then **CMYK Color**. Many inkjet printers are CMYK as well.

7 Click the Green channel.

■ The amount of green in the image is displayed.

8 Click the Blue channel.

■ The amount of blue in the image is displayed.

9 Click the RGB channel to return to the full-color image.

■ Working with channels can be useful when correcting color casts, or when masking low-contrast areas of an image.

CONVERT A COLOR IMAGE TO GRAYSCALE

You can remove the color from your image by converting it to grayscale mode. This can give an image an old-fashioned look. *Grayscale* images are made up of pixels that are white, gray, and black.

CONVERT A COLOR IMAGE TO GRAYSCALE

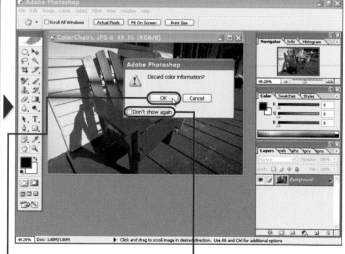

■1 Click **Image**.

■2 Click **Mode**.

■3 Click **Grayscale**.

■ Photoshop displays an alert box.

■4 Click **OK**.

■ You can click the **Don't Show Again** check box (☐ changes to ☑) to avoid the alert in the future.

**How do I make just part of my
image grayscale?**

Define the area you want to turn
gray with a selection tool and
click **Image**, **Adjust**, and
then **Desaturate**. See
Chapter 4 for more about
the selection tools.

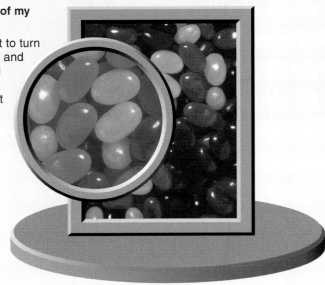

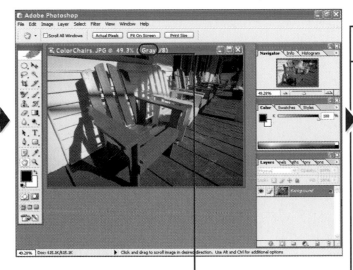

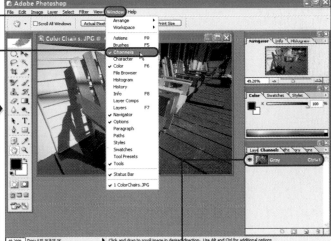

■ Every pixel in the image is
converted to one of 256
shades of gray.

■ *Gray* is displayed in the
image title bar.

5 Click **Window**.

6 Click **Channels**.

■ Grayscale images have a
single channel (compared to
an RGB image's three —
see "Work in RGB Mode"),
so grayscale image files take
up less space than RGB
images.

CREATE A DUOTONE

You can convert a grayscale image to a duotone. This is an easy way to add some color to a black-and-white photo.

A *duotone* is essentially a grayscale image with a color tint.

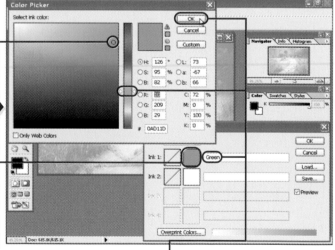

1 If you are working with a color image, convert it to grayscale.

Note: See the section "Convert a Color Image to Grayscale."

2 Click **Image**.

3 Click **Mode**.

4 Click **Duotone**.

5 Click ![v] ([⇕]) and click **Duotone**.

6 Click the first color swatch to open the Color Picker dialog box.

7 Click inside the window to select your first duotone color.

■ You can click and drag the slider to change the color selection.

8 Click **OK**.

9 Type a name for the color.

How can I use duotones?

Duotones offer a quick and easy way to add color to a Web page or printed publication when all you have available are grayscale images.

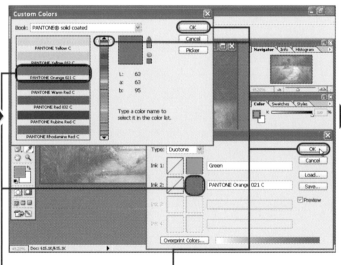

10 Click the second color swatch to open the Custom Colors dialog box.

11 Click inside the window to select your second duotone color.

■ You can click and drag the slider to change the color selection.

12 Click **OK**.

13 Click **OK** in the Duotone Options dialog box.

■ Photoshop uses the two selected colors to create the tones in the image.

CREATE A BITMAP IMAGE

You can convert a grayscale image to a bitmap image. This can produce a photocopied effect. In Photoshop, a bitmap image is made up of only black pixels and white pixels.

The term *bitmap* is also used to describe any image made up of pixels. There is a file format called *bitmap,* abbreviated BMP, as well.

CREATE A BITMAP IMAGE

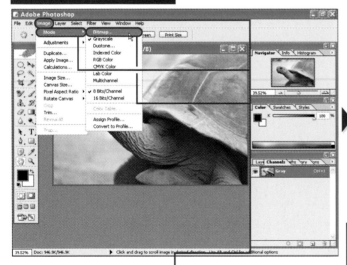

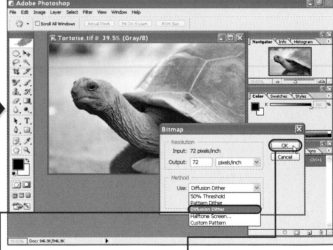

1 If you are working with a color image, convert it to grayscale.

Note: See the section "Convert a Color Image to Grayscale."

2 Click **Image**.

3 Click **Mode**.

4 Click **Bitmap**.

5 Click ⌄ ( ) and select an option for simulating the grayscale tones with black pixels and white pixels.

6 Click **OK**.

How can I convert just part of my image to black and white pixels?

Select an area of the image and click **Image**, **Adjust**, and then **Threshold**. Photoshop converts the selected pixels to black pixels and white pixels. You can adjust the slider in the Threshold dialog box to achieve different effects.

| 0 | 63 | 126 | 189 | 255 |

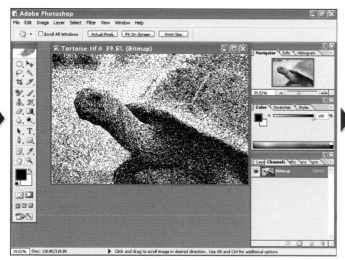

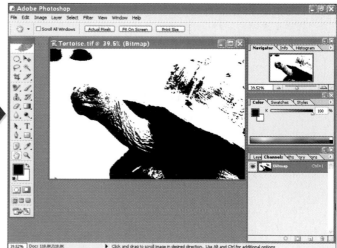

■ Photoshop converts the image to bitmap mode.

■ This figure shows the Diffusion Dither option, in which a random mixture of black pixels and white pixels simulate the grayscale tones.

■ This figure shows the 50% Threshold option, in which pixels that are less than 50% black turn to white and pixels that are 50% or more black turn to black.

CHAPTER 7

Painting and Drawing with Color

Want to add splashes, streaks, or solid areas of color to your image? Photoshop offers a variety of tools with which you can add almost any color imaginable. This chapter introduces you to those tools and shows you how to choose your colors.

Select the Foreground and
  Background Colors.........................100

Select a Web-Safe Color 102

Select a Color with the
  Eyedropper Tool...........................103

Select a Color with the
  Swatches Palette 104

Add a Color to the Swatches Palette....105

Using the Paintbrush Tool 106

Change Brush Styles 108

Create a Custom Brush 110

Using the Pencil Tool.......................112

Apply a Gradient 114

Using the Paint Bucket Tool 116

Fill a Selection 118

Stroke a Selection..........................120

Using the Clone Stamp 122

Using the Pattern Stamp 124

Using the Healing Brush 126

Using the Patch Tool 128

Using the History Brush 130

Using the Eraser.............................132

Replace a Color 134

SELECT THE FOREGROUND AND BACKGROUND COLORS

You can select two colors to work with at a time in Photoshop — a foreground color and a background color. Painting tools such as the Paintbrush apply foreground color. You apply the background color when you use the Eraser tool, enlarge the image canvas, or cut pieces out of your image.

SELECT THE FOREGROUND COLOR

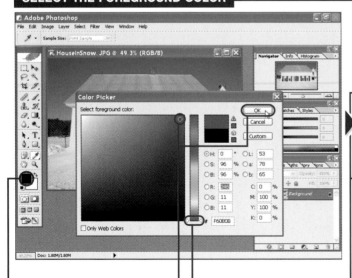

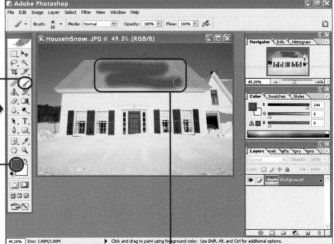

1 Click the Foreground Color box.

■ The Color Picker dialog box appears.

■ To change the range of colors that appears in the color box, click and drag the slider (▷).

2 To select a foreground color, click the color you want in the color box.

3 Click **OK**.

■ The selected color appears in the Foreground Color box.

4 Click a painting tool in the toolbox.

■ This example uses the Paintbrush tool (✐).

Note: For more about painting tools, see the section "Using the Paintbrush Tool."

5 Click and drag to apply the color.

How do I reset the foreground and background colors?

Click the Default icon (■) to the lower left of the Foreground and Background icons. Doing so resets the colors to black and white.

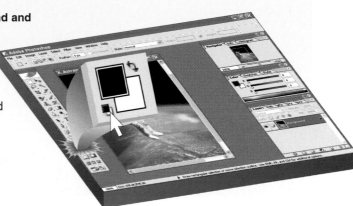

SELECT THE BACKGROUND COLOR

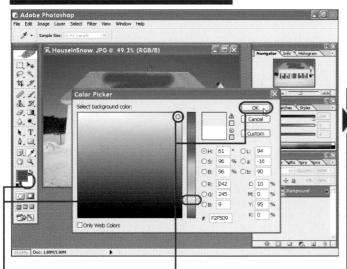

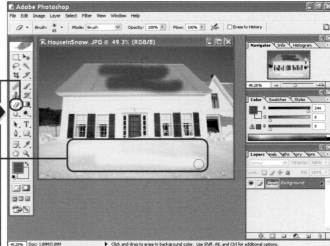

1 Click the Background Color box.

■ To change the range of colors that appears in the color box, click and drag ▷.

2 To select a background color, click the color you want in the color box.

3 Click **OK**.

4 Click the Eraser tool (⬚).

5 Click and drag your cursor (○).

■ The tool "erases" by painting with the background color.

Note: Erasing occurs only in the Background layer; in other layers, the eraser turns pixels transparent. See Chapter 9 for a full discussion of layers.

SELECT A WEB-SAFE COLOR

You can select one of the 216 Web-safe colors as a foreground or background color. A Web-safe color displays accurately in all Web browsers, no matter what type of color monitor or operating system a user has.

See Chapter 15 for information about saving images for the Web.

SELECT A WEB-SAFE COLOR

1 Click the Foreground Color box.

■ Alternatively, to select a Web-safe background color, you can click the Background Color box.

■ The Color Picker dialog box appears.

2 Click **Only Web Colors** (☐ changes to ☑).

■ Photoshop displays only Web-safe colors in the color picker window.

3 Click a color.

■ The hex-code value for the selected color appears here.

4 Click **OK**.

■ The color appears in the Foreground Color box.

SELECT A COLOR WITH THE EYEDROPPER TOOL

You can select a color from an open image with the Eyedropper tool. The Eyedropper tool enables you to paint using a color already present in your image.

SELECT A COLOR WITH THE EYEDROPPER TOOL

1 Click the Eyedropper tool (📷).

2 Place 🖋 over an open image.

■ If you click the **Info** palette tab, you can see color values as you move 🖋.

3 Click to select the color of the pixel beneath the tip of the 🖋.

■ The color becomes the new foreground color.

■ To select a new background color, you can press Alt (option) as you click in step **3**.

You can select a color with the Swatches palette. The Swatches palette lets you choose from a small set of commonly used colors.

SELECT A COLOR WITH THE SWATCHES PALETTE

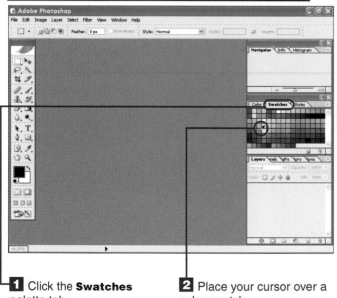

1 Click the **Swatches** palette tab.

2 Place your cursor over a color swatch.

■ ⌖ changes to 🖋.

3 Click a color swatch to select a foreground color.

■ The color becomes the new foreground color.

■ To select a background color, press **Alt** (**option**) as you click in step **3**.

You can add custom
colors to the Swatches
palette. This enables you
to easily select these
colors later.

ADD A COLOR TO THE SWATCHES PALETTE

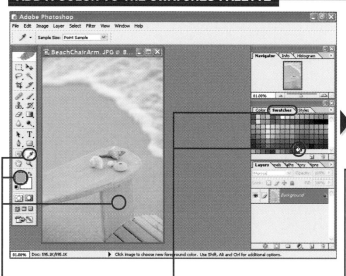

1 Click 🖋.

2 Click inside the image to
select a color.

■ The color appears in the
Foreground Color box.

3 Click the **Swatches**
palette tab.

4 Place 🖋 over an empty
area of the Swatches palette
(🖋 changes to 🖐).

5 Click to add the color.

■ The Color Swatch Name
dialog box appears.

6 Type a name for the new
color swatch.

7 Click **OK**.

■ Photoshop adds the color
as a new swatch.

■ You can remove a swatch
by clicking it and dragging it
to 🗑.

USING THE PAINTBRUSH TOOL

You can use the Paintbrush tool to add color to your image. You may find the paintbrush useful for applying bands of color.

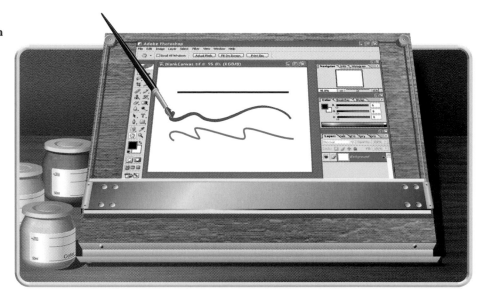

To limit where the paintbrush applies color, create a selection before painting. For details, see Chapter 4.

USING THE PAINTBRUSH TOOL

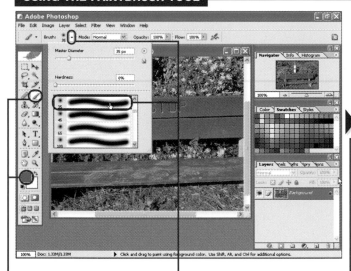

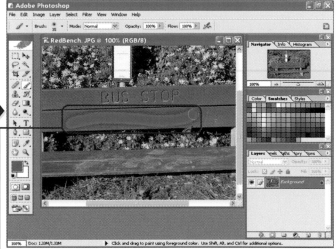

1 Click the Paintbrush tool (☐).

2 Click the Foreground Color box to select a color with which to paint.

Note: For details, see the section "Select the Foreground and Background Colors."

3 Click the Brush ⊡ and select a brush size and type.

4 Click and drag to apply the foreground color to the image.

■ To undo the most recent brush stroke, you can click **Edit** and then **Undo Paintbrush**.

Note: To undo more than one brush stroke, see Chapter 2 for more about the History palette.

What is the Airbrush tool?

You can convert your paintbrush to an airbrush by clicking the Airbrush button () in the Options bar. The Airbrush paints soft lines that get darker the longer you hold down your mouse button.

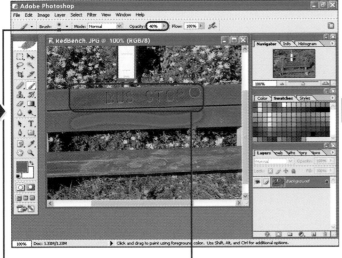

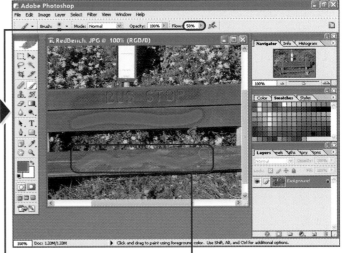

5 Type a percentage value to change the opacity of the brush strokes.

■ Alternatively, you can click the Opacity ▶ and adjust the slider.

6 Click and drag to apply the semitransparent paintbrush.

7 Type a percentage value to change how much color the brush applies.

■ Alternatively, you can click the Flow ▶ and adjust the slider.

8 Click and drag to apply the customized paintbrush.

■ Photoshop applies color per your specifications.

CHANGE BRUSH STYLES

You can select from a variety of predefined brush styles to apply color in different ways. Some of the types of brushes available include calligraphic brushes, texture brushes, and brushes that enable you to add drop shadows to objects.

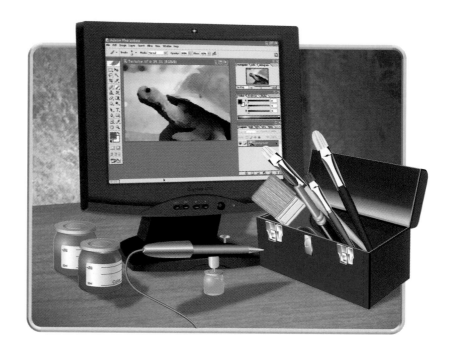

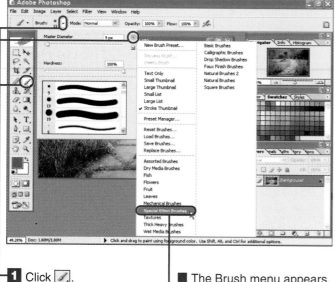

1 Click the brush icon.

2 Click the Brush ⬝.

3 Click ▸.

■ The Brush menu appears.

4 Click a set of brushes.

5 A dialog box appears asking if you want to replace your brushes. Click **OK**.

■ To add the set of brushes to the currently displayed set, click **Append**.

■ If a dialog box appears asking if you want to save the current brush set, click **No**.

Note: You can reset your brushes to the original set by selecting **Reset Brushes** *from the Brush menu.*

How can I make a brush apply scattered dots instead of a line?

Open the Brushes palette by clicking **Window** and then **Brushes**. Click the Scattering checkbox (☐ changes to ☑). Photoshop displays an example of the custom brush stroke at the bottom of the palette. You can change the scattering settings with the controls on the right side of the palette. After closing the Brushes palette, you can apply the customized brush like any other brush.

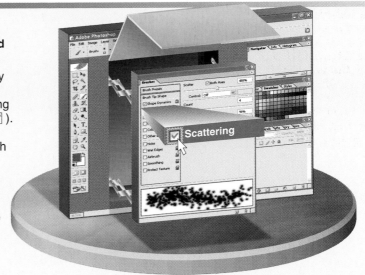

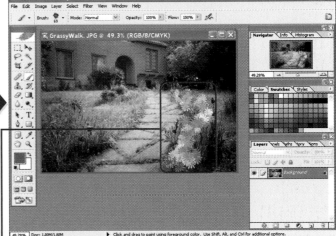

■ The new set appears in the Brush menu.

■ You can click ▒ to view all the brush styles.

6 Click a brush style to select it.

7 Click and drag to apply the new paintbrush.

■ Photoshop applies color with the brush.

■ In this example, the custom brush applies a combination of the foreground and background colors.

CREATE A CUSTOM BRUSH

You can use the Brushes palette to create one-of-a-kind brushes of varying sizes and shapes. You can even specify a brush shape that changes as it paints, to generate a random design.

CREATE A CUSTOM BRUSH

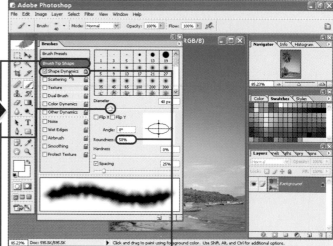

1 Click 🖌.

2 Click the Brush ⋅ and select a brush style to use as a starting point for your custom brush.

3 Click 🗐 to open the Brushes palette.

■ The Brushes palette opens.

4 Click **Brush Tip Shape**.

5 Click and drag the Diameter slider (◻) to change the brush size.

6 Type a Roundness value between 0% and 100%. The lower the number, more oval the brush.

■ You can adjust other settings to further define the tip shape.

7 Click **Shape Dynamics** (◻ changes to ☑).

How do I save my custom brush in the Brush drop-down menu?

Click the Brush ⬝ and then click ▦. A dialog box appears and asks you to name your custom brush. Type a name and then click **OK** to add your brush to the Brush menu.

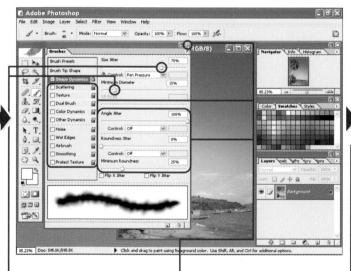

8 Click and drag the Size Jitter slider to specify the amount your brush varies in size as it paints.

9 Click and drag the Minimum Diameter slider to specify the smallest size to which the brush scales when Size Jitter is enabled.

10 Click and drag the other sliders to control how the brush angle and roundness change.

■ You can click other categories to define other settings.

11 Click ☒ (⬤) to close the Brushes palette.

12 Click and drag to apply the custom brush.

USING THE PENCIL TOOL

You can use the Pencil tool to draw hard-edged lines of color. Its lines are more jagged than the paintbrush's.

USING THE PENCIL TOOL

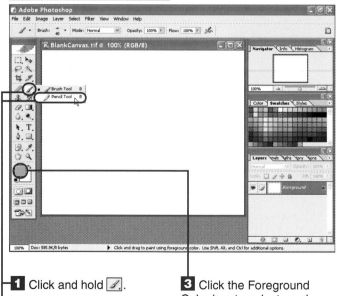

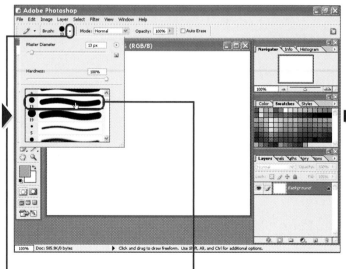

1 Click and hold ✏.

2 From the list that appears, select the Pencil tool (✏).

3 Click the Foreground Color box to select a color with which to draw.

Note: For details, see the section "Select the Foreground and Background Colors."

4 Click the Brush ⊡.

5 Click to select a brush size and type.

What is the Auto Erase function?

If you click **Auto Erase**
(☐ changes to ☑) in the
Options bar, the Pencil tool acts
like an eraser when you click and
drag it over the foreground color
in your image. If you first click
colors other than the foreground
color, it acts like a regular pencil.
For more about the Eraser tool,
see the section "Using the
Eraser" in this chapter.

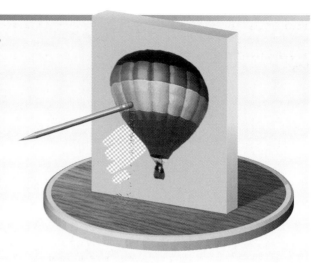

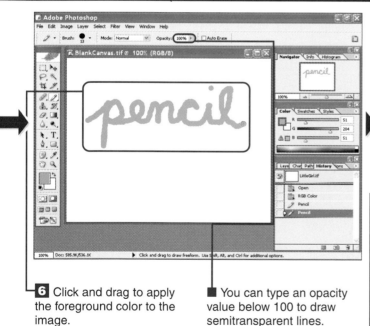

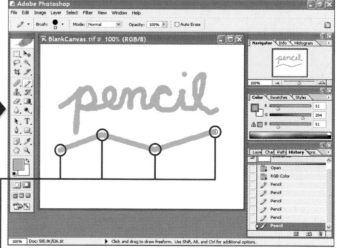

6 Click and drag to apply
the foreground color to the
image.

■ You can type an opacity
value below 100 to draw
semitransparent lines.

DRAW STRAIGHT LINES

7 Press and hold Shift.

8 Click several places
inside your image, without
dragging.

■ Photoshop draws straight
lines between the clicked
points.

APPLY A GRADIENT

You can apply a gradient, which is a transition from one color to another. This can give objects or areas in your image a shaded or 3D look.

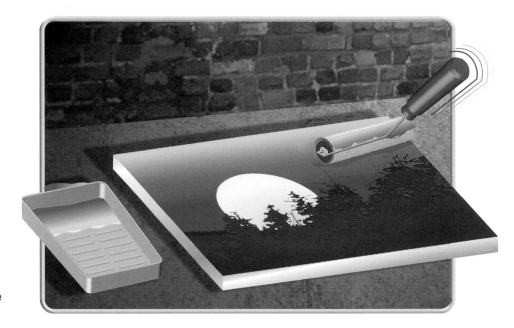

For another way to add a gradient to your image, see Chapter 9.

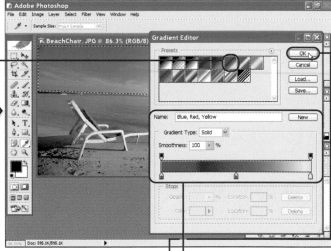

1 Make a selection.

Note: See Chapter 4 for more about making selections.

2 Click the Gradient tool ( ).

■ A linear gradient is the default. You can select different geometries in the Options bar.

3 Click the gradient swatch.

■ The Gradient Editor appears.

4 Select a preset gradient type from the top list box.

■ Photoshop shows the settings for the selected gradient below.

■ You can customize the gradient using the settings.

5 Click **OK**.

114

How can I add a rainbow gradient to my image?

Click a rainbow swatch in the Gradient Editor. When you click and drag the Gradient tool, it applies the spectrum of colors from red to violet.

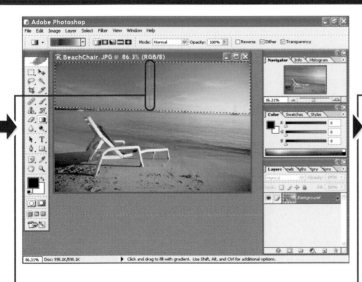

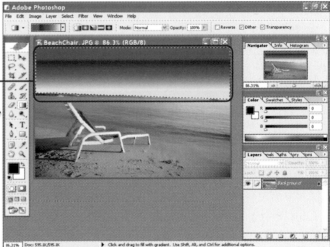

6 Click and drag inside the selection.

Note: This defines the direction and transition of the gradient. Dragging a long line with the tool produces a gradual transition. Dragging a short line with the tool produces an abrupt transition.

■ Photoshop generates a gradient inside the selection.

USING THE PAINT BUCKET TOOL

You can fill areas in your image with solid color using the Paint Bucket tool.

The Paint Bucket tool affects only adjacent pixels in the image. You can set the Paint Bucket's Tolerance value to determine what range of colors the paint bucket affects in the image when you apply it.

To fill the pixels of a selected area, rather than just adjacent pixels, see the section "Fill a Selection."

USING THE PAINT BUCKET TOOL

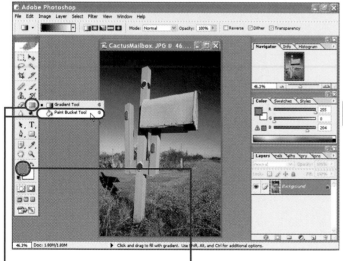

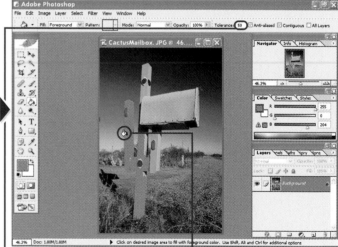

1 Click and hold ▣.

2 From the list that appears, select the Paint Bucket tool (⬛).

3 Click the Foreground Color box to select a color for painting.

Note: For details, see the section "Select the Foreground and Background Colors."

4 Type a Tolerance value from 0 to 255.

■ With a low value, the tool fills only adjacent colors that are very similar to that of the clicked pixel. A high value fills a broader range of colors.

5 Click inside the image.

■ Photoshop fills an area of the image with the foreground color.

How can I reset a tool to its default settings?

Right-click (Control +click) the tool's icon on the far left side of the Options bar and select **Reset Tool** from the menu that appears.

ADJUST OPACITY

6 To fill an area with a semitransparent color, type a percentage value of less than 100 in the Opacity field.

7 Click inside the image.

■ Photoshop fills an area with see-through paint.

CONSTRAIN THE COLOR

8 To constrain where you apply the color, make a selection before clicking.

■ In this example, the opacity was reset to 100%.

9 Click inside the selection.

■ The fill effect stays within the boundary of the selection.

FILL A SELECTION

You can fill a selection using the Fill command. The Fill command is an alternative to the Paint Bucket tool. The Fill command differs from the Paint Bucket tool in that it fills the entire selected area, not just adjacent pixels based on a tolerance value.

See the section "Using the Paint Bucket Tool" if you want to fill adjacent pixels rather than a selected area.

FILL A SELECTION

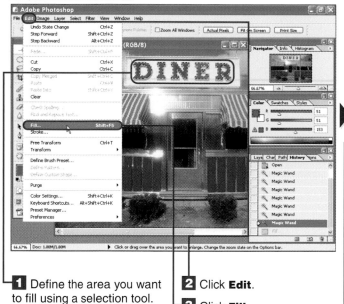

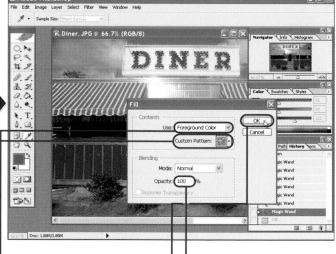

1 Define the area you want to fill using a selection tool.

Note: See Chapter 4 for more about using the selection tools.

2 Click **Edit**.

3 Click **Fill**.

4 Click ∨ (🔽) and select with what you want to fill.

■ To use the Custom Pattern option, use the Rectangular Marquee tool (▭) to select an area of the image with which you want to fill. Next, click **Edit** and then **Define Pattern**.

■ You can decrease the opacity to fill with a semi-transparent color or pattern.

5 Click **OK**.

How do I apply a "ghosted" white layer over part of an image?

Use a selection tool to define the area of the image that you want to cover. Then apply the Fill command with white selected and the opacity set to less than 50%.

What does the Preserve Transparency option in the Fill dialog box do?

If you click Preserve Transparency (☐ changes to ☑) and perform a fill, Photoshop only fills pixels that are not transparent in the layer. Photoshop leaves transparent pixels alone. This option lets you easily color objects that exist by themselves in a layer.

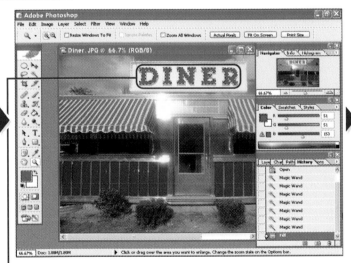

■ Photoshop fills the area.

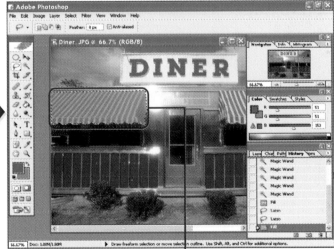

■ You can select other areas and fill them with different colors.

■ This example uses a fill with the background color set to 60% opacity.

STROKE A SELECTION

You can use the Stroke command to draw a line along the edge of a selection. This can help you highlight objects in your image.

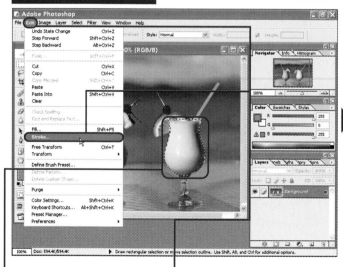

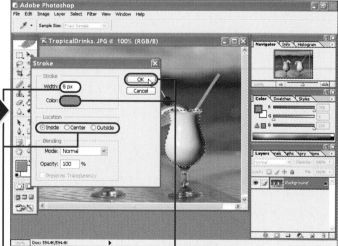

1 Select an area of the image with a selection tool.

Note: See Chapter 4 for more about using the selection tools.

2 Click **Edit**.

3 Click **Stroke**.

■ The Stroke dialog box appears.

4 Type a width.

5 Click **Inside** to stroke a line on the inside of the selection, **Center** to stroke a line straddling the selection, or **Outside** to stroke a line on the outside of the selection (○ changes to ◉).

■ You can click the Color box to define the color of the stroke.

6 Click **OK**.

**How do I add a colored
border to my image?**

Click **Select** and then **All**.
Then apply the Stroke
command, clicking
Inside as the Location
(◯ changes to ◉).
Photoshop adds a
border to the image.

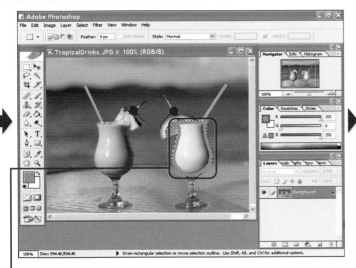

■ Photoshop strokes a line
along the selection.

■ You can select other
areas and stroke them using
different settings.

■ This stroke was applied to
the outside of the selection
at 50% opacity.

USING THE CLONE STAMP

You can clean up small flaws or erase elements in your image with the Clone Stamp tool. This tool copies information from one area of an image to another.

For other ways to correct defects in your image, see the sections "Using the Healing Brush" and "Using the Patch Tool."

USING THE CLONE STAMP

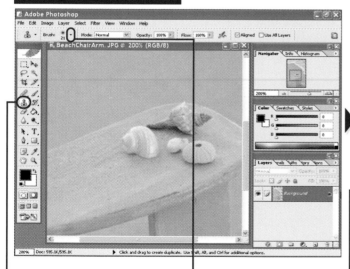

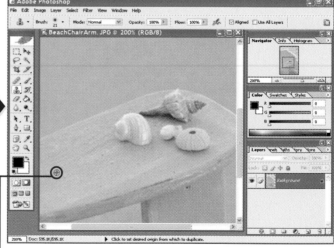

1 Click the Clone Stamp tool (⬚).

2 Click the Brush ⬚ and select a brush size and type.

3 Press and hold **Alt** (**option**) and click the area of the image from which you want to copy.

■ You do not need to select an area inside the current image; you can click another open image.

■ This example uses the tool to select an empty area of a chair.

How can I make the clone stamp's effects look seamless?

To erase elements from your image with the clone stamp without leaving a trace, try the following:

■ Clone between areas of similar color and texture.

■ To apply the clone stamp more subtly, lower its opacity in the Options bar.

■ After you click the Brush ▪, choose a soft-edged brush shape.

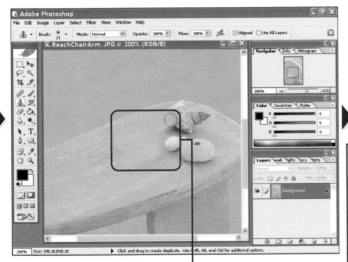

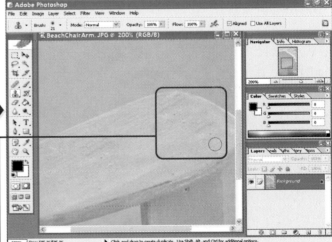

4 Release the Alt (option) key.

5 Click and drag to apply the clone stamp.

■ Photoshop copies the previously clicked area to where you click and drag.

6 Click and drag repeatedly over the image to achieve the desired effect.

■ As you apply the tool, you can press Alt (option) and click again to select a different area from which to copy.

USING THE PATTERN STAMP

You can paint with a pattern using the Pattern Stamp tool. This tool gives you a free-form way to add repeating elements to your images.

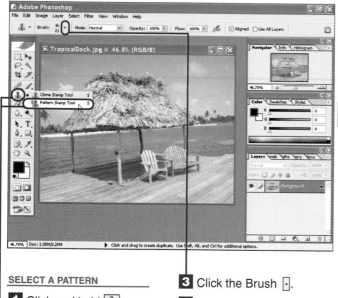

SELECT A PATTERN

1 Click and hold ![stamp icon].

2 From the list that appears, select the Pattern Stamp tool (![icon]).

3 Click the Brush ![].

4 Select a brush size and type.

5 Click the Pattern ![].

6 Select a pattern to apply.

■ You can click **Aligned** (☐ changes to ☑) to make your different strokes paint the pattern as contiguous tiles.

How do I define my own custom patterns?

Select what you want to use as a pattern in the image window with the Rectangular Marquee tool (▢), click **Edit**, and then click **Define Pattern**. A dialog box appears and asks you to name the new pattern. You can click **OK** to add the new pattern to the Pattern menu. For more about the Rectangular Marquee tool and how to select objects, see Chapter 4.

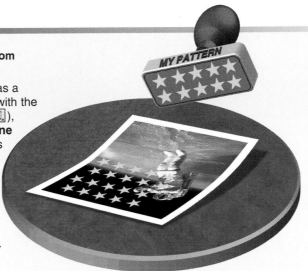

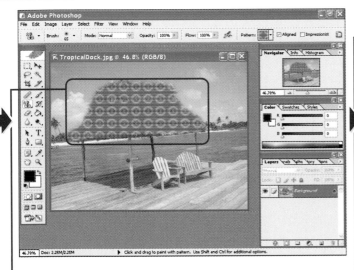

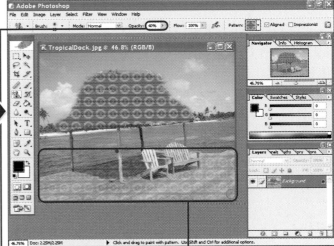

7 Click and drag to apply the pattern.

■ Photoshop applies the pattern to where you click and drag.

APPLY A DIFFERENT OPACITY

8 Type a value of less than 100 in the Opacity box.

9 Click and drag inside the selection to apply the pattern.

■ Decreasing the opacity causes the brush to apply a semi-transparent pattern.

USING THE HEALING BRUSH

You can correct defects in your image using the Healing Brush. The Healing Brush is similar to the Clone Stamp in that it copies pixels from one area of the image to another. However, the Healing Brush takes into account the texture and lighting of the image as it works, which can make its modifications more convincing.

USING THE HEALING BRUSH

1 Click the Healing Brush tool ().

2 Click the Brush ⬇ and specify your brush settings.

■ Make sure **Sampled** is selected (○ changes to ◉).

3 Press and hold `Alt` (`option`) and click the area of the image with which you want to heal.

What does the Healing Brush's Pattern option do?

You can use it to correct defects in your image by painting over them with a predefined pattern. This can be useful if you want to apply a specific texture over defects, rather than pixels cloned from somewhere in the image.

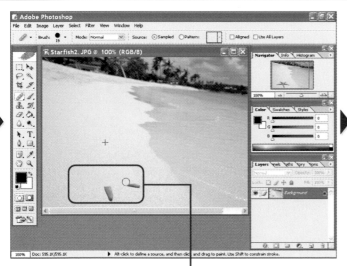

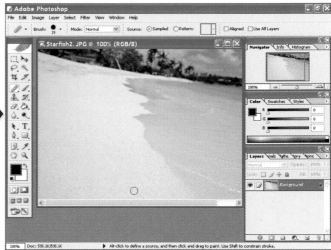

4 Release the Alt (option) key.

5 Click and drag inside the selection to apply the healing stamp.

■ Photoshop copies the selected area to where you click and drag.

6 Stop dragging and release the mouse button.

■ Photoshop adjusts the copied pixels to account for the lighting and texture present in the image.

USING THE PATCH TOOL

The Patch tool lets you correct defects in your image by selecting them and dragging the selection to an unflawed area of your image. This can be useful if there is a large part of your image that is without flaws.

For other ways to correct defects in your image, see the sections "Using the Clone Stamp" and "Using the Healing Brush."

USING THE PATCH TOOL

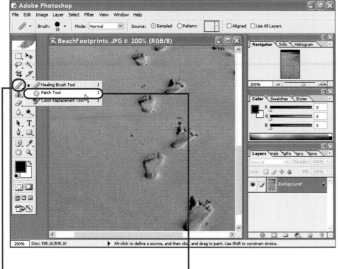

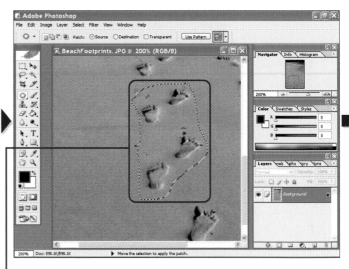

1 Click the Healing Brush tool (🖌️).

2 From the list that appears, click the Patch tool (🩹).

3 Click and drag to select the part of your image that contains the defects that you want to patch.

■ When making selections, the Patch tool works similarly to the Lasso tool. See Chapter 4 for more about the Lasso tool.

How does the Patch tool determine what are defects in my selection?

It does it by comparing what color and texture are the same in the two selections, and what color and texture are different. The tool then tries to eliminate the differences — the defects — while retaining the overall color and texture.

Before

After

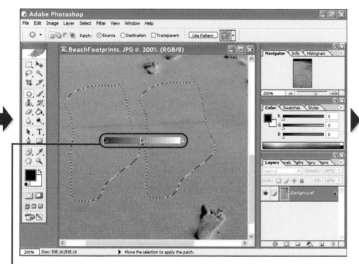

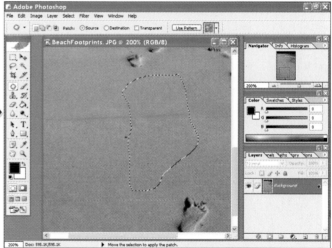

4 Click inside the selection and drag it to an area that does not have defects.

■ Photoshop uses pixels from the destination selection to patch the defects in the source selection.

■ You can click **Destination** (○ changes to ◉) to patch defects in the reverse order — flaws in the destination selection are corrected with the pixels from the source selection.

USING THE HISTORY BRUSH

You can use the History brush to paint a previous state of your image from the History palette into the current image. This can be useful if you want to revert just a part of your image.

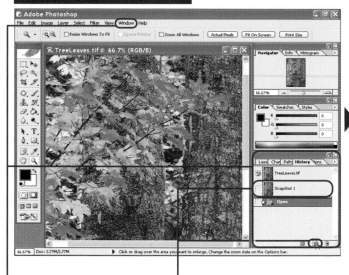

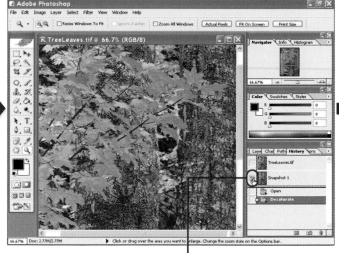

1 Click **Window**.

2 Click **History**.

■ The History palette opens.

3 Click the New Snapshot button (■) in the History palette.

■ Photoshop puts a copy of the current state of the image into the History palette.

4 Modify your image to make it different from the newly created snapshot.

■ In this example, the image was desaturated.

5 Click to the left side of the snapshot to select it as the History brush source.

130

How do I paint onto a blank image with the History brush?

Start with a photographic image, take a snapshot of it with the New Snapshot button (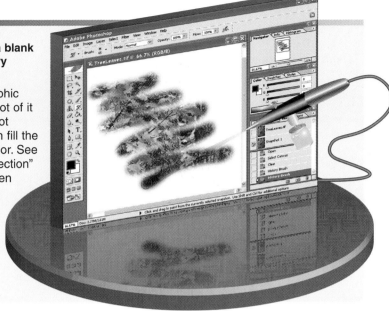), and then fill the image with a solid color. See the section "Fill a Selection" for details. You can then use the History brush (📷) to paint in the photographic content.

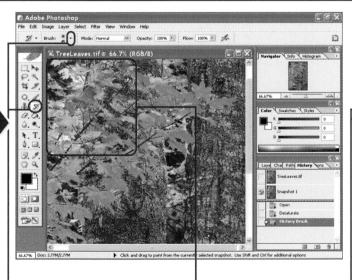

6 Click the History brush (📷).

7 Click the Brush ⬝ and specify your brush settings.

8 Click and drag inside the image.

■ Pixels from the previous snapshot are painted into the image.

USING THE ART HISTORY BRUSH

1 Click and hold 📷 and select the Art History brush(📷).

■ With the Art History brush, you can paint in snapshot information with an added impressionistic effect.

2 Click the Brush ⬝ to specify the settings for the brush.

3 Click and drag to apply an artistic effect.

USING THE ERASER

You can delete elements from your images using the Eraser tool. This can be useful when you are trying to separate elements from their backgrounds.

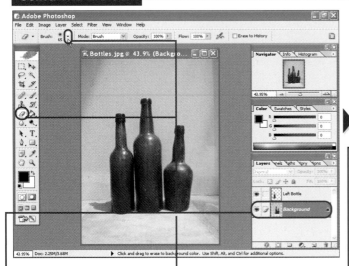

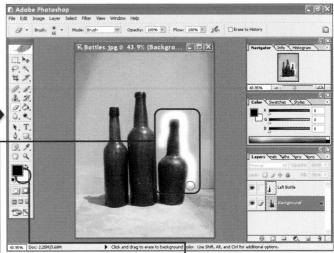

IN THE BACKGROUND LAYER

1 Click the Background layer in the Layers palette.

■ If you start with a newly scanned image, the Background layer is the only layer.

Note: See Chapter 9 for more about layers.

2 Click the Eraser tool ( ).

3 Click the Brush and select a brush size and type.

4 Click and drag inside the image.

■ Photoshop erases the image by painting with the background color.

How can I erase areas of similar color in my image quickly?

If you click and hold  in the toolbox, a list appears, and you can select the Background Eraser (⬚) or the Magic Eraser (⬚). The Background Eraser works by sampling the pixel color beneath the center of the brush and erasing similar colors that are underneath the brush. The Magic Eraser also samples the color beneath the cursor but erases similar pixels throughout the layer. You can adjust the Tolerance of both tools in the Options bar to control how much they erase.

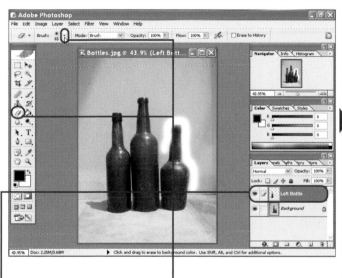

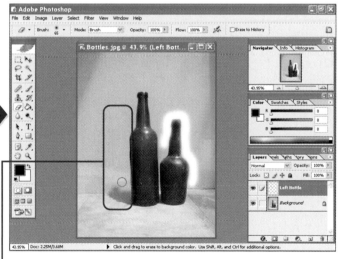

IN A REGULAR LAYER

1 Click a nonbackground layer in the Layers palette.

Note: See Chapter 9 for more about layers.

2 Click the Eraser tool (⬚).

3 Click the Brush ⬚ and select a brush size and type.

4 Click and drag inside the image.

■ Photoshop erases elements in the layer by making pixels transparent.

REPLACE A COLOR

You can replace colors in your image with the current foreground color using the Color Replacement tool. This gives you a free-form way of recoloring objects in your image.

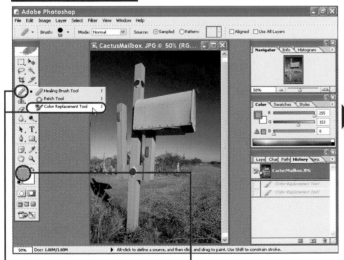

1 Click and hold 🖌.

2 From the list that appears, select the Color Replacement tool (🖌).

3 Click the Foreground Color box to select a color for painting.

Note: For details, see the section "Select the Foreground and Background Colors."

4 Click the Brush ⬚ and select a brush size and type.

5 Click ⬚ (🔀) and select a sampling method.

■ **Continuous** samples different colors to replace as you paint.

■ **Once** samples only the first color you click.

How does the Color Replacement tool decide what colors to replace?

When you click inside your image, the Color Replacement tool samples the color beneath the cross symbol at the center of the cursor. It then replaces any colors inside the brush that are similar to the sampled color. Photoshop determines similarity based on the Tolerance setting of the tool.

How can I replace more than one color?

You can press Shift and then click inside your image to add other colors to your selection. The white area inside the Selection box increases as you click. To deselect colors from your selection, press Alt (option) and then click a color inside your image.

6 Type a tolerance from 1% to 100%.

■ The greater the tolerance, the greater the range of colors the tool replaces.

7 Click and drag in your image to replace color.

8 Continue to click and drag in your image to replace more color.

CHAPTER 8

Adjusting Colors

Do you want to fine-tune the colors in your image — darken them, lighten them, or remove them completely? This chapter introduces the tools that do the trick.

Change Brightness and Contrast 138

Using the Dodge and Burn Tools 140

Using the Blur and Sharpen Tools......142

Adjust Levels 144

Adjust Hue and Saturation................146

Using the Sponge Tool 148

Adjust Color Balance 150

Using the Variations Command 152

Match Colors Between Images..........154

Correct Shadows and Highlights 156

CHANGE BRIGHTNESS AND CONTRAST

The Brightness/Contrast command provides a simple way to make adjustments to the highlights and shadows of your image.

To change the brightness or contrast of small parts of your image, use the Dodge or Burn tool. See the section "Using the Dodge and Burn Tools" in this chapter for details.

If you make a selection before performing the Brightness/Contrast command, changes affect only the selected pixels. Similarly, if you have a multilayered image, your adjustments affect only the selected layer. See Chapter 4 to make a selection, and Chapter 9 for more about layers.

CHANGE BRIGHTNESS AND CONTRAST

1 Click **Image**.

2 Click **Adjustments**.

3 Click **Brightness/Contrast**.

■ The Brightness/Contrast dialog box appears with sliders set to 0.

4 To display your adjustments in the image window as you make them, click **Preview** (□ changes to ☑).

5 Click and drag the Brightness slider (📷).

■ Drag 📷 to the right to lighten the image, or to the left to darken the image.

■ You can also lighten the image by typing a number from 1 to 100, or darken the image by typing a negative number from −1 to −100.

How can I adjust the contrast of an image automatically?

Click **Image**, **Adjustments**, and then **Auto Contrast**. Photoshop converts the very lightest pixels in the image to white and the very darkest pixels in the image to black. Making the highlights brighter and the shadows darker boosts the contrast, which can improve the appearance of poorly exposed photographs.

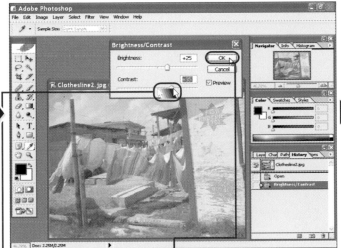

6 Click and drag the Contrast slider ( ).

■ Drag to the right to increase the contrast, or to the left to decrease the contrast.

Note: Increasing contrast can bring out details in your image. Decreasing it can soften the details.

■ You can also increase the contrast by typing a number from 1 to 100, or decrease the contrast by typing a negative number from –1 to –100.

7 Click **OK**.

■ Photoshop applies the new brightness and contrast values.

USING THE DODGE AND BURN TOOLS

You can use the Dodge and Burn tools to brighten or darken a specific area of an image, respectively.

Dodge is a photographic term that describes the diffusing of light when developing a film negative. *Burn* is a photographic term that describes the focusing of light when developing a film negative.

These tools are an alternative to the Brightness/Contrast command, which affects the entire image. To brighten or darken the entire image, see the section "Change Brightness and Contrast."

USING THE DODGE TOOL

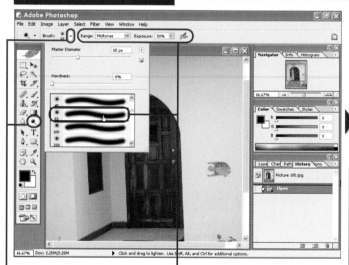

1 Click the Dodge tool (🔍).

2 Click the Brush ⏷.

3 Click the brush that you want to use.

■ You can also select the range of colors you want to affect and the tool's exposure, or strength.

4 Click and drag over the area that you want to lighten.

■ Photoshop lightens the area.

How do I invert the bright and dark colors in an image?

Click **Image**, **Adjustments**, and then **Invert**. This makes the image look like a film negative. Bright colors become dark, and vice versa.

How can I add extra shadows to the bottom of an object?

Applying the Burn tool ( ) with the Range set to Shadows offers a useful way to add shadows to the shaded side of an object. Likewise, you can use the Dodge tool ( ) with the Range set to Highlights to add highlights to the lighter side of an object.

USING THE BURN TOOL

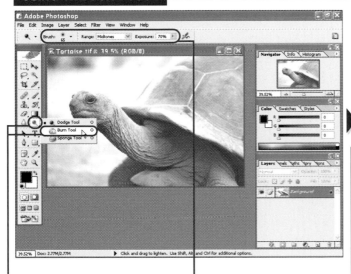

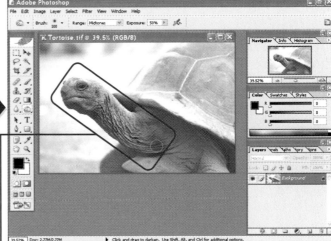

1 Click and hold the Dodge tool ( ).

2 Click the Burn tool ( ) in the list that appears.

■ You can select the brush, the range of colors you want to affect, and the tool's exposure, or strength.

3 Click and drag over the area that you want to darken.

■ Photoshop darkens the area.

USING THE BLUR AND SHARPEN TOOLS

You can sharpen or blur specific areas of your image with the Sharpen and Blur tools. This allows you to emphasize or de-emphasize objects in a photo.

You can blur or sharpen the entire image by using one of the Blur or Sharpen commands located in Photoshop's Filter menu. See Chapter 11 for more information.

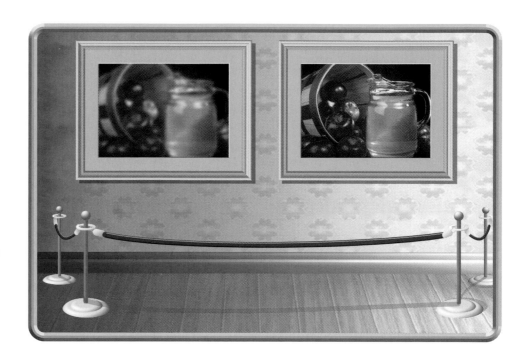

USING THE BLUR TOOL

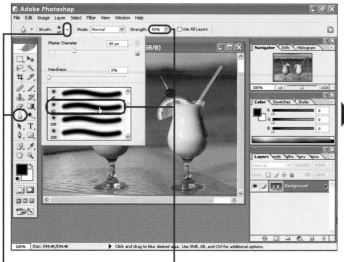

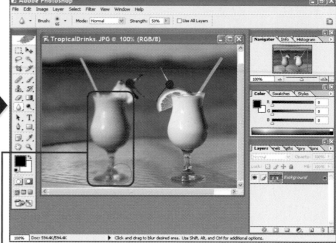

1 Click the Blur tool ().

2 Click the Brush ⏷.

3 Select the brush that you want to use.

■ To change the strength of the tool, type a value from 1% to 100%.

4 Click and drag to blur an area of the image.

What is the Smudge tool?

The Smudge tool ( ) is
another tool in the Photoshop
toolbox. It simulates dragging
a finger through wet paint,
shifting colors and blurring
your image. You can access
it by clicking and holding the
 tool.

USING THE SHARPEN TOOL

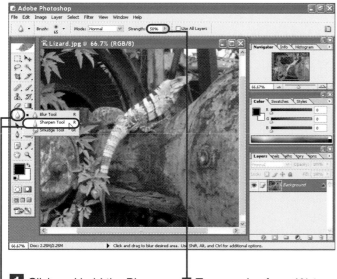

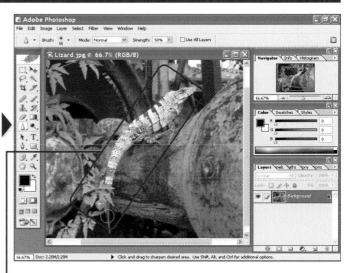

1 Click and hold the Blur
tool ( ).

2 Click the Sharpen tool
( ) in the list that appears.

■ Type a value from 1% to
100% to set the strength of
the tool.

3 Click and drag to
sharpen an area of the
image.

ADJUST LEVELS

You can use the Levels command to make fine adjustments to the highlights, midtones, or shadows of an image.

Although more difficult to use, the Levels command offers more control over brightness than the Brightness/Contrast command covered in the section "Change Brightness and Contrast."

To affect only selected pixels, select them before performing the Levels command. Similarly, in a multilayered image, your adjustments affect only the selected layer.

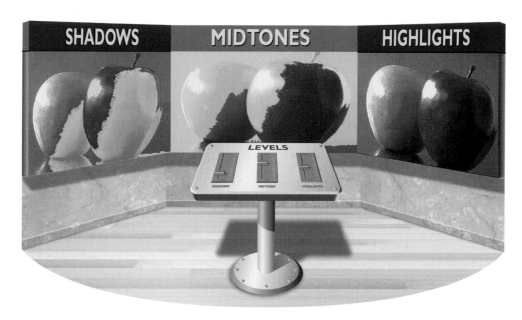

ADJUST LEVELS

1 Click **Image**.

2 Click **Adjustments**.

3 Click **Levels**.

■ The Levels dialog box appears.

4 To display your adjustments in the image window as you make them, click **Preview** (☐ changes to ☑).

■ Use the Input sliders to adjust an image's brightness, midtones, and highlights.

5 Click and drag ▲ to the right to darken shadows and increase contrast.

6 Click and drag △ to the left to lighten the bright areas of the image and increase contrast.

7 Click and drag ▲ to adjust the midtones of the image.

How do you adjust the brightness levels of an image automatically?

Click **Image**, **Adjustments**, and then **Auto Levels**. Photoshop converts the very lightest pixels in the image to white and the very darkest pixels in the image to black. This command is similar to the Auto Contrast command and can quickly improve the contrast of an overly gray photographic image. See the section "Change Brightness and Contrast" for more information.

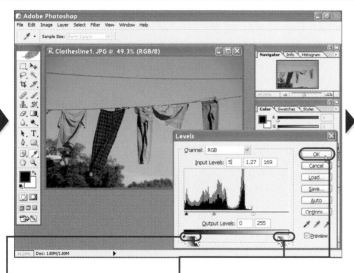

■ You can use the Output sliders to decrease the contrast while either lightening or darkening the image.

8 Click and drag 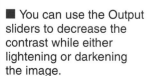 to the right to lighten the image.

9 Click and drag △ to the left to darken the image.

10 Click **OK**.

■ Photoshop makes brightness and contrast adjustments to the image.

ADJUST HUE AND SATURATION

You can change the hue to shift the component colors of an image. You can change the saturation to adjust the color intensity in an image.

If you make a selection before performing the Hue/Saturation command, you affect only the selected pixels. Similarly, if you have a multilayered image, your adjustments affect only the selected layer. See Chapter 4 to make a selection, and Chapter 9 for more about layers.

Hue   Original   Saturation

ADJUST HUE AND SATURATION

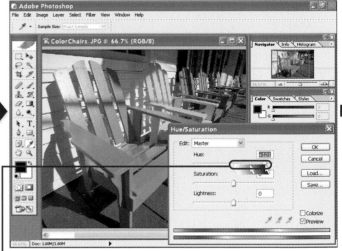

1 Click **Image**.

2 Click **Adjustments**.

3 Click **Hue/Saturation**.

■ The Hue/Saturation dialog box appears.

4 To display your adjustments in the image window as you make them, click **Preview** (☐ changes to ☑).

5 Click and drag the Hue slider (◯) to shift the colors in the image. See the tip on the next page for details.

■ Dragging ◯ left or right shifts the colors in different, and sometimes bizarre, ways.

■ In this example, adjusting the hue has changed the red chair to green.

How does the adjustment of an image's hues work?

When you adjust an image's hues in Photoshop, its colors shift according to their position on the color wheel. The color wheel is a graphical way of presenting all the colors in the visible spectrum.

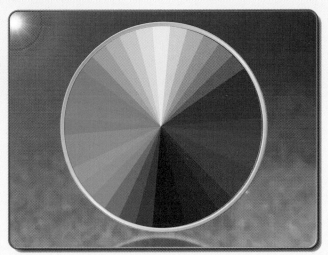

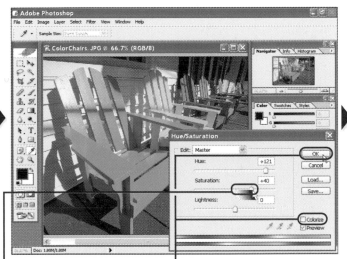

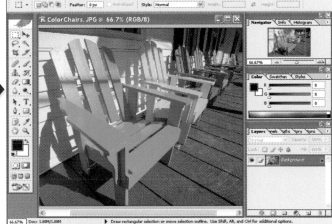

6 Click and drag the Saturation slider (⌂).

■ Dragging ⌂ to the right or to the left increases or decreases the intensity of the image's colors, respectively.

■ Clicking **Colorize** (☐ changes to ☑) turns the image into a monotone, or one-color, image. You can adjust the color with the sliders.

7 Click **OK**.

■ Photoshop makes the color adjustments to the image.

USING THE SPONGE TOOL

You can use the Sponge tool to adjust the color saturation, or color intensity, of a specific area of an image. This can help bring out the colors in washed-out areas of photos.

USING THE SPONGE TOOL

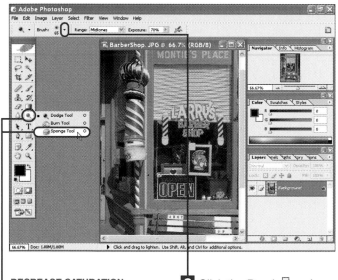

DECREASE SATURATION

1 Click and hold the Dodge tool ( ).

2 Click the Sponge tool ( ) in the list that appears.

3 Click the Brush and select the brush that you want to use.

4 Click ( ) and select **Desaturate**.

5 Click and drag the mouse ( ) to decrease the saturation of an area of the image.

How can I easily convert a color image to a black-and-white image?

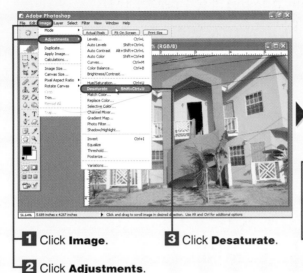

1 Click **Image**.

2 Click **Adjustments**.

3 Click **Desaturate**.

■ Photoshop sets the saturation value of the image to 0, effectively converting it to a black-and-white image.

INCREASE SATURATION

1 Perform steps **1** to **3** on the previous page.

2 Click ⌄ (↕) and select **Saturate**.

3 Click and drag ○ to increase the saturation of an area of the image.

■ You can adjust the strength of the Sponge tool by changing the Flow setting from 1% to 100%.

ADJUST COLOR BALANCE

You can use the Color Balance command to change the amounts of specific colors in your image. This can be useful if you need to remove a color cast introduced by a scanner or by age.

If you make a selection before performing the Color Balance command, you affect only the selected pixels. Similarly, if you have a multilayered image, your adjustments affect only the selected layer. See Chapter 4 to make a selection, and Chapter 9 for more about layers.

ADJUST COLOR BALANCE

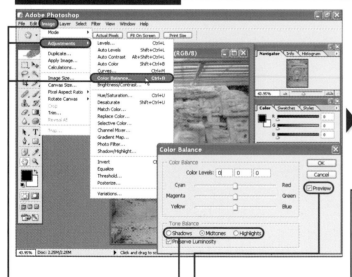

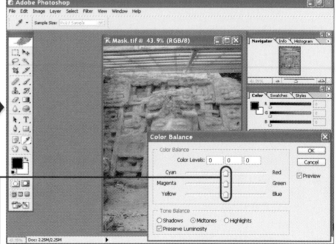

1 Click **Image**.

2 Click **Adjustments**.

3 Click **Color Balance**.

■ The Color Balance dialog box appears.

4 To display your adjustments in the image window as you make them, click **Preview** (☐ changes to ☑).

5 Select the tones in the image that you want to affect (○ changes to ◉).

6 Click and drag a color slider (⌂) toward the color you want to add more of.

■ To add a warm cast to your image, you can drag a slider toward red or magenta. To add a cool cast, you can drag a slider toward blue or cyan.

How can the color balance command help me improve poorly lit digital photos?

The color balance command can help eliminate a color cast that can sometimes permeate a digital photo. For example, some indoor incandescent or fluorescent lighting can add a yellowish or bluish tint to your images. You can remove these tints by adding blue or red, respectively, to your images using the command.

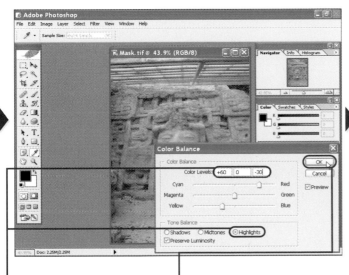

7 Select another tonal range.

8 Type a number from –100 to 100 in one or more of the color level fields.

*Note: Step **8** is an alternative to dragging a slider.*

9 Click **OK**.

■ Photoshop makes color adjustments to the image.

USING THE VARIATIONS COMMAND

The Variations command includes a user-friendly interface that you can use to perform color adjustments in your image.

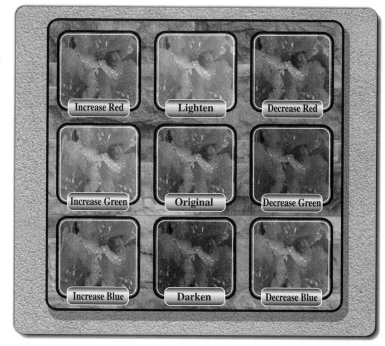

If you make a selection before performing the Variations command, you affect only the selected pixels. Similarly, if you have a multilayered image, your adjustments affect only the selected layer. See Chapter 4 to make a selection, and Chapter 9 for more about layers.

USING THE VARIATIONS COMMAND

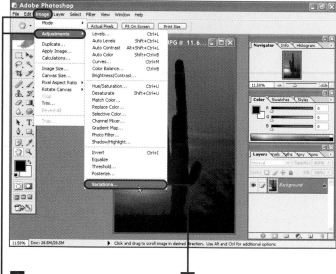

1 Click **Image**.

2 Click **Adjustments**.

3 Click **Variations**.

■ The Variations dialog box appears.

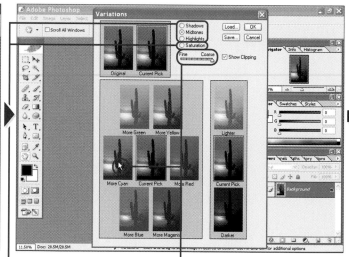

4 Select a tonal range of your image to adjust (○ changes to ◉).

■ Alternatively, you can select **Saturation**, or strength of color (○ changes to ◉).

5 Click and drag ⬜ left to perform small adjustments, or right to make large adjustments.

6 To add a color to your image, click one of the More thumbnails.

How can I undo color adjustments while using the Variations dialog box?

If you clicked one of the More thumbnail images to increase a color, you can click the More thumbnail image opposite to undo the effect.

When you add colors in equal amounts to an image, the colors opposite one another — for example, Green and Magenta — cancel each other out.

Note that clicking the **Original** image in the upper-left corner returns the image to its original state as well.

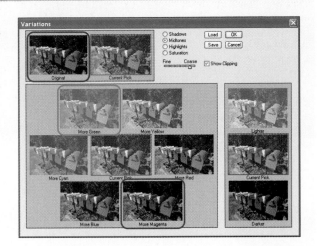

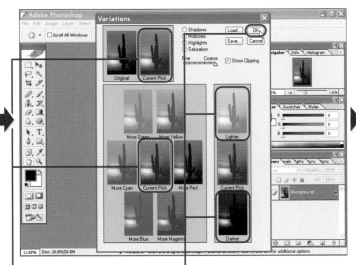

■ The result of the adjustment shows up in the Current Pick thumbnails.

■ To increase the effect, you can click the More thumbnail again.

■ You can decrease the brightness of the image by clicking **Darker**.

■ You can increase the brightness by clicking **Lighter**.

7 Click **OK**.

■ Photoshop makes the color adjustments to the image.

MATCH COLORS BETWEEN IMAGES

You can use the Match Color command to match the colors in one image with the colors from another. For example, you can take the colors from a bluish shoreline image and apply them to a reddish desert image to give the desert image a cooler appearance.

MATCH COLORS BETWEEN IMAGES

1 Open up a source image from which you want to match colors.

2 Open a destination image whose colors you want to change.

3 Click **Image**.

4 Click **Adjustments**.

5 Click **Match Color**.

6 Click ⌄ (⬍) and select the filename of the source image.

How do I match colors using colors from only a selected part of my source image?

Make a selection before performing the Match Color command. Then check the Use Selection in Source to Calculate Colors checkbox (☐ changes to ☑) in the Match Color dialog box. Photoshop uses only colors from inside the selection to determine color replacement.

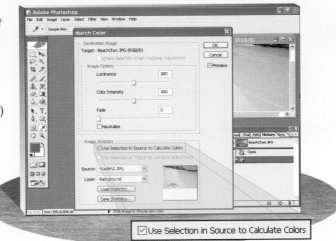

☑ Use Selection in Source to Calculate Colors

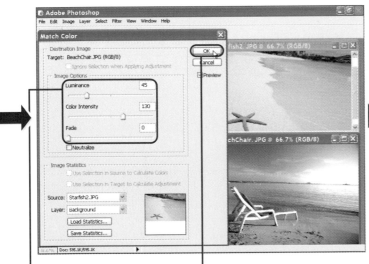

7 Click and drag the sliders (☐) to control how the new colors are applied.

■ **Luminance** controls the brightness.

■ **Color Intensity** controls the saturation.

■ **Fade** controls how much color Photoshop replaces. You can increase the Fade value to greater than 0 to only partially replace the color.

8 Click **OK**.

■ Photoshop replaces the colors in the destination image with those in the source image.

■ In this example, Photoshop changes colors in a bluish beach scene to match a more yellow selection of colors from another beach scene.

CORRECT SHADOWS AND HIGHLIGHTS

You can quickly correct images with overly dark or light areas using the Shadow/Highlight command. This command can help correct photos that have a shadowed subject due to backlighting.

If you make a selection before performing the Shadow/ Highlight command, you affect only the selected pixels. Similarly, if you have a multilayered image, your adjustments affect only the selected layer. See Chapter 4 to make a selection, and Chapter 9 for more about layers.

CORRECT SHADOWS AND HIGHLIGHTS

1 Click **Image**.

2 Click **Adjustments**.

3 Click **Shadow/Highlight**.

■ The Shadow/Highlight dialog box appears.

4 Click and drag the Shadows Amount slider (⬠).

■ The further you drag the ⬠ to the right, the more the shadows lighten.

■ You can also adjust the shadows by typing a number from 0 to 100.

How do I get more control over how my shadows and highlights are affected by the Shadow/Highlight command?

Click the Show More Options checkbox (☐ changes to ☑) in the Shadow/Highlight dialog box. Additional settings appear. Adjusting the Tonal Width sliders helps you control what parts of the image are considered shadows and highlights. The Radius sliders help you control the contrast in your adjusted shadows and highlights.

5 Click and drag the Highlights Amount slider (◖).

■ The further you drag the ◖ to the right, the more the highlights darken.

■ You can also adjust the highlights by typing a number from 0 to 100.

6 Click **OK**.

■ Photoshop adjusts the shadows and highlights in the image.

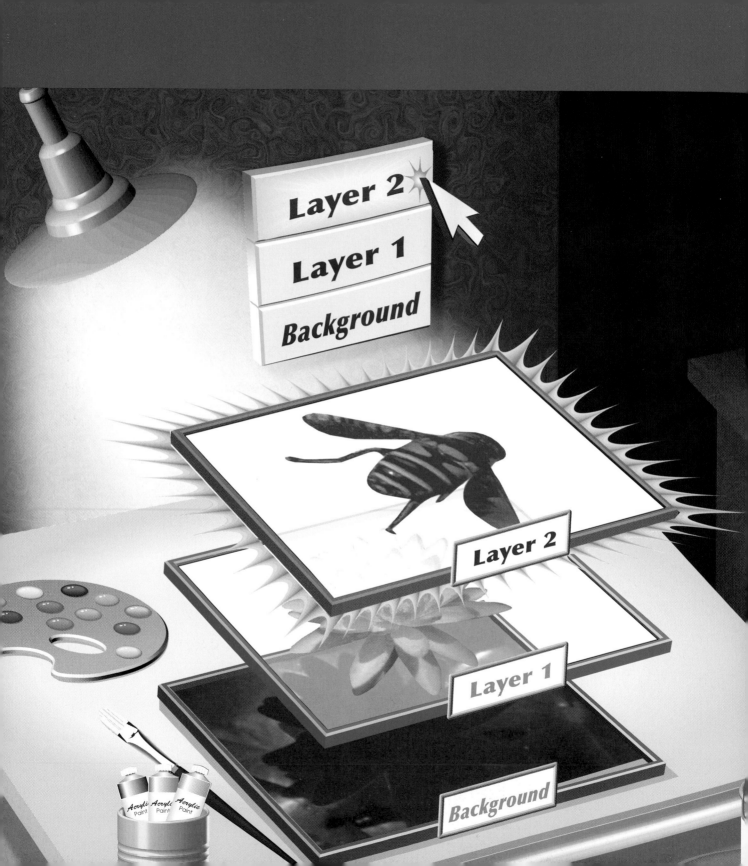

CHAPTER 9

Working with Layers

Do you want to separate the elements in your image so that you can move and transform them independently of one another? You can do this by placing them in different layers.

What Are Layers? 160

Create and Add to a Layer 162

Hide a Layer 164

Move a Layer 165

Duplicate a Layer 166

Delete a Layer 167

Reorder Layers 168

Change the Opacity of a Layer 170

Merge and Flatten Layers 172

Rename a Layer 174

Transform a Layer...........................175

Create a Solid Fill Layer 176

Create a Gradient Fill Layer 178

Create a Pattern Fill Layer 180

Create an Adjustment Layer.............182

Edit an Adjustment Layer 184

Link Layers....................................186

Blend Layers 188

WHAT ARE LAYERS?

A Photoshop image can consist of multiple layers, with each layer containing different objects in the image.

Layer Independence

Layered Photoshop files act like several images combined into one. Each layer of an image has its own set of pixels that you can move and transform independently of the pixels in other layers.

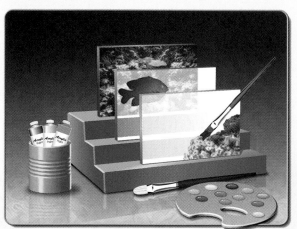

Apply Commands to Layers

Most Photoshop commands affect only the layer that you select. For example, if you click and drag using the Move tool, the selected layer moves while the other layers stay in place; if you apply a color adjustment, only colors in the selected layer change.

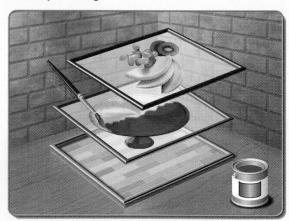

Manipulate Layers

You can combine, duplicate, and hide layers in an image. You can shuffle the order in which you stack layers. You can also link particular layers so that they move in unison.

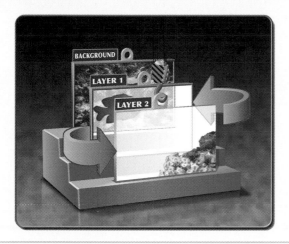

Transparency

Layers can have transparent areas, where the elements on the layers below can show through. When you perform a cut or erase command on a layer, the affected pixels become transparent.

Adjustment Layers

Adjustment layers are special layers that contain information about color or tonal adjustments. An adjustment layer affects the pixels in all the layers below it. You can increase or decrease an adjustment layer's strength to get precisely the effect you want.

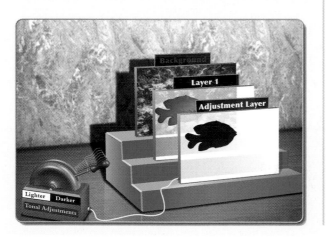

Save Layered Files

You can only save multilayered images in the Photoshop, PDF, and TIFF file formats. To save a layered image in another file format — for example, PICT, BMP, GIF, or JPEG — you must combine the image's layers into a single layer, a process known as *flattening*. For more information about saving files, see Chapter 15.

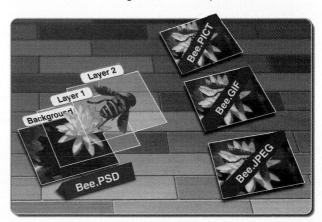

CREATE AND ADD TO A LAYER

To keep elements in your image independent from one another, you can create separate layers and add objects to them.

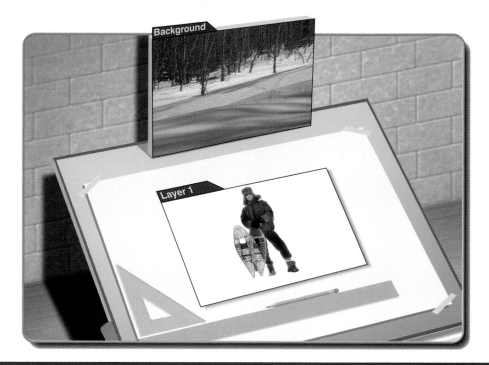

CREATE A LAYER

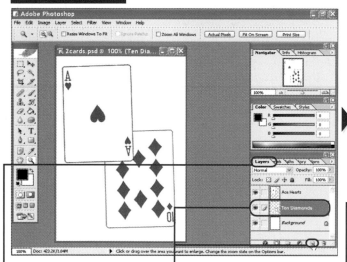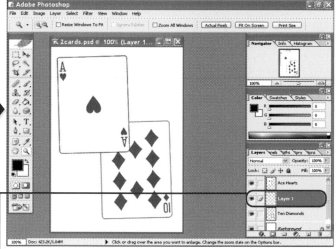

1 Click the **Layers** tab to select the Layers palette.

■ If the Layers tab is hidden, you can click **Window** and then **Layers** to open the Layers palette.

2 Click the layer above which you want to add the new layer.

3 In the Layers palette, click the New Layer button (▣).

■ Alternatively, you can click **Layer**, **New**, and then **Layer**.

■ Photoshop creates a new, transparent layer.

Note: To change the name of a layer, see the section "Rename a Layer."

What is the Background layer?

The Background layer is the default bottom layer that appears when you create a new image that has a non-transparent background color or when you import an image from a scanner or digital camera. You can create new layers on top of a Background layer, but not below it. Unlike other layers, a Background layer cannot contain transparent pixels.

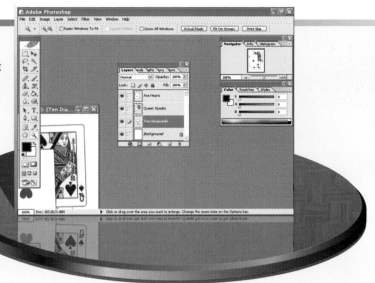

COPY AND PASTE INTO A LAYER

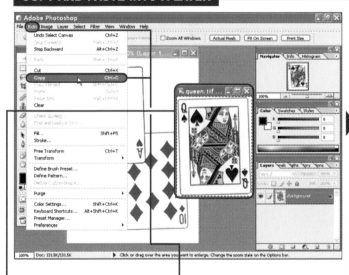

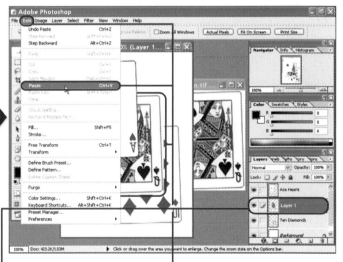

Note: This example shows adding content to the new layer by copying and pasting from another image file.

1 Open another image.

2 Using a selection tool, select the content you want to copy in the other image.

Note: See Chapter 1 for more about opening an image. See Chapter 4 for more about the selection tools.

3 Click **Edit**.

4 Click **Copy**.

5 Click the image window where you created the new layer.

6 Click the new layer in the Layers palette.

7 Click **Edit**.

8 Click **Paste**.

■ The selected content from the other image appears in the new layer.

HIDE A LAYER

You can hide a layer to temporarily remove elements in that layer from view.

Hidden layers do not display when you print or use the Save for Web command.

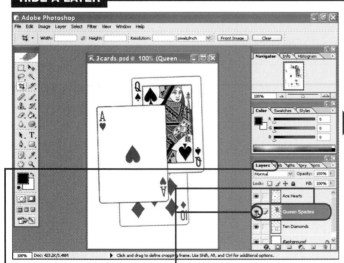

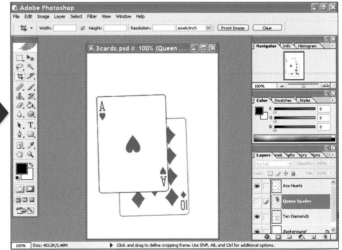

1 Click the **Layers** tab to select the Layers palette.

■ If the Layers tab is hidden, you can click **Window** and then **Layers** to open the Layers palette.

2 Click a layer.

3 Click the Eye icon (👁) for the layer. The icon disappears.

■ Photoshop hides the layer.

■ To show one layer and hide all the others, you can press Alt (option) and click the 👁 for the layer you want to show.

Note: You can also delete a layer. See the section "Delete a Layer" for more information.

164

You can use the Move tool to reposition the elements in one layer without moving those in others.

MOVE A LAYER

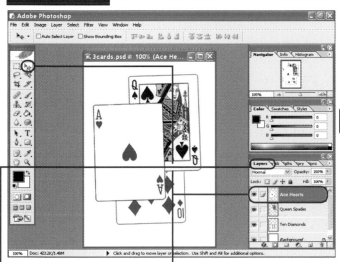

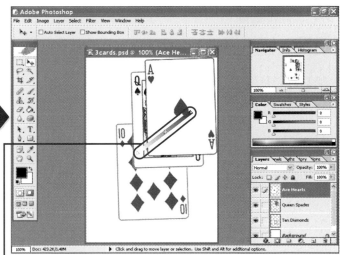

1 Click the **Layers** tab to select the Layers palette.

■ If the Layers tab is hidden, you can click **Window** and then **Layers** to open the palette.

2 Click a layer.

3 Click the Move tool (⊕).

4 Click and drag inside the window.

■ Content in the selected layer moves.

■ Content in the other layers does not move.

Note: To move several layers at the same time, see the section "Link Layers."

DUPLICATE A LAYER

By duplicating a layer, you can manipulate elements in an image while keeping a copy of their original state.

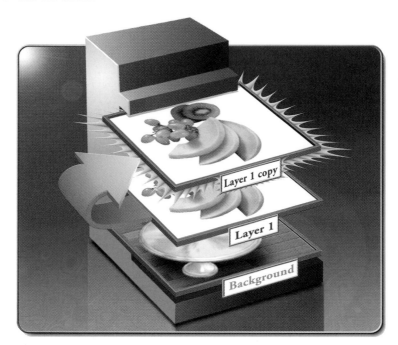

DUPLICATE A LAYER

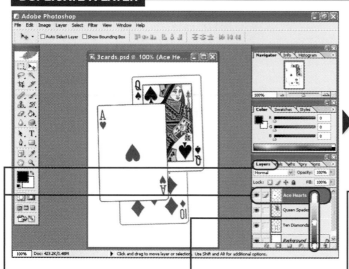

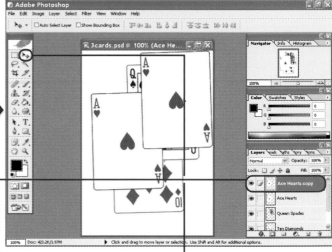

1 Click the **Layers** tab to select the Layers palette.

■ If the Layers tab is hidden, you can click **Window** and then **Layers** to open the Layers palette.

2 Click a layer.

3 Click and drag the layer to 🔲.

■ Alternatively, you can click **Layer** and then **Duplicate Layer**, in which case a dialog box appears, asking you to name the layer you want to duplicate.

■ Photoshop duplicates the selected layer.

Note: To rename the duplicate layer, see the section "Rename a Layer."

■ You can see that Photoshop has duplicated the layer by selecting the new layer, clicking ➕, and clicking and dragging the layer.

You can delete a layer
when you no longer have
a use for its contents.

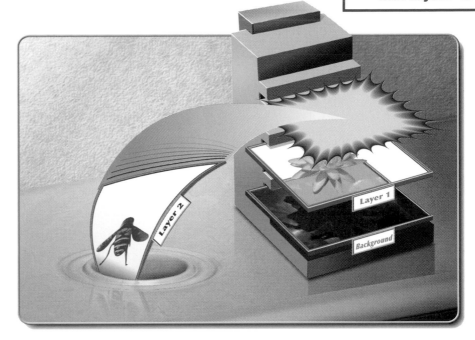

DELETE A LAYER

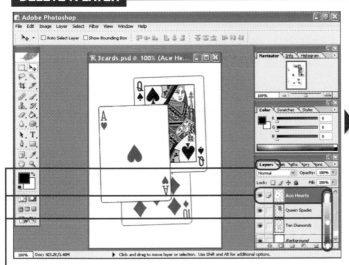

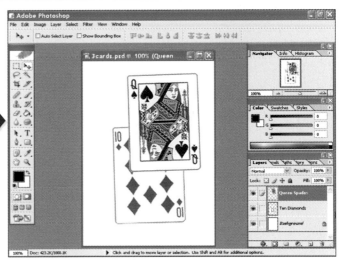

1 Click the **Layers** tab to
select the Layers palette.

2 Click a layer.

3 Click and drag the layer
to 🗑.

■ Alternatively, you can click
Layer and then **Delete
Layer**, in which case a
confirmation dialog box
appears.

■ Photoshop deletes
the selected layer, and
the content in the layer
disappears from the image
window.

*Note: You can also hide a layer. See
the section "Hide a Layer" for more
information.*

REORDER LAYERS

You can change the stacking order of layers to move elements forward or backward in your image.

REORDER LAYERS

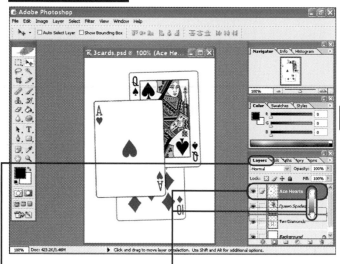

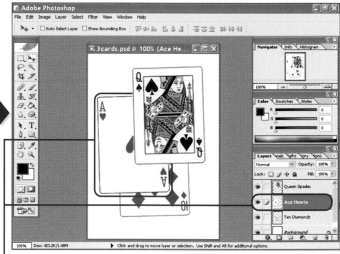

USING THE LAYERS PALETTE

1 Click the **Layers** tab to select the Layers palette.

■ If the Layers tab is hidden, you can click **Window** and then **Layers** to open the palette.

2 Click a layer.

3 Click and drag the layer to change its arrangement in the stack.

■ The layer assumes its new position in the stack.

Are there shortcuts for changing the order of layers?

You can shift a layer forward one step in the stack by pressing Ctrl +] (⌘+]). You can shift a layer backward by pressing Ctrl + [(⌘+[). Pressing Shift + Ctrl +] (Shift+⌘+]) or Shift + Ctrl + [(Shift+⌘+[) moves a layer to the very front or very back of the stack, respectively.

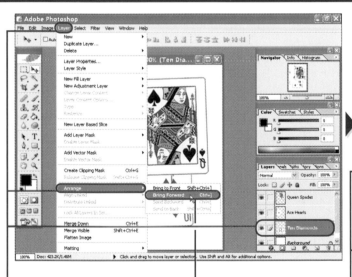

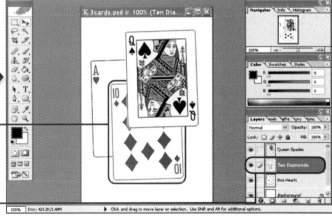

USING THE ARRANGE COMMANDS

1 Click a layer.

2 Click **Layer**.

3 Click **Arrange**.

4 Click the command for how you want to move the layer: **Bring to Front**, **Bring Forward**, **Send Backward**, or **Send to Back**.

■ The layer assumes its new position in the stack.

Note: You cannot move a layer in back of the default Background layer.

CHANGE THE OPACITY OF A LAYER

Adjusting the opacity of a layer can let elements in the layers below show through. *Opacity* is the opposite of transparency. Decreasing the opacity of a layer increases its transparency.

CHANGE THE OPACITY OF A LAYER

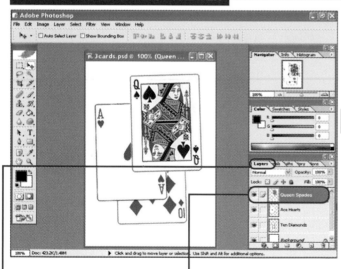

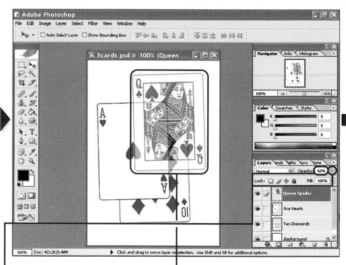

1 Click the **Layers** tab to select the Layers palette.

■ If the Layers tab is hidden, you can click **Window** and then **Layers** to open the Layers palette.

2 Click a layer other than the Background layer.

Note: You cannot change the opacity of the Background layer.

■ The default opacity is 100%, which is completely opaque.

3 Type a new value in the Opacity field and press Enter (Return).

■ Alternatively, you can click and drag the slider.

■ A layer's opacity can range from 0% to 100%.

■ The layer changes in opacity.

What is the Fill setting in the Layers palette?

It is similar to the opacity setting, except that lowering it does not affect any blending options or layer styles applied to the layer. Lowering the Opacity *does* affect these settings. For more about blending options, see the section "Blend Layers." For more about layer styles, see Chapter 10.

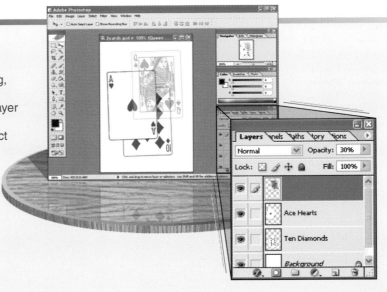

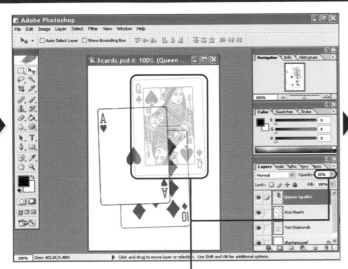

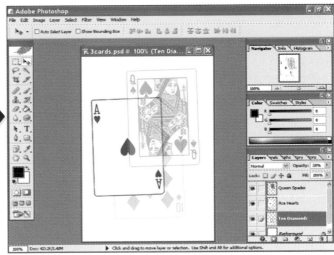

■ A shortcut for changing layer opacity is to click the layer and type a number key.

■ In this example, **3** was typed, which changes the opacity to 30%.

■ You can make multiple layers in your image semitransparent by changing their opacities.

■ In this example, both the Queen Spades and Ten Diamonds layers are semitransparent.

MERGE AND FLATTEN LAYERS

Merging layers lets you permanently combine information from two or more separate layers. Flattening layers combines all the layers of an image into one.

MERGE LAYERS

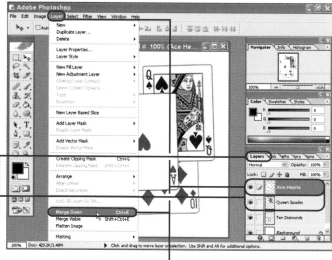

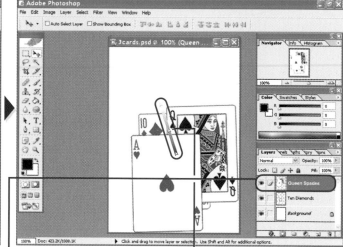

1 Click the **Layers** tab to select the Layers palette.

2 Place the two layers you want to merge next to each other.

Note: See the section "Reorder Layers" to change stacking order.

3 Click the topmost of the two layers.

4 Click **Layer**.

5 Click **Merge Down**.

■ The two layers merge.

■ Photoshop keeps the name of the lower layer.

■ To see the result of the merge, select the new layer, click [ ], and click and drag the merged layer. The elements that were previously in separate layers now move together.

Why would I want to merge layers?

Merging layers enables you to save computer memory. The fewer layers a Photoshop image has, the less space it takes up in RAM and on your hard drive when you save it. Merging layers also lets you permanently combine elements of your image when you are happy with how you have arranged them relative to one another. If you want the option of rearranging all the original layers in the future, save a copy of your image before you merge layers.

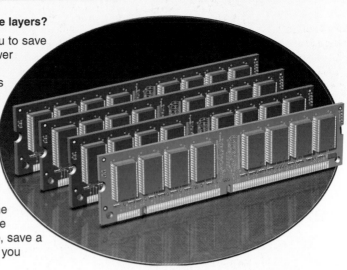

FLATTEN LAYERS

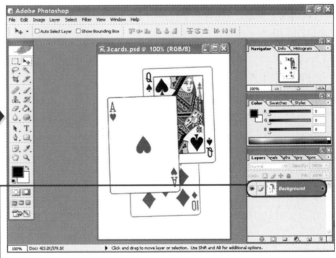

1 Click **Layer**.

2 Click **Flatten Image**.

■ All the layers merge into one.

RENAME A LAYER

You can rename a layer
to give it a name that
describes its content.

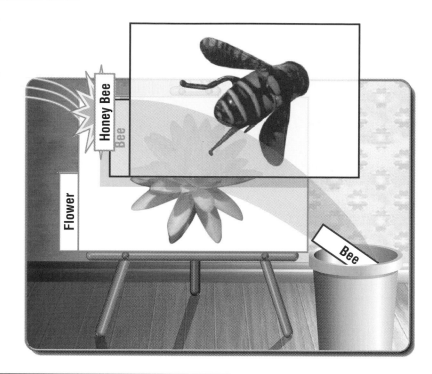

RENAME A LAYER

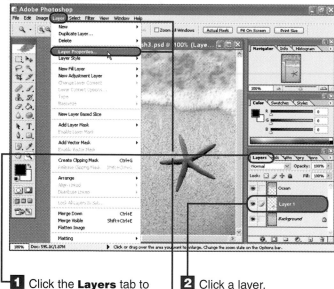

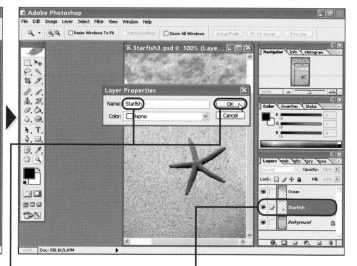

1 Click the **Layers** tab to
select the Layers palette.

■ If the Layers tab is hidden,
you can click **Window** and
then **Layers** to open the
Layers palette.

2 Click a layer.

3 Click **Layer**.

4 Click **Layer Properties**.

■ The Layer Properties
dialog box appears.

5 Type a new name for the
layer.

6 Click **OK**.

■ The name of the layer
changes in the Layers
palette.

■ You can also double-click
the name of the layer in the
Layers palette to edit the
name in place.

TRANSFORM A LAYER

You can use a transform tool to change the shape of the objects in a layer. When you transform a layer, the rest of your image remains unchanged.

TRANSFORM A LAYER

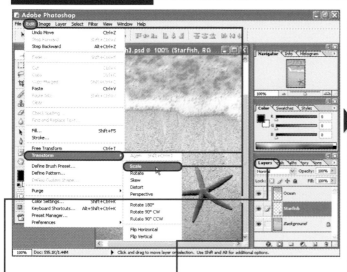

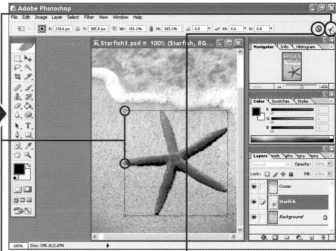

1 Click the **Layers** tab to select the Layers palette.

■ If the Layers tab is hidden, you can click **Window** and then **Layers** to open the Layers palette.

2 Click **Edit**.

3 Click **Transform**.

4 Click a transform command.

5 Click and drag the side and corner handles to transform the shape of the layer.

6 Click ✓ or press **Enter** (**Return**) to apply the change.

■ You can click ⊘ or press **Esc** (⌘ + .) to cancel the change.

Note: For more about transforming your images, see Chapter 5.

175

CREATE A SOLID FILL LAYER

You can create a solid fill layer to place an opaque layer of color throughout your image.

CREATE A SOLID FILL LAYER

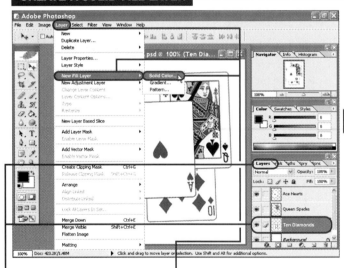

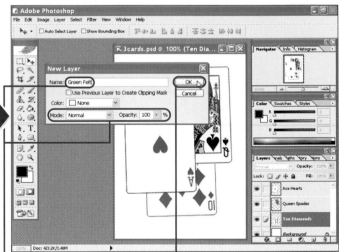

1 Click the **Layers** tab to select the Layers palette.

■ If the Layers tab is hidden, you can click **Window** and then **Layers** to open the Layers palette.

2 Click the layer above which you want to add solid color.

3 Click **Layer**.

4 Click **New Fill Layer**.

5 Click **Solid Color**.

■ You can also click the Create new fill or adjustment layer button ( ) and select Solid Color.

■ The New Layer dialog box appears.

6 Type a name for the layer.

■ You can specify a blend mode or opacity setting for the layer.

Note: See the section "Blend Layers" or "Change the Opacity of a Layer" for details.

7 Click **OK**.

176

How do I add solid color to just part of a layer?

Make a selection with a selection tool before creating the solid fill layer. Photoshop adds color only inside the selection.

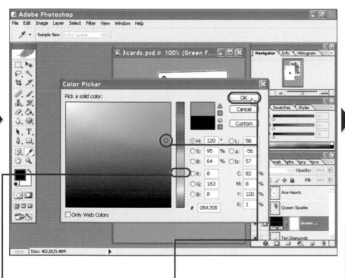

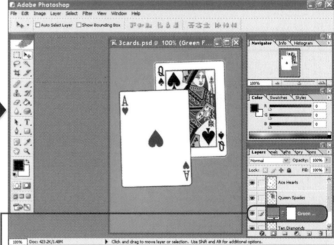

■ The Color Picker dialog box appears.

8 To change the range of colors that appears in the window, click and drag the slider (▷).

9 To select a fill color, click in the color window.

10 Click **OK**.

■ Photoshop creates a new layer filled with a solid color.

■ Layers above the new layer are not affected.

CREATE A GRADIENT FILL LAYER

You can create a gradient fill layer to place color transition throughout your image.

For another way to add a gradient to your image, see Chapter 7.

CREATE A GRADIENT FILL LAYER

1 Click the **Layers** tab to select the Layers palette.

■ If the Layers tab is hidden, you can click **Window** and then **Layers** to open the Layers palette.

2 Click the layer above which you want to add a pattern.

3 Click **Layer**.

4 Click **New Fill Layer**.

5 Click **Gradient**.

■ You can also click the Create new fill or adjustment layer button ( ) and select **Gradient**.

■ The New Layer dialog box appears.

6 Type a name for the layer.

■ You can specify a blend mode or opacity setting for the layer.

Note: See the section "Blend Layers" or "Change the Opacity of a Layer" for details.

7 Click **OK**.

Can I convert one type of fill layer to another?

Yes. Select the layer in the Layers palette. Click **Layer**, **Change Layer Content**, and then a different layer type.

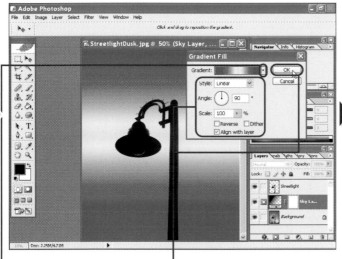

■ The Gradient Fill dialog box appears.

8 Click ⊡.

9 Click a set of gradient colors from the menu that appears.

10 Select your other gradient settings.

■ You can select a style to specify the shape.

■ You can select an angle to specify the direction.

11 Click **OK**.

■ Photoshop creates a new layer filled with the specified gradient.

■ Layers above the new layer remain unaffected.

CREATE A PATTERN FILL LAYER

You can create a pattern fill layer to place a repeating design throughout your image.

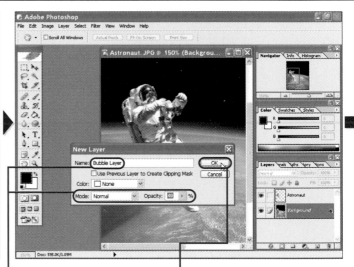

1 Click the **Layers** tab to select the Layers palette.

■ If the Layers tab is hidden, you can click **Window** and then **Layers** to open the Layers palette.

2 Click the layer above which you want to add a pattern.

3 Click **Layer**.

4 Click **New Fill Layer**.

5 Click **Pattern**.

■ You can also click the Create new fill or adjustment layer button ( ) and select Pattern.

■ The New Layer dialog box appears.

6 Type a name for the layer.

■ You can specify a blend mode or opacity setting for the layer.

Note: See the section "Blend Layers" or "Change the Opacity of a Layer" for more details.

7 Click **OK**.

180

How do I change the applied pattern after creating the layer?

Double-click the layer thumbnail in the Layers palette. The Pattern Fill dialog box appears and enables you to change the pattern.

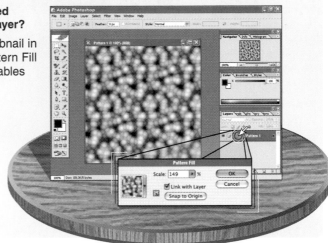

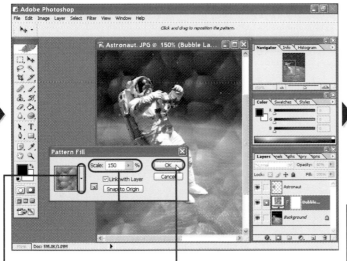

■ The Pattern Fill dialog box appears.

8 Click ⊡.

9 Click a pattern.

10 To determine how often the pattern repeats, type a value between 1 and 1000.

11 Click **OK**.

■ Photoshop creates a new layer filled with a pattern.

■ Layers above the new layer remain unaffected.

CREATE AN ADJUSTMENT LAYER

Adjustment layers let you store color and tonal changes in a layer, rather than having them permanently applied to your image.

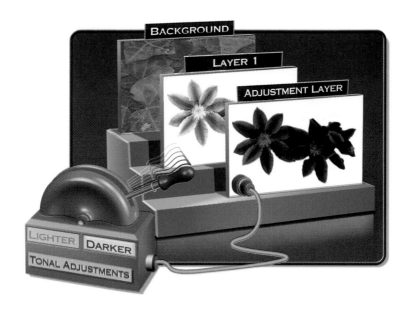

CREATE AN ADJUSTMENT LAYER

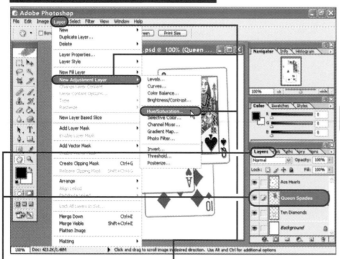

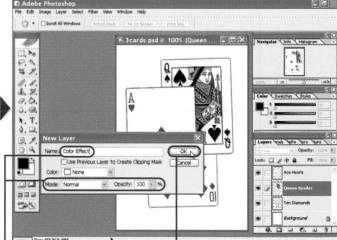

1 Click the **Layers** tab to select the Layers palette.

■ If the Layers tab is hidden, you can click **Window** and then **Layers** to open the Layers palette.

2 Click a layer.

3 Click **Layer**.

4 Click **New Adjustment Layer**.

5 Click an adjustment command.

■ You can also click the Create new fill or adjustment layer button ( ) and select an adjustment command.

■ The New Layer dialog box appears.

6 Type a name for the adjustment layer.

■ You can specify a blend mode or opacity setting for the layer.

Note: See the section "Blend Layers" or "Change the Opacity of a Layer" for details.

7 Click **OK**.

■ Photoshop places the new adjustment layer above the currently selected layer.

182

How do I apply an adjustment layer to only part of my image canvas?

Make a selection with a selection tool before creating the adjustment layer. See Chapter 4 for more about the selection tools.

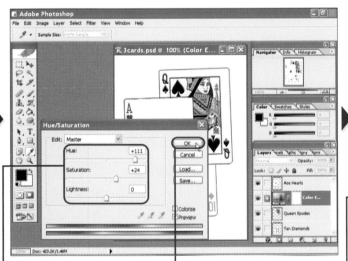

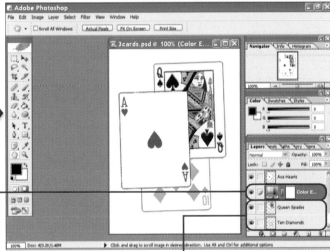

■ The dialog box for the adjustment command appears.

8 Click and drag the sliders (⬜) and type values to adjust the settings.

■ In this example, an adjustment layer is created that changes the hue and saturation.

9 Click **OK**.

■ Photoshop creates an adjustment layer.

■ Photoshop applies the effect to the layers below the adjustment layer.

■ In this example, Photoshop affects the card layers below the adjustment layer while leaving the card layer above it unaffected.

EDIT AN ADJUSTMENT LAYER

You can change the color and tonal changes that you defined in an adjustment layer. This lets you fine-tune your adjustment layer to get the effect you want.

EDIT AN ADJUSTMENT LAYER

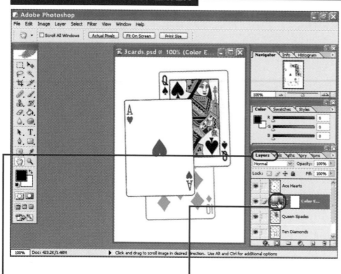

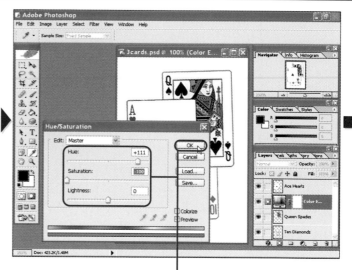

1 Click the **Layers** tab to select the Layers palette.

■ If the Layers tab is hidden, you can click **Window** and then **Layers** to open the Layers palette.

2 Double-click the adjustment layer icon 🖼 in the Layers palette.

■ The settings dialog box corresponding to the adjustment command appears.

3 Click and drag the sliders (🔺) to change the settings in the dialog box.

4 Click **OK**.

How do I merge an adjustment layer with a regular layer?

Place the adjustment layer over the layer with which you want to merge it and then click **Layer** and **Merge Down**. When you merge the layers, Photoshop applies the adjustment layer's effects only to the layer with which you merged. The other layers below it remain unaffected.

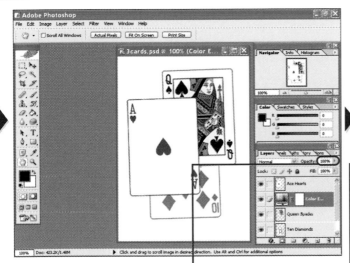

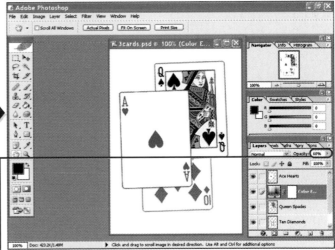

■ Photoshop applies your changes.

■ In this example, the saturation was reduced to the minimum, which removed the color in the layers below the adjustment layer.

■ You can lessen the affect of an adjustment layer by decreasing the layer's opacity to less than 100%.

■ In this example, the opacity was decreased to 60%, which reverses the decrease in saturation. Some of the original color in the cards returns.

LINK LAYERS

Linking causes different layers to move in unison when you move them with the Move tool. You may find linking useful when you want to keep elements of an image aligned with one another, but do not want to merge their layers. See the section "Merge and Flatten Layers" for more about merging. Keeping layers unmerged lets you apply effects independently to each.

LINK LAYERS

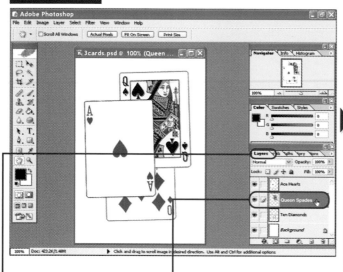

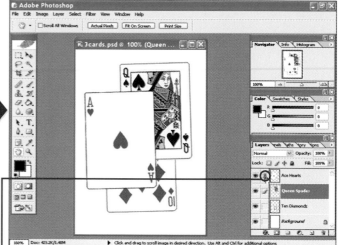

CREATE A LINK

1 Click the **Layers** tab to select the Layers palette.

■ If the Layers tab is hidden, you can click **Window** and then **Layers** to open the Layers palette.

2 Click one of the layers you want to link.

3 Click the box next to the other layer that you want to link.

■ Doing so turns on a linking icon ( ).

■ The layers link together.

How do I keep from changing a layer after I have it the way I want it?

You can lock the layer by selecting the layer and clicking the Lock icon (⬚) located on the Layers palette. You cannot move, delete, or otherwise edit a locked layer. You can click the box to the left of the Transparency icon (⬚) if you just want to prevent a user from editing the transparent pixels in the layer.

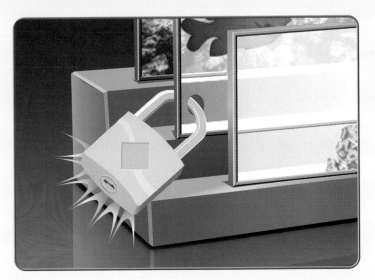

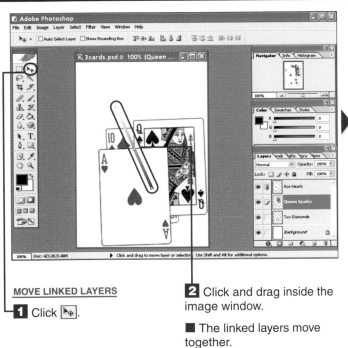

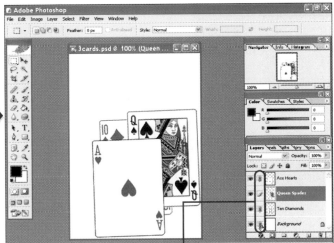

MOVE LINKED LAYERS

1 Click ⊕.

2 Click and drag inside the image window.

■ The linked layers move together.

■ You can link as many layers as you want.

■ In this example, all the layers have been linked, including the Background layer.

BLEND LAYERS

Blend Layer

Layer 1

Background

You can use Photoshop's blending modes to specify how pixels in a layer blend with the layers below it.

Blending Modes
Multiply
Screen
Color
Luminosity

BLEND LAYERS

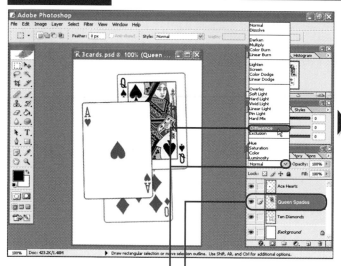

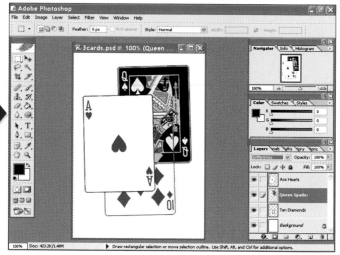

BLEND A REGULAR LAYER

1 Click the **Layers** tab to select the Layers palette.

■ If the Layers tab is hidden, you can click **Window** and then **Layers** to open the Layers palette.

2 Click the layer that you want to blend.

3 Click ☑ (⬍).

4 Click a blend mode.

■ Photoshop blends the selected layer with the layers below it.

■ This example shows the Difference mode, which creates a photo-negative effect where the selected layer overlaps other layers.

What effects do some of the different blending modes have?

The Multiply mode darkens the colors where the selected layer overlaps layers below it. The Screen mode is the opposite of Multiply; it lightens colors where layers overlap. Color takes the selected layer's colors and blends them with the details in the layers below it. Luminosity is the opposite of Color; it takes the selected layer's details and mixes them with the colors below it.

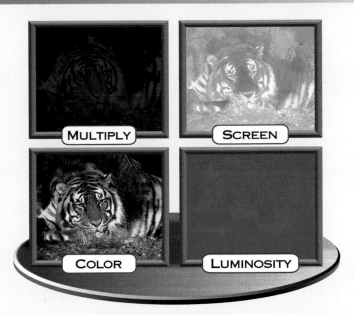

MULTIPLY   SCREEN

COLOR   LUMINOSITY

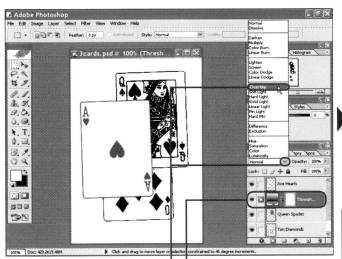

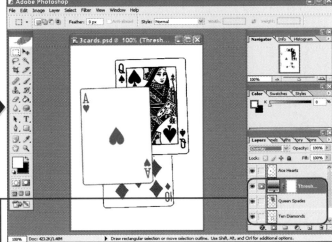

BLEND AN ADJUSTMENT LAYER

1 Click the **Layers** tab to select the Layers palette.

■ If the Layers tab is hidden, you can click **Window** and then **Layers** to open the Layers palette.

2 Click an adjustment layer that you want to blend.

3 Click ⌄ (⊞).

4 Click a blend mode.

■ Photoshop blends the selected layer with the layers below it.

■ This example shows the Overlay mode applied to a Threshold adjustment layer, which lets some of the original color through.

APPLY
OUTER
GLOW?

OUTER GLOW

NIGHT CLUB

...APPLYING DROP SHADOW...

ANGLE

LOCK

DISTAN

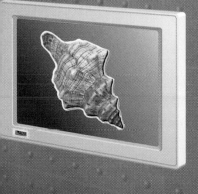

CHAPTER 10

Applying Layer Effects

You can apply special effects to layers by applying Photoshop's built-in layer effects. With these effects, you can add shadows, glows, and 3D appearances to your layers. Photoshop's Styles palette lets you easily apply predefined combinations of effects to your image.

Apply a Drop Shadow 192

Apply an Outer Glow 194

Apply Beveling and Embossing 196

Apply Multiple Effects to a Layer 198

Edit a Layer Effect............................200

Apply a Style 202

APPLY A DROP SHADOW

You can apply a drop shadow to make a layer look as though it is raised off the image canvas.

APPLY A DROP SHADOW

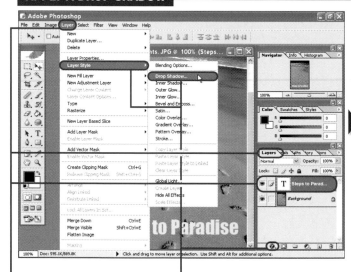

1 Click the **Layers** tab to select the Layers palette.

2 Click the layer to which you want to add the effect.

3 Click **Layer**.

4 Click **Layer Style**.

5 Click **Drop Shadow**.

■ You can also click the Add a layer style button (🔲) and select **Drop Shadow**.

Note: Perform steps 6 to 11 if you want to enter your own settings. If you want to use the default settings, you can skip to step 12.

6 Type an Opacity value to specify the shadow's transparency.

7 Click the color swatch to select a shadow color.

Note: The default shadow color is black.

8 Type an Angle value to specify in which direction the shadow is displaced.

**How do I add an inner shadow
to a layer?**

Click a layer and click **Layer**,
Layer Style, and then **Inner
Shadow**. An inner shadow
creates a "cut out" effect,
with the selected layer
appearing to drop
behind the image
canvas.

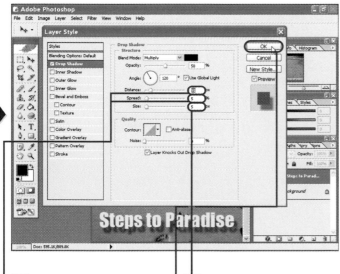

9 Type a Distance value to
specify how far the shadow
is displaced.

10 Type a Spread value to
specify the fuzziness of the
shadow's edge.

11 Type a Size value to
specify the size of the
shadow edge.

12 Click **OK**.

■ Photoshop creates a
shadow in back of the
selected layer.

■ The effect appears below
the selected layer in the
Layers palette.

*Note: In this example, the effect
was applied to a text layer. For
more information about type,
see Chapter 13.*

APPLY AN OUTER GLOW

The outer glow effect adds faint coloring to the outside edge of a layer.

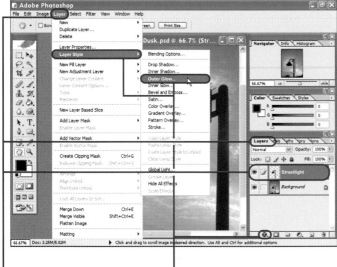

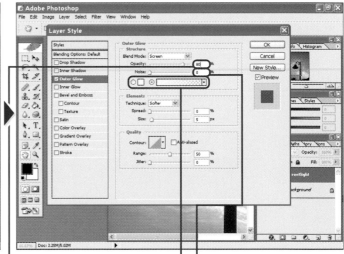

1 Click the **Layers** tab to select the Layers palette.

2 Click the layer to which you want to add the effect.

3 Click **Layer**.

4 Click **Layer Style**.

5 Click **Outer Glow**.

■ You can also click and select **Outer Glow**.

Note: Perform steps 6 to 10 if you want to enter your own Outer Glow settings. If you want to use the default settings, you can skip to step 11.

6 Type an Opacity value to specify the glow's darkness.

7 Specify a Noise value to add speckling to the glow.

8 Click the color swatch to choose the color of the glow (○ changes to ◉). Or, you can choose from a series of preset color gradients by clicking ⯆.

194

How do I give elements in a layer an inner glow?

Click a layer and click **Layer**, **Layer Style**, and then **Inner Glow**. An inner glow adds color to the inside edge of a layer.

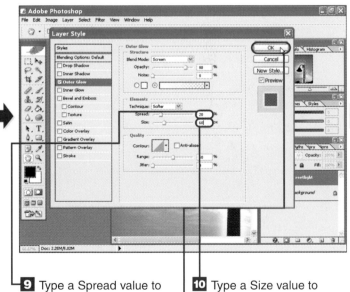

9 Type a Spread value to determine the fuzziness of the glow.

10 Type a Size value to specify a size of the glow.

11 Click **OK**.

■ Photoshop creates a glow around the outer edge of the selected layer.

APPLY BEVELING AND EMBOSSING

You can bevel and emboss a layer to give it a three-dimensional look. This can make objects in the layer stand out and seem to rise off the screen.

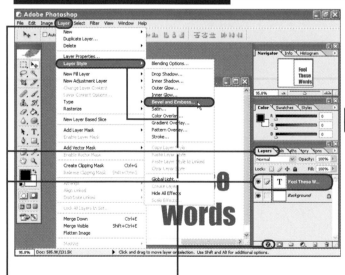

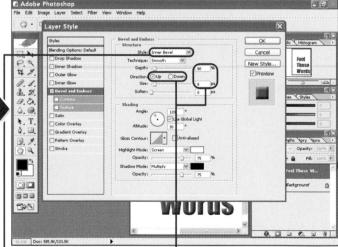

1 Click the **Layers** tab to select the Layers palette.

2 Click the layer to which you want to add the effect.

3 Click **Layer**.

4 Click **Layer Style**.

5 Click **Bevel and Emboss**.

■ You can also click and select **Bevel and Emboss**.

Note: Perform steps 6 to 9 if you want to enter your own settings. If you want to use the default settings, you can skip to step 10.

6 Select an effect style. Clicking **Inner Bevel** creates a three-dimensional look.

7 Specify the direction of the effect's shadowing (◯ changes to ◉).

8 Type Depth and Size values to control the magnitude of the effect.

196

When would I use the Bevel and Emboss effect?

The effect can be useful for creating three-dimensional buttons for Web pages or multimedia applications. For example, to create a 3D button, you can apply Bevel and Emboss to a colored rectangle and then add type over it.

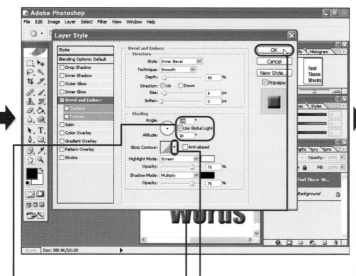

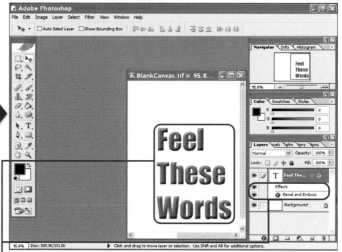

9 Specify the direction of the shading with the Angle and Altitude values.

■ You can click ⋅ and select one of the Gloss Contour settings to apply abstract effects to your layer.

10 Click **OK**.

■ Photoshop applies the bevel and emboss settings to the layer.

■ The effect appears below the selected layer in the Layers palette.

Note: In this example, the effect was applied to a text layer. For more about type, see Chapter 13.

LAPPLY MULTIPLE EFFECTS TO A LAYER

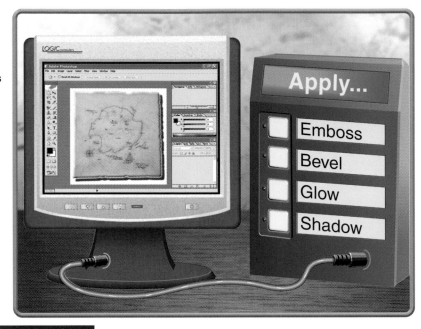

You can apply multiple layer effects to layers in your image. This enables to you to style your layers in complex ways.

APPLY MULTIPLE EFFECTS TO A LAYER

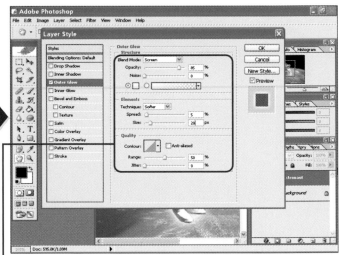

1 Click the **Layers** tab.

■ If the Layers tab is hidden, you can click **Window** and then **Layers**.

■ In this example, Drop Shadow and Color Overlay effects are applied.

APPLY THE FIRST EFFECT

2 Click **Layer**.

3 Click **Layer Style**.

4 Click the name of the first effect that you want to apply.

5 Specify the settings for the first effect.

■ In this example, a yellow outer glow is applied to the layer.

How do I turn off layer effects that I have applied?

When you apply an effect to a layer, Photoshop adds the effect to the Layers palette. You may have to click ▶ to see a layer's effects (▶ changes to ▼). You can temporarily turn off an effect by clicking 👁 in the Layers palette. You can turn the effect on by clicking the now-empty box again to make 👁 reappear.

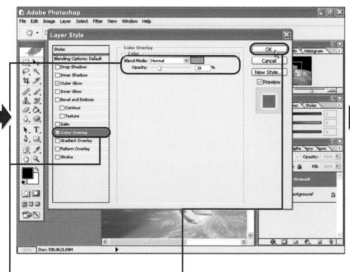

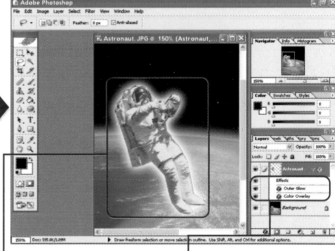

APPLY THE SECOND EFFECT

6 Click the next effect you want to apply (☐ changes to ☑).

7 Specify the settings for this effect.

■ In this example, a semitransparent green overlay is also applied to the layer.

■ You can apply other effects to the layer by repeating steps **6** and **7**.

8 Click **OK**.

■ Photoshop applies the effects to the layer.

■ The effects appear below the selected layer in the Layers palette.

You can edit a layer effect that you have applied to your image. This lets you fine-tune the effect to achieve an appearance that suits you.

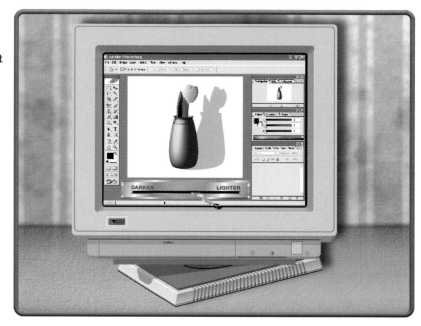

EDIT A LAYER EFFECT

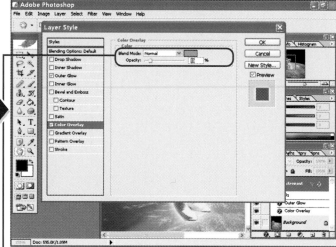

1 Click the **Layers** tab.

■ If the Layers tab is hidden, you can click **Window** and then **Layers**.

■ This example shows editing the color overlay of a layer object.

2 Click **Layer**.

3 Click **Layer Style**.

4 Click the effect you want to edit.

■ You can also double-click the effect in the Layers palette.

■ Photoshop displays the current configuration values for the effect.

How do I keep a layer effect from accidentally being changed?

You can lock a layer and its effects by selecting the layer and clicking 🔒 in the Layers palette — the button depresses and becomes highlighted. The layer is then locked, which means that you cannot change its styles or apply any more Photoshop commands to it. You can also click ☒, ✏, or ⊕ to lock a layer's transparent pixels, all of its pixels, or its position, respectively.

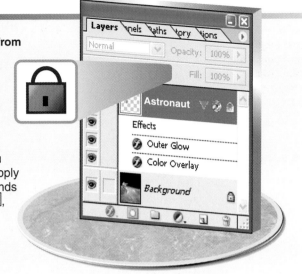

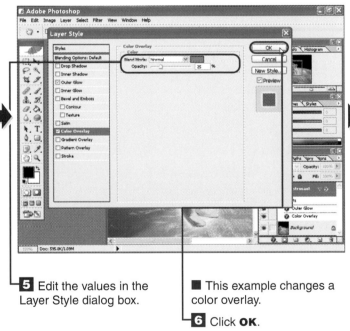

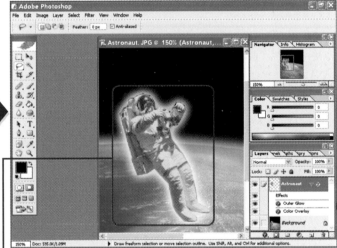

5 Edit the values in the Layer Style dialog box.

■ This example changes a color overlay.

6 Click **OK**.

■ Photoshop applies the edited effect to the layer.

■ You can edit an effect as many times as you want.

APPLY A STYLE

You can apply a Photoshop style to a layer to give the layer a colorful or textured look. Styles are predefined combinations of Photoshop effects that are stored in the Styles palette.

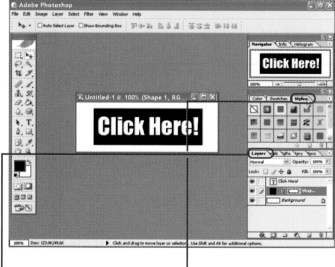

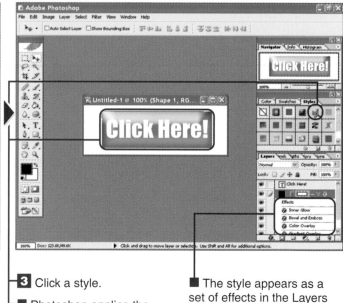

1 Click the **Layers** tab to select the Layers palette.

■ If the Layers tab is hidden, you can click **Window** and then **Layers** to open the Layers palette.

2 Click the **Styles** tab to display Photoshop's styles.

■ If the Styles tab is hidden, you can click **Window** and then **Styles** to open the Styles palette.

3 Click a style.

■ Photoshop applies the style to the selected layer.

■ The style appears as a set of effects in the Layers palette.

How do I create my own custom styles?

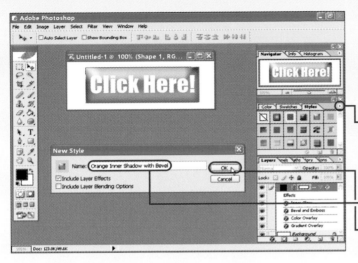

1 Repeat steps **1** to **3** on the opposite page below to apply one or more effects to a layer in your image.

■ Alternatively, you can apply any styles — such as Drop Shadow, Outer Glow, and others — to a layer in your image.

2 Select the layer in the Layers palette.

3 Click the Styles ⊙ and click **New Style** from the menu that appears.

■ The New Style dialog box appears and asks you to name your custom style.

4 Type a name for your new style.

5 Click **OK**.

■ An icon for your new style appears in the Styles palette.

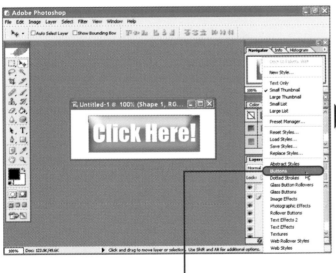

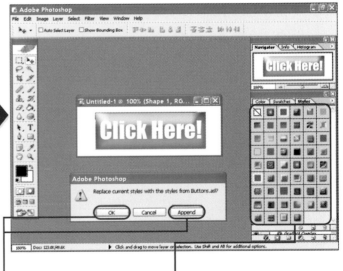

ACCESS MORE STYLES

1 Click the Styles ⊙.

2 Click a set of styles.

■ A dialog box appears and asks if you want to replace the current styles with the new set or append the new set.

3 Click **OK** or **Append**.

■ Photoshop places the new styles in the Styles palette.

■ In this example, the new styles have been appended to the current ones.

CHAPTER 11

Applying Filters

With Photoshop's filters, you can quickly and easily apply enhancements to your image, including artistic effects, texture effects, and distortions. Filters can help you correct defects in your images or let you turn a photograph into something resembling an impressionist painting. Photoshop comes with more than 100 filters; this chapter highlights only a few. For details about all the filters, see the Help documentation.

Turn an Image Into a Painting 206

Blur an Image 208

Sharpen an Image 210

Distort an Image.............................212

Add Noise to an Image 214

Turn an Image Into Shapes 216

Turn an Image Into
   a Charcoal Sketch 218

Apply Glowing Edges to an Image....220

Add Texture to an Image.................222

Offset an Image 224

Using the Liquify Filter......................226

Apply Multiple Filters 228

Generate a Pattern 230

TURN AN IMAGE INTO A PAINTING

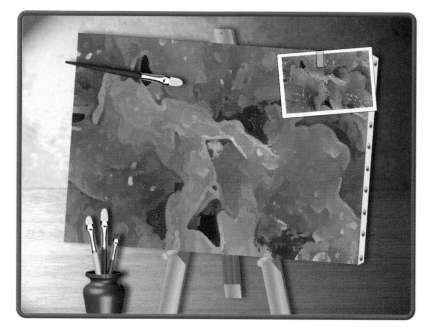

You can use many of Photoshop's artistic filters to make your image look as though it was created with a paintbrush. The Dry Brush filter, for example, applies a painted effect by converting similarly colored areas in your image to solid colors.

The Dry Brush filter uses the Filter Gallery interface. For more information about the Filter Gallery, see the section "Apply Multiple Filters."

TURN AN IMAGE INTO A PAINTING

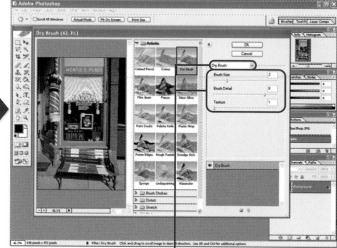

■ **1** Select the layer to which you want to apply the filter.

■ To apply the filter to just part of your image, make a selection with a selection tool.

■ In this example, the image has a single Background layer.

2 Click **Filter**.

3 Click **Artistic**.

4 Click **Dry Brush**.

■ The Dry Brush dialog box appears.

■ The left pane displays a preview of the filter's effect.

■ The middle pane enables you to select a different artistic filter.

■ You can also select a different filter by clicking the ⌄ in the right pane.

5 Fine-tune the filter effect by typing values for the Brush Size, Brush Detail, and Texture.

What does the Sponge filter do?

The Sponge filter reduces detail and modifies the shapes in an image to create the effect you get when applying a damp sponge to a wet painting. Apply it by clicking **Filter**, **Artistic**, and then **Sponge**. Note that this effect is different from what the Sponge tool (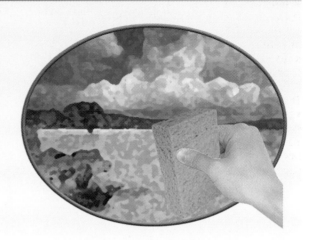) applies. See Chapter 8 for more about the Sponge tool.

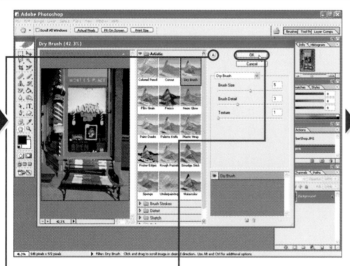

■ You can close the middle pane by clicking ⚐.

■ This example shows how to thicken the dry-brush effect by increasing Brush Size and decreasing Brush Detail.

6 Click **OK**.

■ Photoshop applies the filter.

Note: For more about layers, see Chapter 9. See Chapter 4 to use the selection tools.

BLUR AN IMAGE

Photoshop's Blur filters reduce the amount of detail in your image. The Gaussian Blur filter has advantages over the other Blur filters in that you can control the amount of blur added.

BLUR AN IMAGE

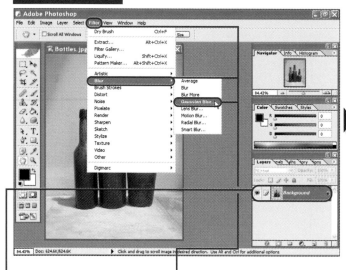

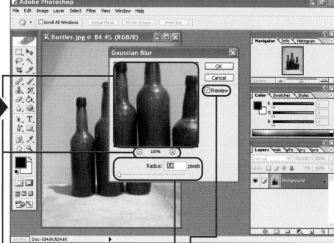

1 Select the layer to which you want to apply the filter.

■ To apply the filter to just part of your image, make a selection with a selection tool.

■ In this example, the image has a single Background layer.

2 Click **Filter**.

3 Click **Blur**.

4 Click **Gaussian Blur**.

■ The Gaussian Blur dialog box appears.

■ A preview of the filter's effect appears here.

■ Click 🔲 or 🔳 to zoom out or in.

5 Click **Preview** to preview the effect in the main window (🔲 changes to ☑).

6 Click and drag the Radius slider (△) to control the amount of blur added.

How do I add directional blurring to an image?

You can add directional blur to your image with the Motion Blur filter. This can add a sense of motion to your image. Apply it by selecting **Filter**, **Blur**, and then **Motion Blur**.

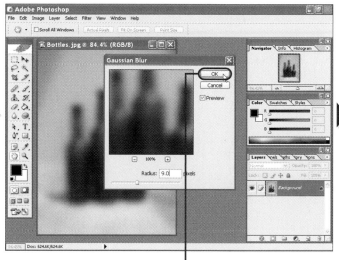

■ In this example, the amount of blur has been increased by boosting the Radius value.

7 Click **OK**.

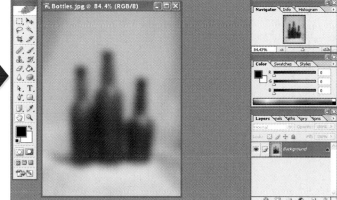

■ Photoshop applies the filter.

Note: For more about layers, see Chapter 9. To use the selection tools, see Chapter 4.

SHARPEN AN IMAGE

Photoshop's Sharpen filters intensify the detail and reduce blurring in your image. The Unsharp Mask filter has advantages over the other Sharpen filters in that you can control the amount of sharpening you apply.

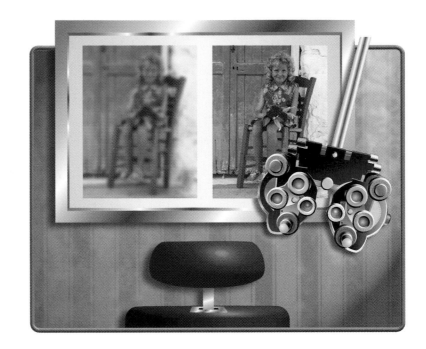

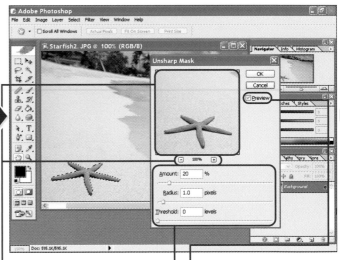

1 Select the layer to which you want to apply the filter.

■ To apply the filter to just part of your image, make a selection with a selection tool.

■ In this example, the filter is applied to a selection.

2 Click **Filter**.

3 Click **Sharpen**.

4 Click **Unsharp Mask**.

■ The Unsharp Mask dialog box appears.

■ A preview of the filter's effect appears here.

■ Click ⊟ or ⊞ to zoom out or in.

5 Click **Preview** to preview the effect in the main window (☐ changes to ☑).

6 Click and drag the sliders (△) to control the amount of sharpening you apply to the image.

When should I apply sharpening?

It is a good idea to sharpen an image after you have changed its size because changing an image's size adds blurring. Applying the Unsharp Mask filter can also help clarify scanned images.

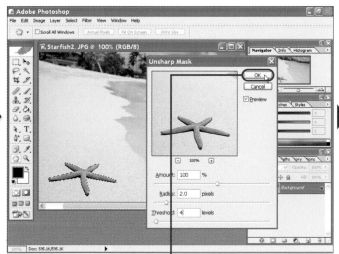

■ **Amount** controls the overall amount of sharpening.

■ **Radius** controls whether sharpening is confined to edges in the image — low Radius setting — or added across the entire image — high Radius setting.

■ **Threshold** controls how much contrast you must have present for an edge to be recognized and sharpened.

7 Click **OK**.

■ Photoshop applies the filter.

Note: For more about layers, see Chapter 9. To use the selection tools, see Chapter 4.

DISTORT AN IMAGE

Photoshop's Distort filters stretch and squeeze areas of your image. For example, the Spherize filter produces a fun-house effect. It makes your image look like it is being reflected in a mirrored sphere.

You can also distort an image by using the Distort command, located under the Image menu. See Chapter 5 for more information.

DISTORT AN IMAGE

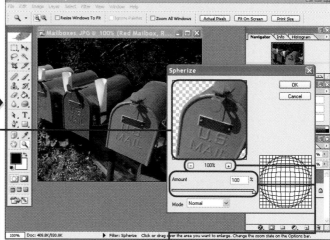

1 Select the layer to which you want to apply the filter.

■ To apply the filter to just part of your image, make a selection with a selection tool.

2 Click **Filter**.

3 Click **Distort**.

4 Click **Spherize**.

■ The Spherize dialog box appears.

■ A preview of the filter's effect appears here.

■ Click ⊟ or ⊞ to zoom out or in.

5 Click and drag the Amount slider (◻) to control the amount of distortion added.

What happens when I type a negative value in the Amount field of the Spherize dialog box?

A negative value "squeezes" the shapes in your image instead of expanding them. The Pinch filter — which you can also find under the **Filter** and **Distort** menu selections — produces a similar effect.

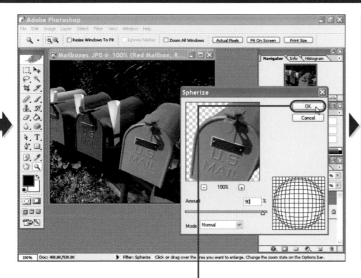

How can I quickly add wild special effects to my images?

Many of the filters in the Stylize menu produce out-of-this-world effects. The Emboss and Solarize filters are two examples. Click **Filter** and then **Stylize** to access them.

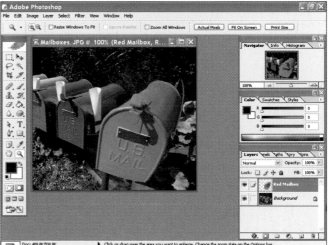

■ In this example, the intensity of the spherize effect has been decreased.

6 Click **OK**.

■ Photoshop applies the filter.

Note: For more about layers, see Chapter 9. See Chapter 4 to use the selection tools.

ADD NOISE TO AN IMAGE

Filters in the Noise menu add or remove graininess in your image. You can add graininess with the Add Noise filter.

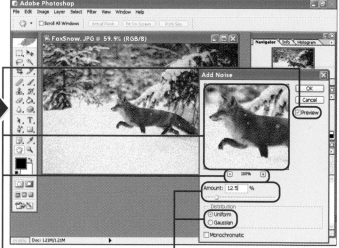

1 Select the layer to which you want to apply the filter.

■ To apply the filter to just part of your image, make a selection with a selection tool.

■ This image has a single Background layer.

2 Click **Filter**.

3 Click **Noise**.

4 Click **Add Noise** to open the Add Noise dialog box.

■ A preview appears here.

■ Click 🔲 or 🔳 to zoom out or in.

5 Click **Preview** to preview the effect in the main window (☐ changes to ☑).

6 Click and drag the 🔲 to control the amount of noise added.

7 Select the way you want the noise distributed (◯ changes to ◉). Uniform spreads the noise more evenly than Gaussian.

What does the Monochromatic setting in the Add Noise dialog box do?

If you click **Monochromatic** (☐ changes to ☑), Photoshop adds noise by lightening or darkening pixels in your image. Pixel hues stay the same. At high settings with the Monochromatic setting on, the filter produces a television-static effect.

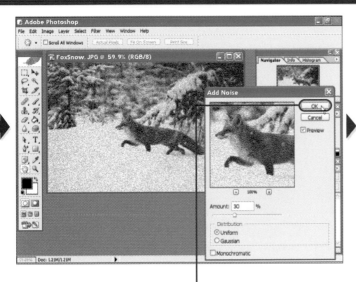

■ In this example, the Amount value has been increased.

8 Click **OK**.

■ Photoshop applies the filter.

Note: For more about layers, see Chapter 9. See Chapter 4 to use the selection tools.

TURN AN IMAGE INTO SHAPES

The Pixelate filters divide areas of your image into solid-colored dots or shapes. The Crystallize filter, one example of a Pixelate filter, re-creates your image using colored polygons.

TURN AN IMAGE INTO SHAPES

1 Select the layer to which you want to apply the filter.

■ To apply the filter to just part of your image, make a selection with a selection tool.

■ In this example, the image has a single Background layer.

2 Click **Filter**.

3 Click **Pixelate**.

4 Click **Crystallize**.

■ The Crystallize dialog box appears.

■ A preview of the filter's effect appears here.

■ Click ⊟ or ⊞ to zoom out or in.

5 Click and drag the Cell Size slider (⬜) to adjust the size of the shapes.

■ The size can range from 3 to 300.

216

What does the Mosaic filter do?

The Mosaic filter converts your image to a set of solid-color squares. You can control the size of the squares in the filter's dialog box. Apply it by clicking **Filter**, **Pixelate**, and then **Mosaic**.

What does the Stained Glass filter do?

The Stained Glass filter converts small areas of your image to different solid-color shapes, similar to those you might see in a stained-glass window. A foreground-color border separates the shapes. Apply it by selecting **Filter**, **Texture**, and then **Stained Glass**.

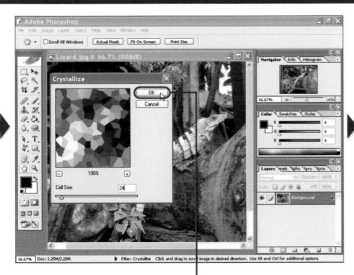

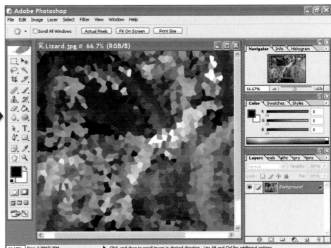

■ In this example, the Cell Size has been slightly increased.

6 Click **OK**.

■ Photoshop applies the filter.

Note: For more about layers, see Chapter 9. To use the selection tools, see Chapter 4.

TURN AN IMAGE INTO A CHARCOAL SKETCH

The Sketch filters add outlining effects to your image. The Charcoal filter, for example, makes an image look as if you have sketched it by using charcoal on paper.

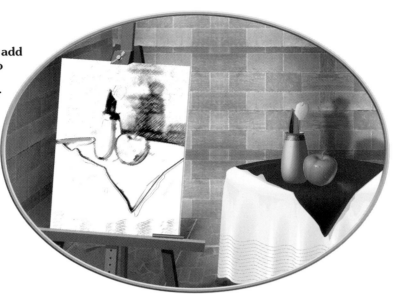

Photoshop uses the foreground and background colors from the toolbox as the charcoal and paper colors, respectively. Changing these changes the filter's effect. See Chapter 8 to adjust color.

The Charcoal filter uses the Filter Gallery interface. For more information about the Filter Gallery, see the section "Apply Multiple Filters."

TURN AN IMAGE INTO A CHARCOAL SKETCH

1 Select the layer to which you want to apply the filter.

■ To apply the filter to just part of your image, make a selection with a selection tool.

■ In this example, the image has a single Background layer.

2 Click **Filter**.

3 Click **Sketch**.

4 Click **Charcoal**.

■ The Charcoal dialog box appears.

■ The left pane displays a preview of the filter's effect.

■ The middle pane enables you to select a different sketch or other type of filter.

■ You can also select a different filter by clicking the ⬇ in the right pane.

5 Click and drag the sliders (⬜) to control the filter's effect.

What does the Photocopy filter do?

The Photocopy filter converts shadows and midtones in your image to the foreground color in the toolbox and highlights in your image to the background color. The result is an image that looks photocopied. You can apply the Photocopy filter by clicking **Filter**, **Sketch**, and then **Photocopy**.

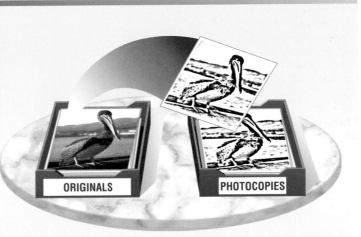

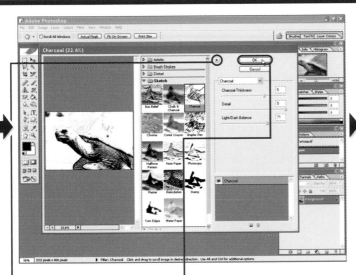

■ You can close the middle pane by clicking [≈].

■ In this example, the thickness of the charcoal strokes has been increased. The Light/Dark Balance setting has also been increased.

6 Click **OK**.

■ Photoshop applies the filter.

Note: For more about layers, see Chapter 9. To use the selection tools, see Chapter 4.

APPLY GLOWING EDGES TO AN IMAGE

The Glowing Edges filter, one example of a Stylize filter, applies a neon effect to the edges in your image. Areas between the edges turn black. Other Stylize filters produce similarly extreme artistic effects.

The Glowing Edges filter uses the Filter Gallery interface. For more information about the Filter Gallery, see the section "Apply Multiple Filters."

APPLY GLOWING EDGES TO AN IMAGE

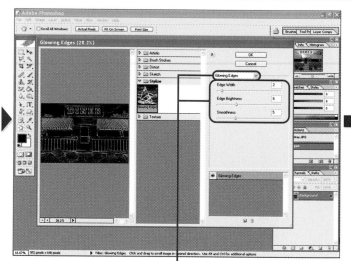

1 Select the layer to which you want to apply the filter.

■ To apply the filter to just part of your image, make a selection with a selection tool.

■ In this example, the image has a single Background layer.

2 Click **Filter**.

3 Click **Stylize**.

4 Click **Glowing Edges**.

■ The Glowing Edges dialog box appears.

■ The left pane displays a preview of the filter's effect.

■ The middle pane enables you to select a different filter.

■ You can also select a different filter by clicking the ⌄ in the right pane.

5 Click and drag the sliders (⌂) to control the intensity of the glow you add to the edges in the image.

What is the Find Edges filter?

The Find Edges filter is similar to the Glowing Edges filter except that it places white pixels between the edges in your image. Find Edges is a one-step filter, which means that you cannot fine-tune its effects in a dialog box before you apply it. To apply the filter:

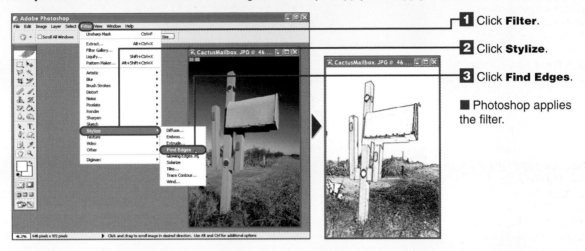

1 Click **Filter**.

2 Click **Stylize**.

3 Click **Find Edges**.

■ Photoshop applies the filter.

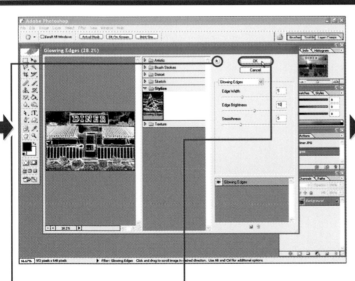

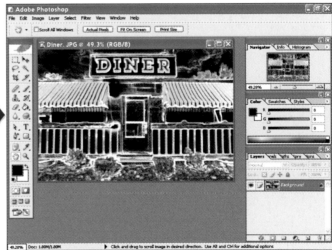

■ You can close the middle pane by clicking ⊗.

■ In this example, the Edge Width and Edge Brightness values have been increased to intensify the neon effect.

6 Click **OK**.

■ Photoshop applies the filter.

Note: For more about layers, see Chapter 9. To use the selection tools, see Chapter 4.

ADD TEXTURE TO AN IMAGE

You can overlay different textures on your image with the Texturizer filter. The other Texture filters let you apply other patterns.

The Texturizer filter uses the Filter Gallery interface. For more information about the Filter Gallery, see "Apply Multiple Filters."

ADD TEXTURE TO AN IMAGE

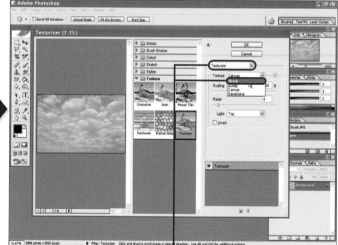

1 Select the layer to which you want to apply the filter.

■ To apply the filter to just part of your image, make a selection with a selection tool.

2 Click **Filter**.

3 Click **Texture**.

4 Click **Texturizer**.

■ The Texturizer dialog box appears.

■ The left pane displays a preview of the filter's effect.

■ The middle pane enables you to select a different texture filter.

■ You can also select a different filter by clicking the ⌄ in the right pane.

5 Click ⌄ (⬦) and select a texture to apply.

What is a lens flare, and how can I add it to an image?

Lens flare is the extra flash of light that sometimes appears in a photo when too much light enters a camera lens. Although photographers try to avoid this effect, you can add it to make your digital image look more like an old-fashioned photograph. To apply the filter:

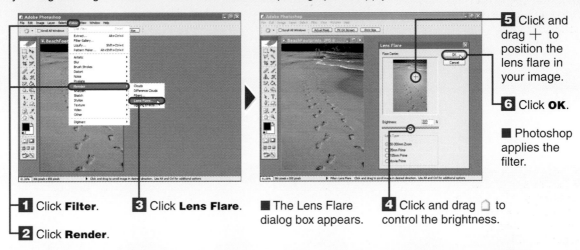

5 Click and drag + to position the lens flare in your image.

6 Click **OK**.

■ Photoshop applies the filter.

1 Click **Filter**.

2 Click **Render**.

3 Click **Lens Flare**.

■ The Lens Flare dialog box appears.

4 Click and drag ⬚ to control the brightness.

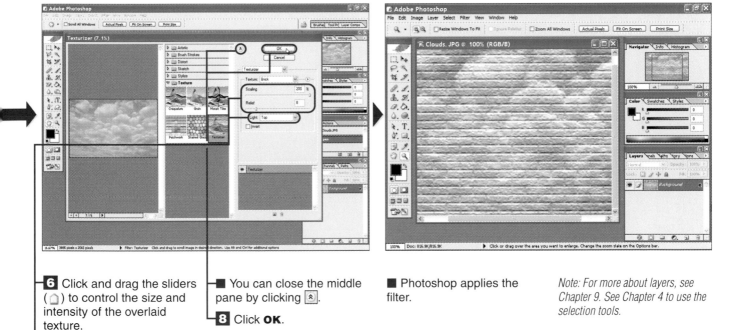

6 Click and drag the sliders (⬚) to control the size and intensity of the overlaid texture.

7 Click ⌄ (◆) and select a Light direction.

■ You can close the middle pane by clicking ⬆.

8 Click **OK**.

■ Photoshop applies the filter.

Note: For more about layers, see Chapter 9. See Chapter 4 to use the selection tools.

OFFSET AN IMAGE

The filters in the Other submenu produce interesting effects that do not fall under the other menu descriptions. For example, you can shift your image horizontally or vertically in the image window using the Other submenu's Offset filter.

OFFSET AN IMAGE

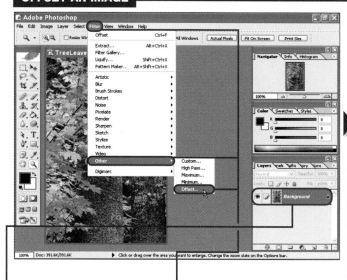

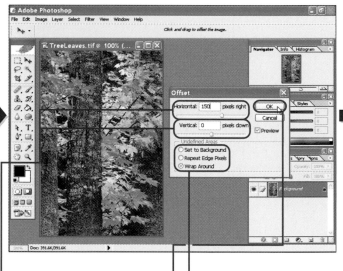

1 Select the layer to which you want to apply the filter.

■ To apply the filter to just part of your image, make a selection with a selection tool.

■ In this example, the image has a single Background layer.

2 Click **Filter**.

3 Click **Other**.

4 Click **Offset**.

■ The Offset dialog box appears.

5 Type a horizontal offset.

6 Type a vertical offset.

7 Select how you want Photoshop to treat pixels at the edge (○ changes to ◉).

8 Click **OK**.

224

How do I make a seamless tile?

Seamless tiles are images that when laid side-by-side leave no noticeable seam where they meet. You often use them as background images for Web pages. To create a seamless tile, start with an evenly textured image; offset the image horizontally and vertically; and, clean up the resulting seams with the Clone Stamp tool (⬚). See Chapter 7 for information on using the Clone Stamp tool. The resulting image tiles seamlessly when you use it as a Web page background.

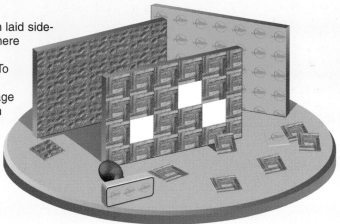

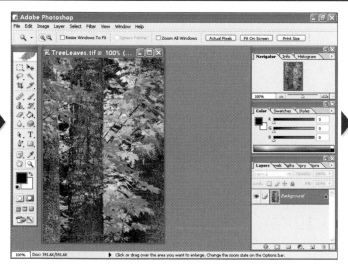

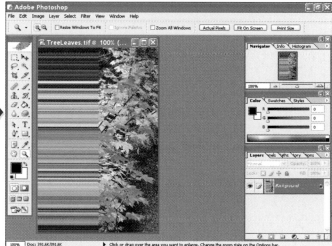

■ In this example, the image has been shifted horizontally to the right by adding a positive value to the horizontal field.

■ Wrap Around was selected in step **7**, so the pixels cropped from the right edge of the image reappear on the left edge.

■ In this example, the same offset was applied but with Repeat Edge Pixels selected in step **7**. This creates a streaked effect at the left edge.

Note: For more about layers, see Chapter 9. See Chapter 4 to use the selection tools.

USING THE LIQUIFY FILTER

Photoshop's Liquify tools enable you to dramatically warp areas of your image. The tools are useful for making your image look like it is melting.

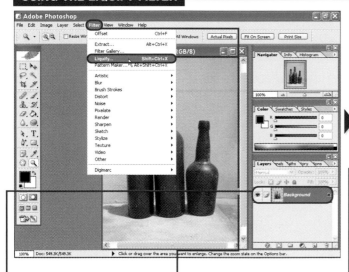

1 Select the layer to which you want to apply the Liquify filter.

■ To apply the filter to just a select part of your image, make a selection with a selection tool.

■ In this example, the image has a single Background layer.

2 Click **Filter**.

3 Click **Liquify**.

■ The Liquify dialog box appears.

4 Type a Brush Size from 1 to 600.

5 Type a Brush Pressure, or strength, from 1 to 100.

6 Click a Liquify tool.

■ This example uses the Forward Warp tool ( ).

What do some of the different Liquify tools do?

	Forward Warp tool	Pushes pixels in the direction you drag
	Reconstruct tool	Restores pixels to their original state
	Twirl Clockwise tool	Twirls pixels clockwise. You can press Alt as you apply it to twirl pixels counterclockwise
	Pucker tool	Pushes pixels toward the brush center
	Bloat tool	Pushes pixels away from the brush center
	Push Left tool	Pushes pixels to the left as you drag up, and to the right as you drag down
	Mirror tool	Reflects pixels as you drag
	Turbulence tool	Mimics a roiling liquid

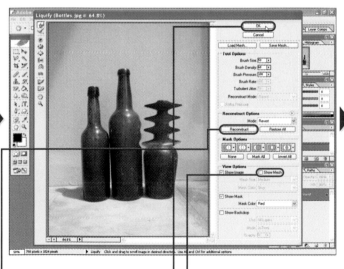

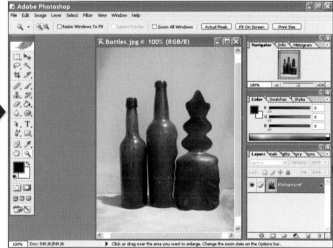

7 Click and drag inside the image preview box.

■ Photoshop liquifies the image where you drag the brush.

■ You can click **Reconstruct** to change the image back to its original state step by step.

■ You can click **Show Mesh** (☐ changes to ☑) to overlay a grid to measure your changes.

8 Click **OK**.

■ Photoshop applies the Liquify effect to your image.

Note: For more about layers, see Chapter 9. See Chapter 4 to use the selection tools.

You can apply more than one filter to an image using the Filter Gallery interface. The interface allows you to view a variety of different filter effects and apply them in combination.

Many filters bring up the Filter Gallery interface when you apply them, including Dry Brush, Charcoal Sketch, Glowing Edges, and Texturizer. See previous sections in this chapter for more information about these filters.

Not all of the effects listed under Photoshop's Filter menu appear in the Filter Gallery.

APPLY MULTIPLE FILTERS

1 Select the layer to which you want to apply the filters.

■ To apply the filters to just part of your image, make a selection with a selection tool.

2 Click **Filter**.

3 Click **Filter Gallery**.

■ The Filter Gallery dialog box appears with the most recently applied filter selected.

■ The left pane displays a preview of the filtered image.

4 Click ▣ to display filters from a category (▣ changes to ▣).

5 Click a thumbnail to apply a filter.

■ The filter appears in the filter list.

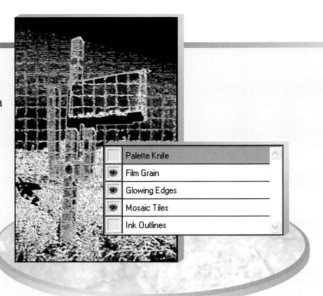

How can I turn off filters in the Filter Gallery?

Currently applied filters appear in a list in the lower right corner of the Filter Gallery. You can click 👁 to temporarily hide a filter in the list. A hidden filter's effects are not applied to the preview in the left pane of the Filter Gallery, nor are they applied to the image when you click OK. You can click 🗑 to delete a filter entirely from the list.

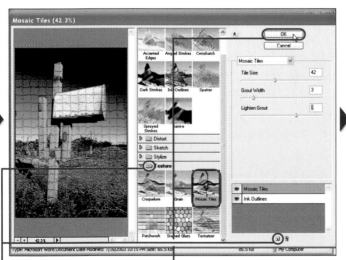

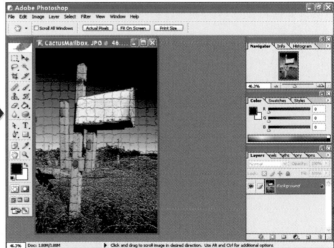

6 Click the New Effect Layer button (🔲).

7 Click 📁 to display filters from another category.

8 Click a thumbnail to apply another filter.

■ You can repeat steps **6** to **8** to apply additional filters.

9 Click **OK**.

■ Photoshop applies the filters.

Note: For more about layers, see Chapter 9. See Chapter 4 to use the selection tools.

GENERATE A PATTERN

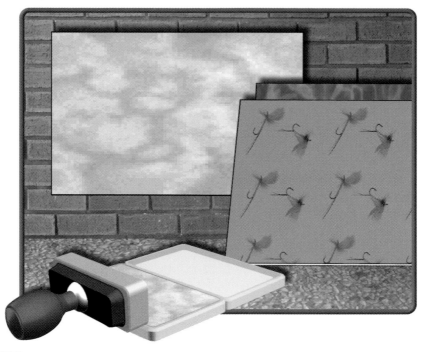

You can generate an abstract pattern based on a selection in your image using Photoshop's Pattern Maker. The Pattern Maker enables you to specify the size, border color, and other settings for your pattern.

You can use your patterns for backgrounds on Web pages.

GENERATE A PATTERN

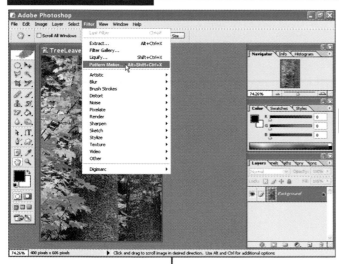

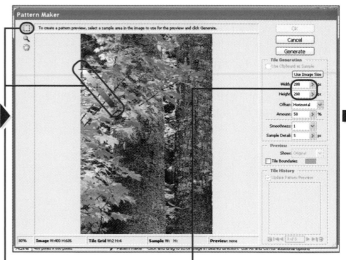

1 Open the image from which you want to generate the pattern.

2 Click **Filter**.

3 Click **Pattern Maker**.

■ The Pattern Maker dialog box appears.

4 Click the Rectangular Marquee tool ([ ]).

5 Click and drag inside the image to select an area from which to generate your pattern.

6 Type the dimensions for your pattern.

■ If the dimensions are smaller than the image dimensions, the pattern repeats.

How can I view patterns that Photoshop has already generated?

When you click **Generate** to create new patterns in the Pattern Maker, Photoshop remembers previous patterns, up to a total of 20. To cycle through previous patterns, you can click the following buttons, located in the Tile History area of the dialog box:

|◀|	Click to view the first pattern.
◀	Click to view the previous pattern.
▶	Click to view the next pattern.
▶|	Click to view the last pattern.

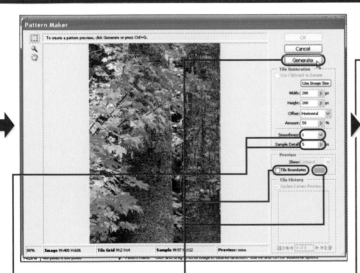

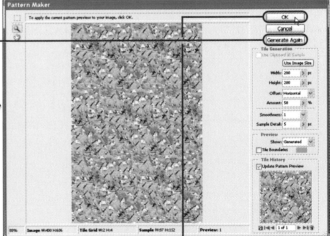

7 Click ☑ (⬍) and specify the smoothness of the pattern.

8 Click ▶ and specify the detail of the pattern.

■ You can click Tile Boundaries to add a border around the pattern (☐ changes to ☑).

■ You can click the color box to select the color of the border.

9 Click **Generate**.

■ Photoshop generates the pattern.

■ You can click **Generate Again** to create a new pattern.

10 Click **OK**.

■ The pattern appears in the image window.

CHAPTER 12

Drawing Shapes

Photoshop offers a variety of tools for drawing geometric and abstract shapes. Other tools let you edit the lines that bound your shapes, or change the colors with which the shapes are filled. You can also use the tools to draw lines that have arrowheads at their ends.

Draw a Shape 234

Draw a Custom Shape 236

Draw a Straight Line........................238

Draw a Shape with the Pen 240

Edit a Shape 242

DRAW A SHAPE

You can create solid shapes in your image using Photoshop's many shape tools. This makes it easy to create solid decorations for your photos or buttons for your Web site.

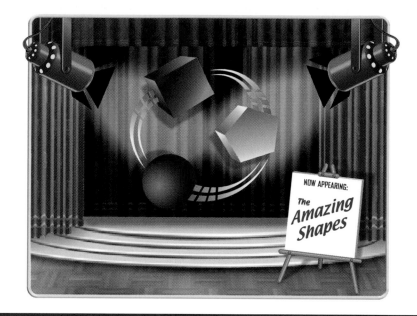

DRAW A SHAPE

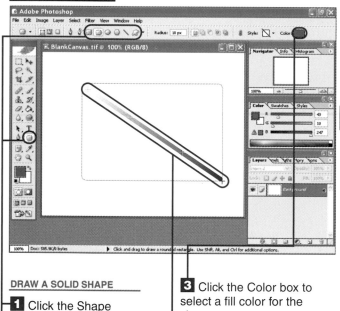

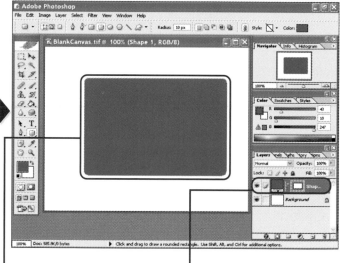

DRAW A SOLID SHAPE

1 Click the Shape tool (□).

Note: The tool icon may differ, depending on the type of shape you drew last.

2 Click a shape in the Options bar.

3 Click the Color box to select a fill color for the shape.

Note: For details on selecting colors, see Chapter 7.

4 Click and drag to draw the shape.

■ Photoshop draws the shape and fills it with the specified color.

■ The shape appears in a new layer in the Layers palette.

How do I resize a shape after I draw it?

Click the shape's layer and then click the Shape tool (). Click **Image**, **Transform Shape**, and then a transform command. You can then resize the shape just as you would a selection. See Chapter 5 for details on transforming selections.

How do I overlap shapes in interesting ways?

To determine how overlapping shapes interact, click one of the following options in the Options bar before drawing:

Add to Shape Area (⬜) adds a shape area to another shape area
Subtract from Shape Area (⬜) subtracts a shape area from another shape area
Intersect Shape Areas (⬜) keeps the area where shapes intersect
Exclude Overlapping Shape Areas (⬜) keeps the area where shapes do not overlap

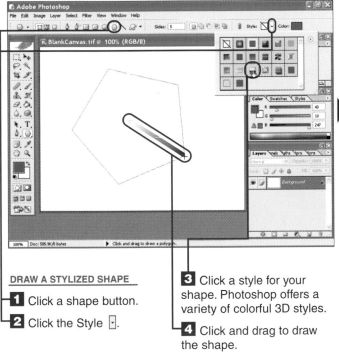

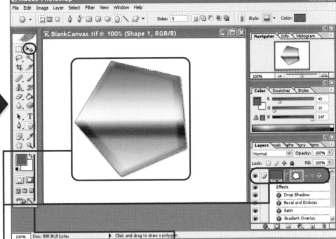

DRAW A STYLIZED SHAPE

1 Click a shape button.

2 Click the Style ▾.

3 Click a style for your shape. Photoshop offers a variety of colorful 3D styles.

4 Click and drag to draw the shape.

■ Photoshop draws the shape and styles it with the specified style.

■ The shape appears in a new layer in the Layers palette.

Note: For more about layers, see Chapter 9. For more about styles, see Chapter 10.

■ You can move the shape by selecting its layer and using the Move tool (⊹).

Note: For more about the Move tool, see Chapter 5.

DRAW A CUSTOM SHAPE

You can use the Custom
Shape tool to draw a
variety of interesting
predefined shapes,
including animals,
frames, and talk bubbles.

DRAW A CUSTOM SHAPE

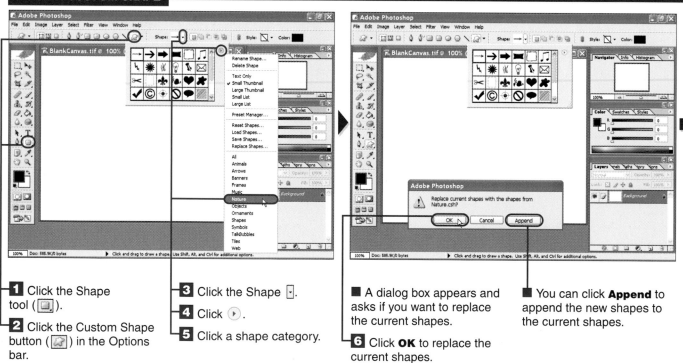

1 Click the Shape
tool (▣).

2 Click the Custom Shape
button (▨) in the Options
bar.

3 Click the Shape ▾.

4 Click ⊙.

5 Click a shape category.

■ A dialog box appears and
asks if you want to replace
the current shapes.

6 Click **OK** to replace the
current shapes.

■ You can click **Append** to
append the new shapes to
the current shapes.

How do I access more custom shapes?

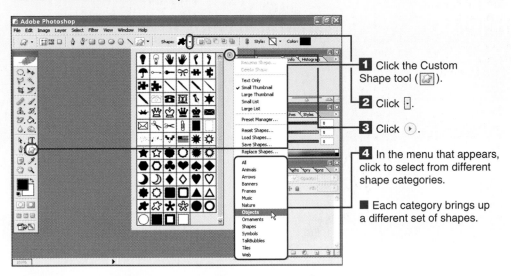

1 Click the Custom Shape tool (📷).

2 Click ·.

3 Click ▸.

4 In the menu that appears, click to select from different shape categories.

■ Each category brings up a different set of shapes.

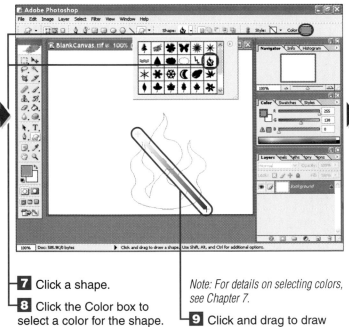

7 Click a shape.

8 Click the Color box to select a color for the shape.

Note: For details on selecting colors, see Chapter 7.

9 Click and drag to draw the shape.

■ Photoshop draws the shape and fills it with the specified color.

■ The shape appears in a new layer in the Layers palette.

Note: For more about layers, see Chapter 9.

■ You can move the shape by selecting its layer and using the Move tool (▶).

Note: For more about the Move tool, see Chapter 5.

DRAW A STRAIGHT LINE

You can draw a straight
line using Photoshop's
Shape tool. You can
customize the line with
arrowheads, giving you
an easy way to point out
elements in your image.

DRAW A STRAIGHT LINE

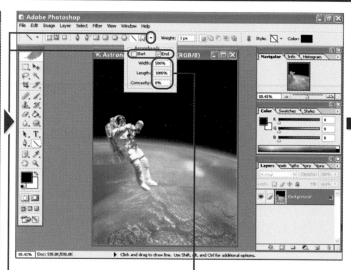

1 Click ▣.

*Note: The tool icon may differ,
depending on the type of shape you
drew last.*

2 Click the Line
button (◥).

3 Click the tool ·.

4 Click **Start** or **End** to
include arrowheads on your
line (☐ changes to ☑).

■ You can also specify
the size and shape of the
arrowheads by typing values
here.

5 Press Enter (Return) to
close the menu.

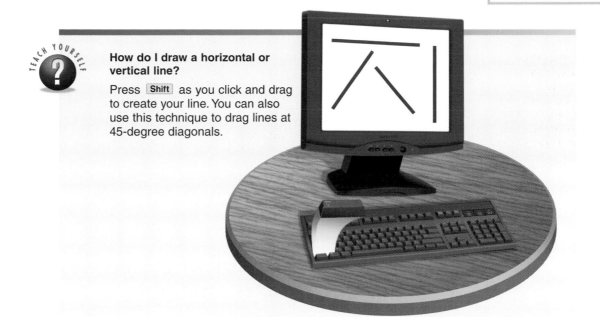

How do I draw a horizontal or vertical line?

Press `Shift` as you click and drag to create your line. You can also use this technique to drag lines at 45-degree diagonals.

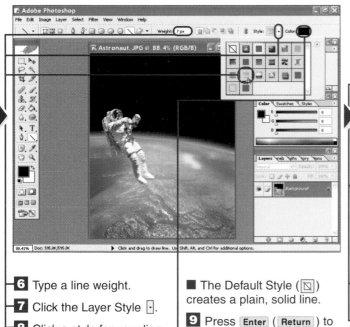

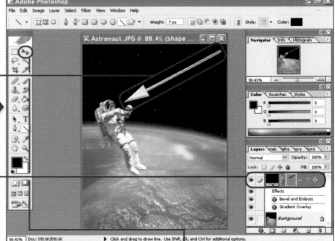

6 Type a line weight.

7 Click the Layer Style ⬝.

8 Click a style for your line.

■ The Default Style (◻) creates a plain, solid line.

9 Press `Enter` (`Return`) to close the menu.

■ You can click the Color box to select a different line color.

10 Click and drag to draw the line.

■ Photoshop places the line in its own layer.

Note: For more about layers, see Chapter 9.

■ You can move the shape by selecting its layer and using the Move tool (⊹).

Note: For more about the Move tool, see Chapter 5.

DRAW A SHAPE WITH THE PEN

The Pen tool lets you create shapes by drawing the lines yourself. This allows you to make shapes that are not in Photoshop's predefined menus.

DRAW A SHAPE WITH THE PEN

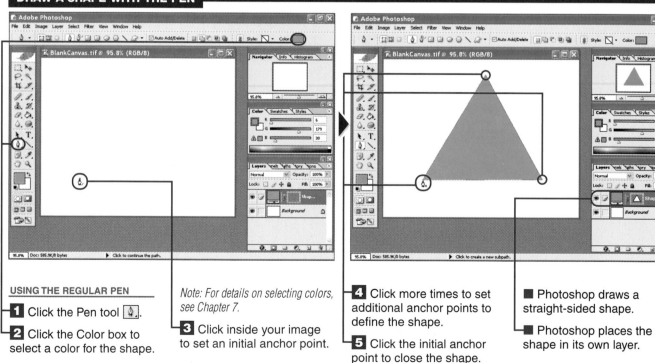

USING THE REGULAR PEN

1 Click the Pen tool (⬧).

2 Click the Color box to select a color for the shape.

Note: For details on selecting colors, see Chapter 7.

3 Click inside your image to set an initial anchor point.

4 Click more times to set additional anchor points to define the shape.

5 Click the initial anchor point to close the shape.

■ Photoshop draws a straight-sided shape.

■ Photoshop places the shape in its own layer.

Can I use the Pen to trace an object?

If the object has well-defined edges, you can trace it using the Freeform Pen tool ( ) with the Magnetic option selected in the Options bar (☐ changes to ☑). The tool works similarly to the Magnetic Lasso tool . For more on using the Magnetic Lasso, see Chapter 4.

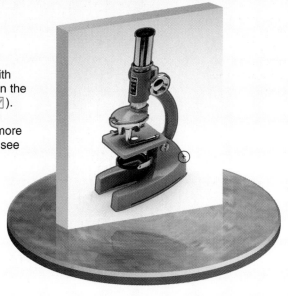

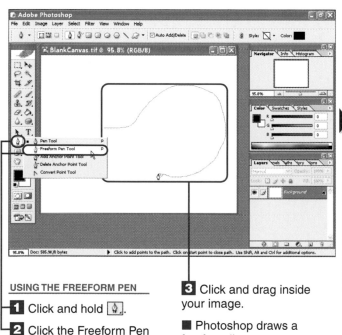

USING THE FREEFORM PEN

1 Click and hold .

2 Click the Freeform Pen tool ( ) from the list that appears.

3 Click and drag inside your image.

■ Photoshop draws a freeform line.

4 Drag to the starting point of the line.

■ Photoshop completes the shape.

■ Alternatively, you can release the mouse, and Photoshop completes your shape with a straight line.

■ Photoshop places the shape in its own layer.

EDIT A SHAPE

You can edit shapes by manipulating their anchor points. This lets you fine-tune the geometries of your shapes.

You can edit shapes drawn with Photoshop's predefined shape tools or the Pen tool.

For more shape-editing techniques, see Photoshop's Help documentation.

EDIT A SHAPE

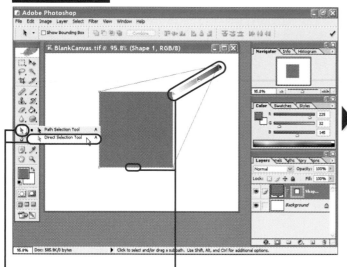

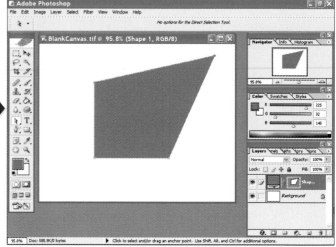

MOVE AN ANCHOR POINT

1 Click and hold the Path Selection tool (⬉).

2 Click the Direct Selection tool (⬉) from the list that appears.

3 Click the edge of a shape to select it.

■ Photoshop shows the anchor points that make up the shape.

4 Click and drag an anchor point.

■ Photoshop moves the anchor point, changing the geometry of the shape.

242

How do I edit curved lines?

If you click an anchor point situated on a curved line with the [▶], direction lines appear to the sides of the anchor point. You can click and drag the ends of the direction lines to edit the curve on each side of the anchor point. You can also click and drag the curves themselves with the [▶].

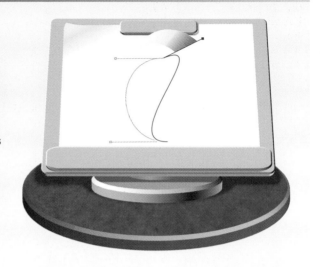

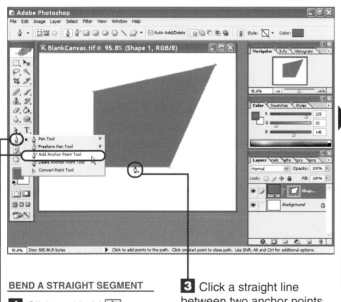

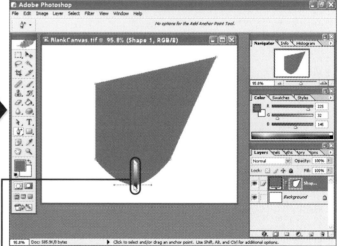

BEND A STRAIGHT SEGMENT

1 Click and hold [✎].

2 Click the Add Anchor Point tool ([✎]) from the list that appears.

3 Click a straight line between two anchor points.

■ Photoshop adds an anchor point to the line.

4 Click the anchor point and drag.

5 Release the mouse.

■ Photoshop turns the straight line into a curved line.

■ You can use this technique to create a concave or convex curve.

SUMMER
VACATION
AIR
SHOW
2003
Acrylic
Paint
color
Acrylic
Paint
color
SUMMER
VACATION

CHAPTER 13

Adding and Manipulating Type

Do you want to add letters and words to your photos and illustrations? Photoshop lets you add type to your images and precisely control the type's appearance and layout. You can also stylize your type using Photoshop's filters and other tools.

Add Type to an Image 246

Add Type in a Bounding Box............248

Change the Formatting of Type 250

Change the Color of Type 252

Apply a Filter to Type 254

Apply an Effect to Type...................256

Warp Type 258

ADD TYPE TO AN IMAGE

Adding type enables you
to label elements in your
image or use letters and
words in artistic ways.

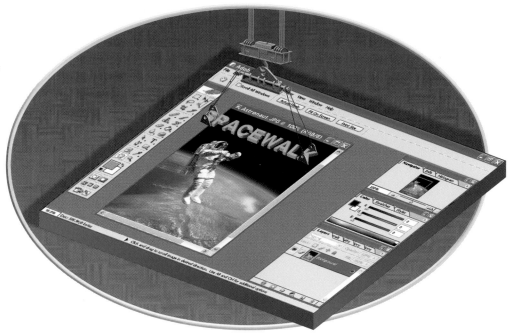

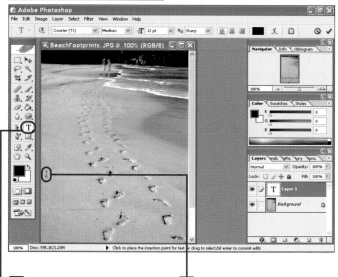

1 Click the Type tool (⊤).

2 Click where you want the new type to appear.

3 Click ∨ and select a font, style, and size for your type.

4 Click the color swatch to select a color for your type.

Note: Photoshop applies the foreground color by default. See Chapter 7 for more about selecting colors.

How do I create vertical type?

If you click and hold T, a list appears with the Vertical Type tool (IT) in it. You can use it to create up-and-down type. When using the regular Type tool, you can click the Change Orientation button (IT) in the Options bar to change horizontal type to vertical, and vice versa. Note that with vertical type, "lines" go from right to left.

How do I reposition my type?

You can move the layer that contains the type with the Move tool (+). Click the layer of type, click +, and then click and drag to reposition your type. For more about moving a layer, see Chapter 9.

5 Type your text.

■ To create a line break, press **Enter** (**Return**).

6 When you finish typing your text, click ✓ or press **Enter** on your keyboard's number pad.

■ Photoshop places the type in its own layer.

■ You can click the alignment buttons to left-align, center, or right-align your type.

ADD TYPE IN A BOUNDING BOX

You can add type inside a *bounding box* to constrain where the type appears and how it wraps.

ADD TYPE IN A BOUNDING BOX

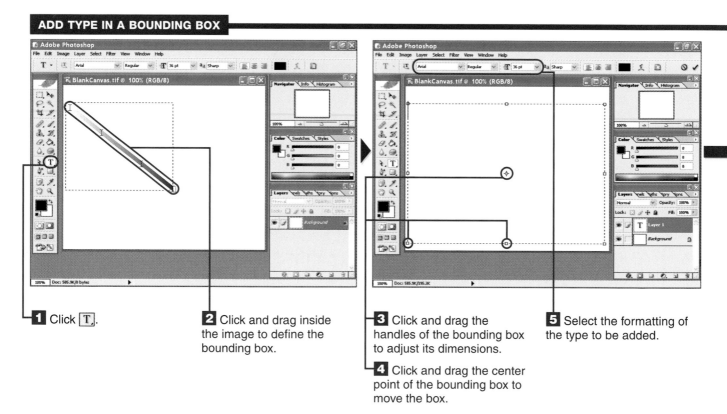

1 Click T.

2 Click and drag inside the image to define the bounding box.

3 Click and drag the handles of the bounding box to adjust its dimensions.

4 Click and drag the center point of the bounding box to move the box.

5 Select the formatting of the type to be added.

How do I format paragraph text inside a bounding box?

With [T] selected, click the text inside the box to highlight it. Then click **Window** and **Paragraph** to display the Paragraph palette. The palette enables you to control the alignment, indenting, and hyphenation of the text inside a bounding box.

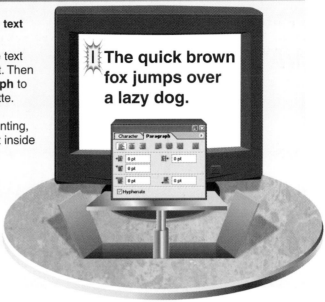

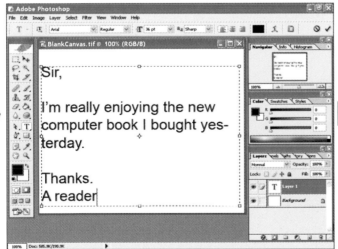

6 Type your text.

■ Your text appears inside the bounding box.

Note: When a line of text hits the edge of the bounding box, it automatically wraps to the next line. Photoshop also automatically adds hyphenation.

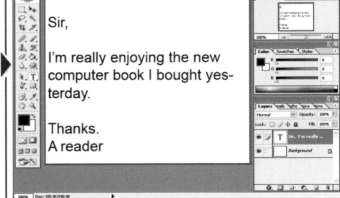

7 When you finish typing your text, click ✔ or press **Enter** on your keyboard's number pad.

■ The bounding box disappears.

■ To make the box reappear in order to change its dimensions, click [T] and click the text.

CHANGE THE FORMATTING OF TYPE

You can change the font, style, size, and other characteristics of your type.

CHANGE THE FORMATTING OF TYPE

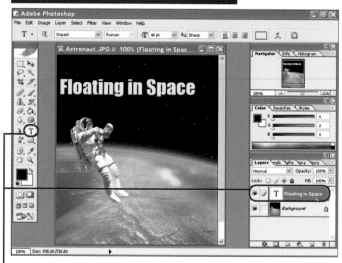

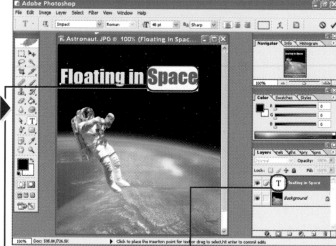

1 Click T.

2 Click the type layer that you want to edit.

■ If the Layers palette is not visible, you can click **Window** and then **Layers** to view it.

3 Click and drag to select some type from the selected layer.

■ You can double-click the layer thumbnail to select all the type.

How do I edit the content of my type?

With the type's layer selected in the Layers palette, you can click inside the type with the T tool. Then you can press Delete to delete letters and type to add new ones. You can press ←, →, ↑, or ↓ to move the cursor inside your type.

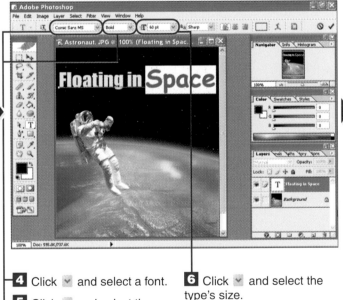

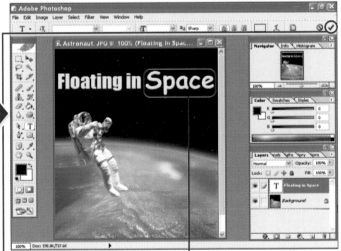

-4 Click ∨ and select a font.

-5 Click ∨ and select the type's style.

6 Click ∨ and select the type's size.

■ You can edit your type in more complex ways by clicking **Window** and then **Character** to open the Character palette.

7 When you finish formatting your text, click ✔ or press Enter on your keyboard's number pad.

■ Photoshop applies the formatting to your type.

CHANGE THE COLOR OF TYPE

You can change the color of your type to make it blend or contrast with the rest of the image.

1 Click T.

2 Click the type layer that you want to edit.

■ If the Layers palette is not visible, you can click **Window** and then **Layers** to view it.

3 Click and drag to select some text.

■ You can double-click the layer thumbnail to select all the type.

4 Click the Color swatch.

252

What is antialiasing?

Antialiasing is the process of adding semitransparent pixels to curved edges in digital images to make the edges appear more smooth. You can apply antialiasing to type to improve its appearance. Text that you do not antialias can sometimes look jagged. You can control the presence and style of your type's antialiasing with the menu in the Options bar.

■ The Color Picker dialog box appears.

5 Click a color.

■ You can click and drag the slider ( ) to change the colors that Photoshop displays in the selection box.

6 Click **OK**.

7 Click ✓ or press **Enter** on your keyboard's number pad.

■ Photoshop changes the text to the new color.

APPLY A FILTER TO TYPE

To apply a filter to type, you must first rasterize it. Rasterizing converts your type layer into a regular Photoshop layer. You can no longer edit rasterized type using the type tools.

For more about filters, see Chapter 11.

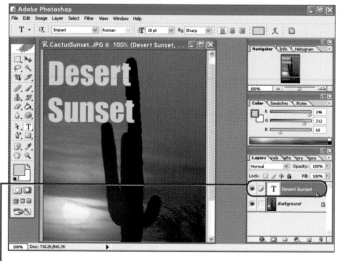

1 Select the type layer to which you want to apply a filter.

■ If the Layers palette is not visible, you can click **Window** and then **Layers** to view it.

2 Click **Layer**.

3 Click **Rasterize**.

4 Click **Type**.

How can I create semitransparent type?

Select the type layer in the Layers palette and then reduce the layer's opacity to less than 100%. This makes the type semitransparent. For details about changing opacity, see Chapter 9.

■ Photoshop converts the type layer to a regular layer.

■ Now you can apply a filter to the type.

■ In this example, a special effect was added to the type by clicking **Filter**, **Sketch**, and then **Bas Relief**.

APPLY AN EFFECT TO TYPE

You can easily apply an effect to type to give it a colorful or 3D appearance. After you apply an effect, you can still edit the type using the type tools.

For more about effects, see Chapter 10.

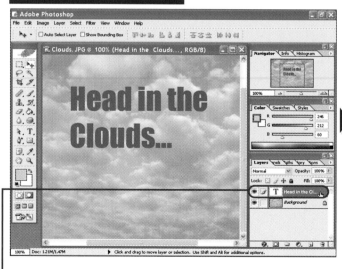

1 Select the type layer to which you want to apply an effect.

■ If the Layers palette is not visible, you can click **Window** and then **Layers** to view it.

2 Click **Layer**.

3 Click **Layer Style**.

4 Click an effect.

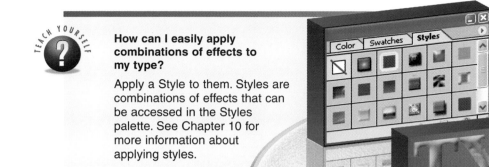

How can I easily apply combinations of effects to my type?

Apply a Style to them. Styles are combinations of effects that can be accessed in the Styles palette. See Chapter 10 for more information about applying styles.

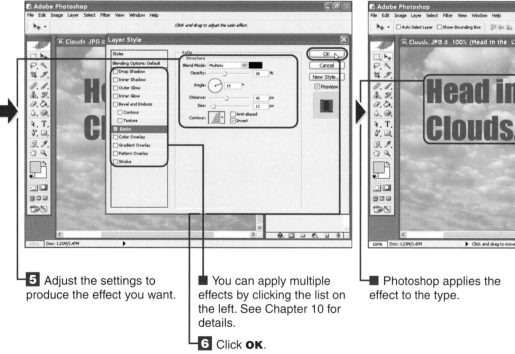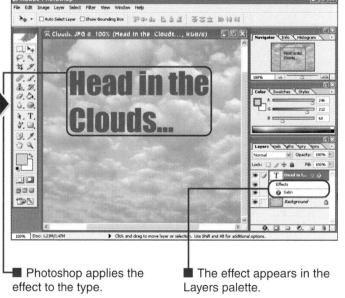

5 Adjust the settings to produce the effect you want.

■ You can apply multiple effects by clicking the list on the left. See Chapter 10 for details.

6 Click **OK**.

■ Photoshop applies the effect to the type.

■ The effect appears in the Layers palette.

WARP TYPE

You can easily bend and distort layers of type with Photoshop's Warp feature. This can make words look wrinkled, or like they are blowing in the wind.

WARP TYPE

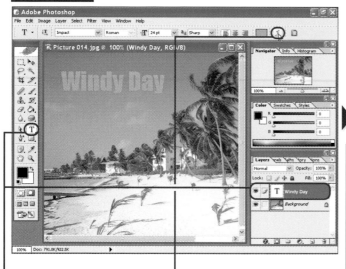

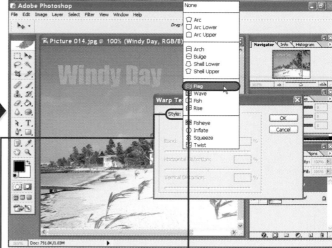

1 Click [T].

2 Click the type layer that you want to warp.

■ If the Layers palette is not visible, you can click **Window** and then **Layers** to view it.

3 Click the Create Warped Text button ([I]).

■ The Warp Text dialog box appears.

4 Click the Style ([ ]).

5 Click a warp style.

258

How do I unwarp text?

Click the type layer that you want to unwarp and click the Create Warped Text button (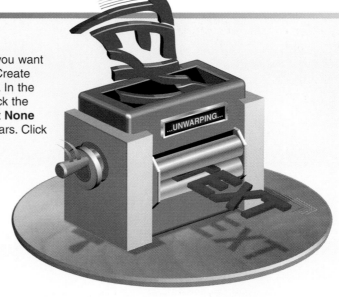). In the Warp Text dialog box, click the Style ⌄ (⬚) and select **None** from the menu that appears. Click **OK** to unwarp the type.

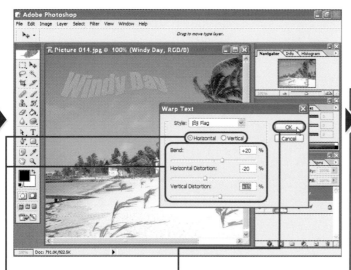

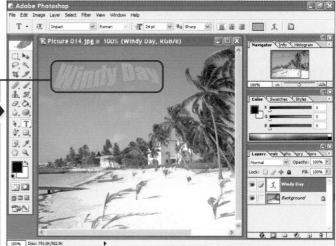

6 Select an orientation for the warp effect (○ changes to ◉).

7 Adjust the Bend and Distortion values by clicking and dragging the sliders (⬚).

■ The Bend and Distortion values determine the strength of the warp. At 0% for all values, no warp is applied.

8 Click **OK**.

■ Photoshop warps the text.

■ You can still edit the format, color, and other characteristics of the type after you apply warp.

CHAPTER 14

Automating Your Work

Sometimes you want to perform the same simple sequence of commands on many different images. With Photoshop's Action commands, you can automate repetitive imaging tasks by saving sequences of commands and applying them automatically to many image files. Other Photoshop commands let you streamline your work by helping you create Web photo galleries, picture packages, and contact sheets.

Record an Action 262

Play an Action 264

Batch Process by Using an Action 266

Create a Contact Sheet....................268

Create a Picture Package 270

Create a Web Photo Gallery 272

Create a Panoramic Image 274

RECORD AN ACTION

You can record a
sequence of commands
as an action and replay
them on other image
files. This can save you
time when you have a
task in Photoshop that
you need to repeat.

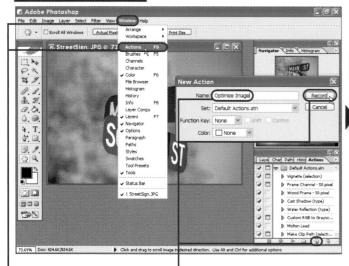

1 Click **Window**.

2 Click **Actions** to open the Actions palette.

3 Click the Create New Action button (🔲) to open the New Action dialog box.

4 Type a name for your action.

5 Click **Record**.

6 Perform the sequence of commands that you want to automate on your images.

■ In this example, the first command, Auto Contrast, is performed by clicking **Image**, **Adjustments**, and then **Auto Contrast**.

Note: See Chapter 8 for more about adjusting colors and contrast.

What if I make a mistake when recording my action?

You can try recording the action again by clicking ⊙ in the Actions palette and clicking **Record Again**. This runs through the same actions, and you can apply different settings in the command dialog boxes. Alternatively, you can select the action, click 🗑 to delete the action, and try rerecording it.

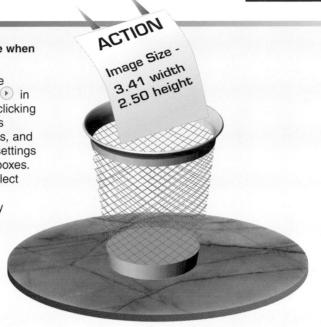

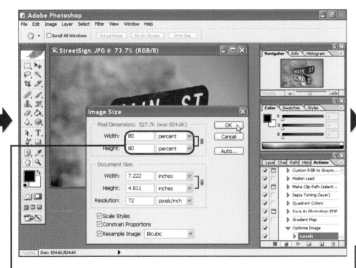

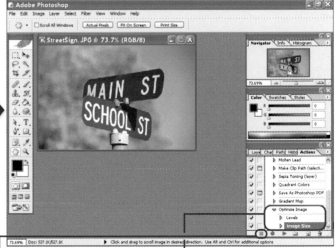

■ In this example, the second command reduces the image size to 80% by clicking **Image** and **Image Size**.

Note: See Chapter 3 for more about resizing images.

7 Click the Stop button (▣) to stop recording.

■ The Actions palette lists the commands performed under the name of the action.

PLAY AN ACTION

You can play an action from the Actions palette on an image. This saves time, because you can execute multiple Photoshop commands with a single click. You can also play a specific command that is part of an action by itself.

PLAY AN ACTION

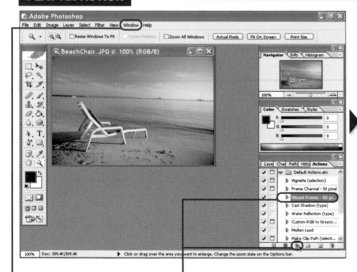

1 Click **Window** and then **Actions** to open the Actions palette.

■ Photoshop comes with several predefined actions in the Actions palette.

Note: To create your own action, see the section "Record an Action."

2 Click the action that you want to play.

3 Click the Play button (▶).

■ Photoshop applies the commands that make up the action to the image.

■ In this example, a wood frame is added around the image.

■ You can undo the multiple commands in an action using the History palette. See Chapter 2 for more information.

How do I assign a special key command to an action?

Click ⊙ to open the Actions palette menu, and then click **Action Options** to open the Action Options dialog box. Select a key command from the Function Key drop-down menu. Then, to perform an action on an image, press the Function key.

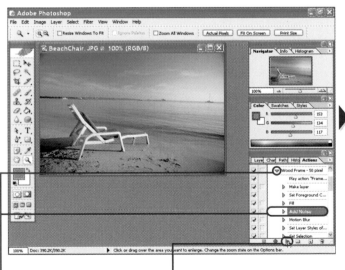

PLAY A COMMAND IN AN ACTION

1 Click ▶ to list the commands that make up an action (▶ changes to ▼).

2 Click the command that you want to execute.

■ You can press Shift +click to select multiple commands.

3 Ctrl +click (⌘ +click) the ▶ button.

■ Photoshop executes the selected command, but no commands before or after it.

■ In this example, the selected command adds noise to the image.

BATCH PROCESS BY USING AN ACTION

You can apply an action to multiple images automatically with Photoshop's Batch command. The command is a great time-saver for tasks such as optimizing large numbers of digital photos.

BATCH PROCESS BY USING AN ACTION

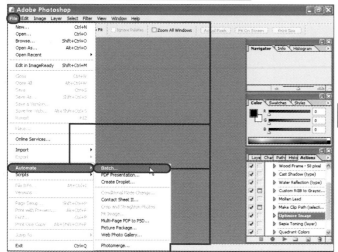

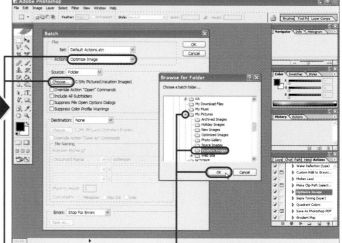

1 Place all the images you want to apply an action to in a source folder.

2 Create a destination folder in which to save your batch-processed files.

Note: To work with folders, see your operating system's documentation.

3 In Photoshop, click **File**.

4 Click **Automate**.

5 Click **Batch**.

6 Click (☑) and select an action to apply.

7 Click **Choose**.

■ The Browse For Folder (Choose a batch folder) dialog box appears.

8 Click ⊞ to open folders on your computer (⊞ changes to ⊟).

9 Click the folder containing your images.

10 Click **OK**.

How can I change the mode — such as RGB Color or Grayscale — of an image during a batch process depending on its current mode?

When you record the original action, click **File**, **Automate**, and then **Conditional Mode Change**. A dialog box appears, and asks you to specify the source modes that should be switched, and a target mode. When the action is run as a batch process, images that are one of the selected source modes will be converted.

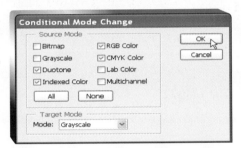

How do I batch process using an action in Mac OS X?

You do this very much like a Windows user would, but with the Open dialog box instead of with the Browse for Folder dialog box. When you click **Choose** in step **7**, the Open-style dialog box appears. Using the file browser in the center of the dialog box, locate the source and destination folders for your batch-processed images.

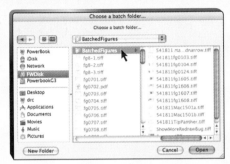

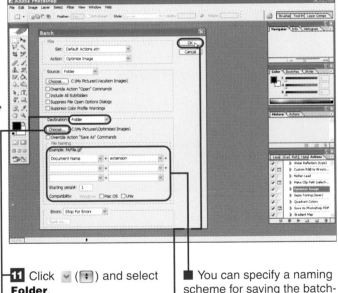

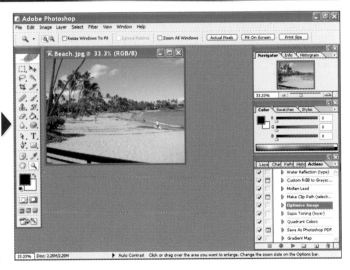

11 Click ☑ (⬍) and select **Folder**.

12 Click **Choose** and repeat steps **8** and **9** to select the folder where you want your batch-processed files to be saved.

■ You can specify a naming scheme for saving the batch-processed files.

13 Click **OK**.

■ Photoshop opens each image in the specified folder one at a time, applies the action, and then saves the files in the destination directory.

CREATE A CONTACT SHEET

Photoshop can automatically create a digital version of a photographer's contact sheet. Useful for keeping a hard-copy record of your digital images, contact sheets consist of miniature versions of images.

For information about printing a contact sheet after you create it, see Chapter 16.

CREATE A CONTACT SHEET

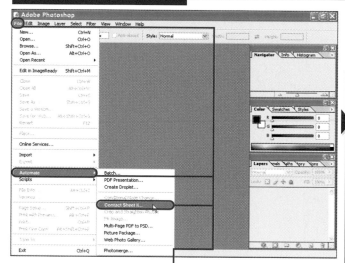

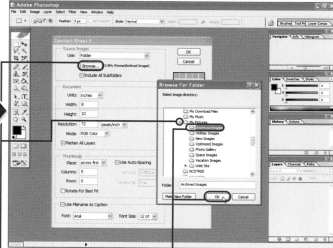

1 Place the images that you want on the contact sheet in a folder.

Note: To work with folders, see your operating system's documentation.

2 Click **File**.

3 Click **Automate**.

4 Click **Contact Sheet II**.

■ The Contact Sheet II dialog box appears.

5 Click **Browse (Choose)**.

■ The Browse For Folder (Select image directory) dialog box appears.

6 In Windows, click ⊞ to open folders on your computer (⊞ changes to ⊟).

■ See the tip in the section "Batch Process by Using an Action" to choose a folder on a Mac.

7 Click the folder containing your images.

8 Click **OK**.

TEACH YOURSELF

How do I make the thumbnail images larger on my contact sheet?

Paper size and the number of rows and columns automatically determine the size of the thumbnails. To increase the thumbnail size, type a smaller number of rows and columns for the sheet in the Columns and Rows boxes in the Contact Sheet II dialog box.

Contact Sheet

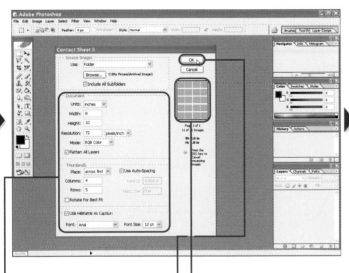

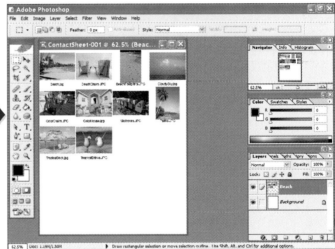

9 Set any contact sheet properties by typing values or by clicking ✔ (⬍) and selecting settings.

■ You can set the contact sheet size and resolution, the order and number of columns and rows in the sheet, as well as the caption font and font size.

■ Photoshop displays a preview of the layout.

10 Click **OK**.

■ Photoshop creates and displays your contact sheet.

■ If there are more images than can fit on a single page, Photoshop creates multiple contact sheets.

Note: To save your contact sheet, see Chapter 15.

CREATE A PICTURE PACKAGE

You can automatically create a one-page layout with one or more selected images at various sizes using the Picture Package command. You may find this useful when you want to print pictures for friends, family, or associates.

For information about printing a picture package after you create it, see Chapter 16.

CREATE A PICTURE PACKAGE

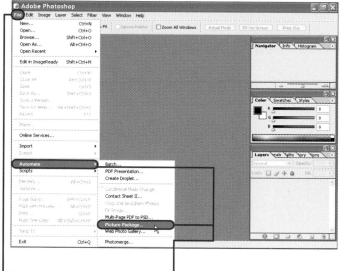

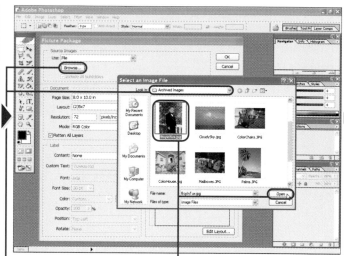

1 Click **File**.

2 Click **Automate**.

3 Click **Picture Package**.

■ The Picture Package dialog box appears.

4 Click **Browse (Choose)**.

■ The Select an Image File dialog box appears.

5 In Windows, click ⌄ (📢) and select the folder that contains the image file.

■ See the tip in the section "Batch Process by Using an Action" to choose a folder on a Mac.

6 Click the image file.

7 Click **Open**.

How do I label my picture package?

At the bottom of the Picture Package dialog box, you can choose labels such as copyright or caption information, the image filename, or custom text that you define. To set copyright and caption information for an image, see Chapter 15.

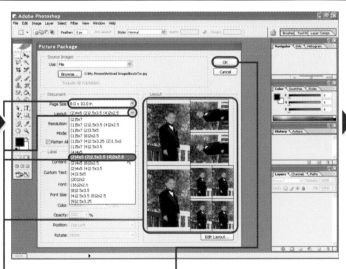

8 Click ⌄ (⬇) and select a paper size.

9 Click the Layout ⌄ (⬇).

10 Click a layout.

■ A preview of the layout appears.

■ You can click individual thumbnails to change the image files.

11 You can select other picture package settings in the dialog box.

12 Click **OK**.

■ Photoshop constructs the picture package step-by-step, and then opens a new image window with the picture package inside it.

Note: To save your picture package, see Chapter 15.

271

CREATE A WEB PHOTO GALLERY

You can have Photoshop create a photo gallery Web site that showcases your images. Photoshop not only sizes and optimizes your image files for the site, but it also creates the Web pages that display the images and links those pages together.

After you create your photo gallery, you can use an FTP program such as WS FTP in Windows or RBrowserLite on a Mac to upload your images to a Web server.

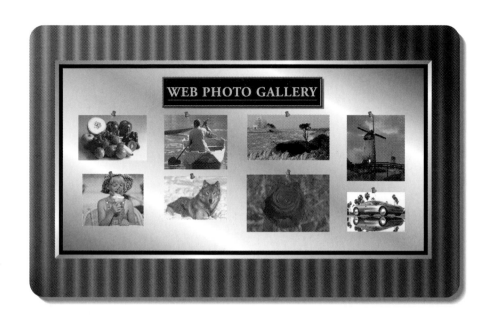

CREATE A WEB PHOTO GALLERY

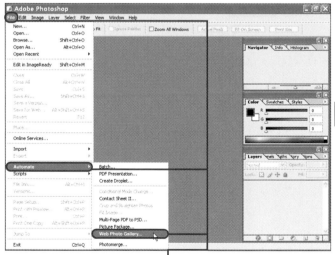

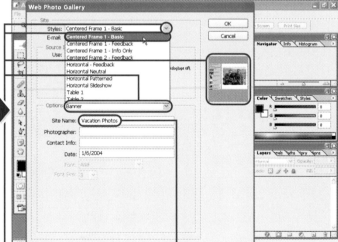

1 Place all the images you want to feature in your Web photo gallery in a folder.

2 Create a separate folder where Photoshop can save all the image files and HTML files necessary for your gallery.

Note: To work with folders, see your operating system's documentation.

3 Click **File**.

4 Click **Automate**.

5 Click **Web Photo Gallery**.

6 Click ▾ (▾) and select a photo gallery style.

■ Photoshop displays a preview of the style.

7 Click ▾ (▾) and click **Banner**.

■ You can select other Options to further customize your gallery.

8 Type the site name for your gallery Web pages.

272

How can I allow viewers the option of sending me feedback from my Web Photo Gallery pages?

In the Web Photo Gallery dialog box, type your e-mail address in the E-mail field. Then, in the Styles menu, select a gallery style that includes "Feedback" in the style name. When Photoshop builds the Web Photo Gallery, it includes an option on the pages that allows viewers to send feedback about the gallery photos. You can check your e-mail to read the feedback.

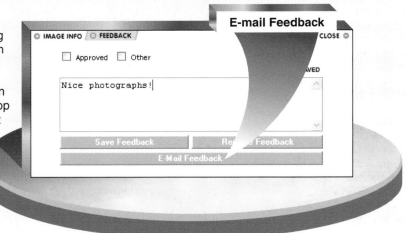

E-mail Feedback

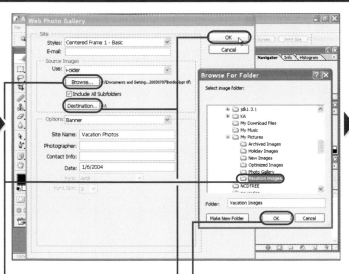

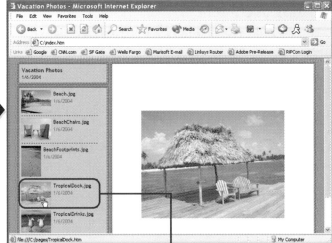

9 Click **Browse (Choose)**.

■ The Browse For Folder (Select image directory) dialog box appears.

10 Select the folder containing your images.

11 Click **OK**.

12 Click **Destination** and repeat steps **10** and **11** to specify the folder in which to save your gallery.

13 Click **OK** in the Web Photo Gallery dialog box.

■ Photoshop opens each image in the specified folder, creates versions for the photo gallery, and generates the necessary HTML.

■ After the processing is complete, Photoshop opens the default Web browser on your computer and displays the home page of the gallery.

■ You can click a thumbnail to see a larger version of the image.

CREATE A PANORAMIC IMAGE

You can use the Photomerge feature in Photoshop to stitch several images together into a single panoramic image. This allows you to capture more scenery than is usually possible in a regular photograph.

CREATE A PANORAMIC IMAGE

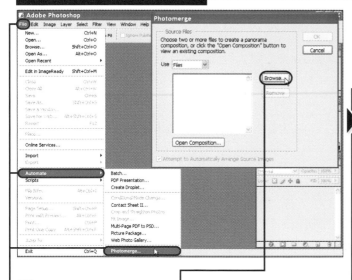

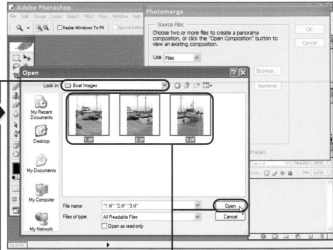

■ 1 Click **File**.

■ 2 Click **Automate**.

■ 3 Click **Photomerge**.

■ The Photomerge dialog box appears.

■ 4 Click **Browse**.

■ The Open dialog box appears.

Note: For more information about the Open dialog box on a Mac, see page 17.

■ 5 Click ⌄ (🔾) and select the folder that contains the images that you want to merge.

■ 6 Press `Ctrl` (⌘) and then click the images you want to merge into a panoramic image.

■ 7 Click **Open**.

How can I create photos that merge successfully?

To merge photos successfully, you need to align and overlap the photos. Here are a few hints:

- Use a tripod to keep your photos level with one another.

- Experiment with the Perspective setting in the Photomerge dialog box. This setting can be useful if you use a tripod to shoot your photos.

- Refrain from using lenses, such as fisheye lenses, that distort your photos.

- Shoot your photos so that they overlap at least 30%.

For more tips, see the Photoshop Help documentation.

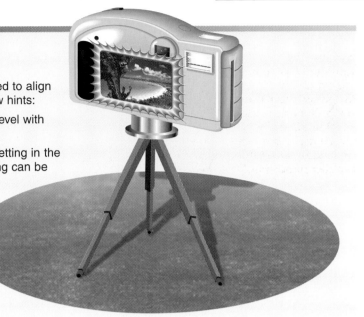

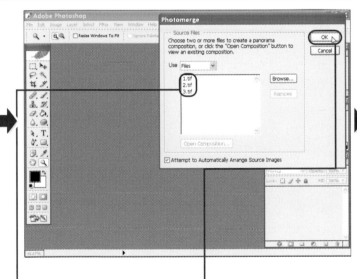

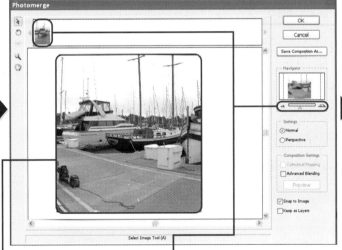

■ The filenames of the images appear in the Source Files list.

8 Click **OK** to build the panoramic image.

■ Photoshop attempts to merge the images together into a single panoramic image.

■ Thumbnails of the images that it cannot merge appear in a lightbox area.

■ You can click and drag ◢ to zoom the panoramic image in and out.

CONTINUED

CREATE A PANORAMIC IMAGE

The Photomerge dialog box allows you to interactively align the images that make up your panorama.

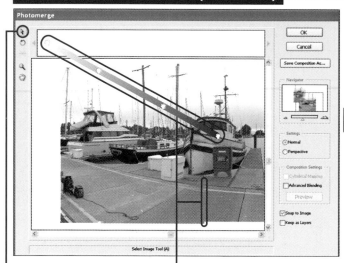

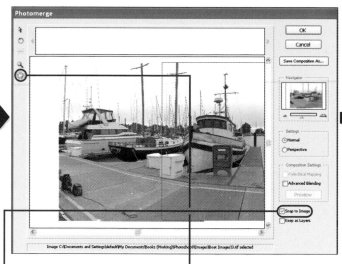

9 Click the Select Image Tool ( ).

10 Click and drag an image from the lightbox to the work area.

11 Place the image so that it lines up with its neighboring image in the panorama.

■ If you select **Snap to Image** (changes to), Photoshop tries to merge the image edges after you click and drag.

■ You can use the Move View tool ( ) to adjust the placement of the entire panoramic image inside the main window.

12 Repeat steps **9** to **11** for any other images in the lightbox so that they overlap and match one another.

How do I apply perspective to my panorama?

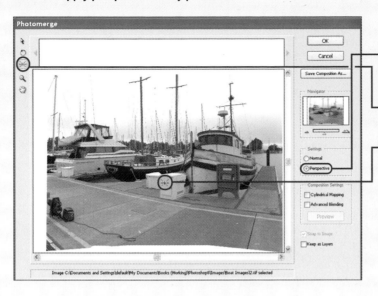

1 In the Photomerge dialog box, click the **Perspective** option (○ changes to ⊙).

2 Click the Vanishing Point tool ( ).

3 Click the part of the image to serve as the central focal point for your panorama.

■ When you apply this option, Photoshop warps the area next to the vanishing point slightly to provide the correct perspective.

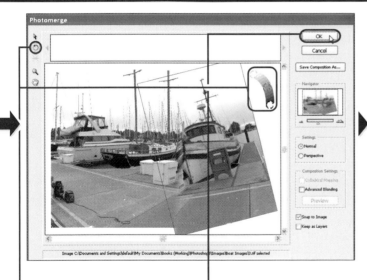

■ You can click the Rotate Image tool ( ) and click and drag with it to align image seams that are not level with one another.

13 Click **OK**.

■ Photoshop merges the images and opens the new panorama in a new image window.

Note: To save the panorama, see Chapter 15. To print the panorama, see Chapter 16.

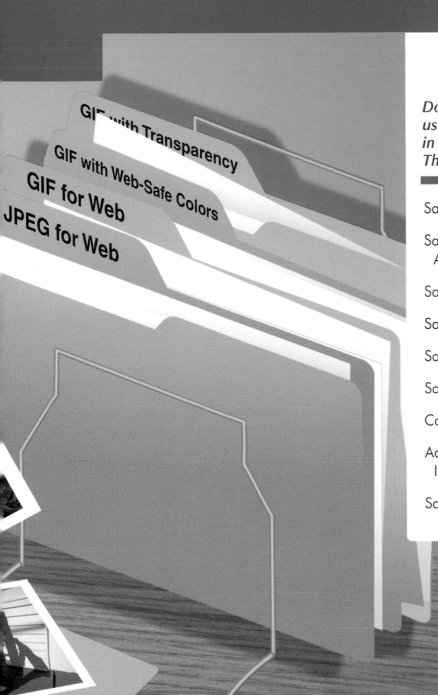

GIF with Transparency

GIF with Web-Safe Colors

GIF for Web

JPEG for Web

CHAPTER 15

Saving Images

Do you want to save your images for use later, or so that you can use them in another application or on the Web? This chapter shows you how.

Save in the Photoshop Format 280

Save an Image for Use in Another
Application 282

Save a JPEG for the Web 284

Save a GIF for the Web 286

Save a GIF with Transparency 288

Save a GIF with Web-Safe Colors 290

Compare File Sizes 292

Add Descriptive and Copyright
Information 294

Save a Sliced Image.......................296

SAVE IN THE PHOTOSHOP FORMAT

You can save your image in Photoshop's native image format. This format enables you to retain multiple layers in your image, if it has them. This is the best format in which to save your images if you still need to edit them.

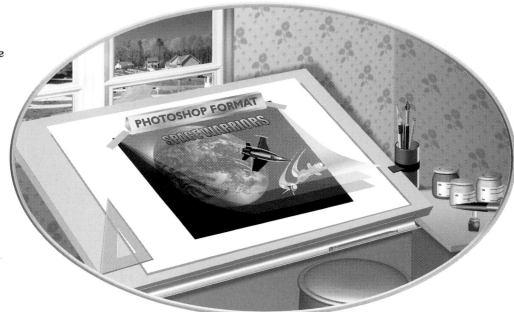

The Photoshop PDF and TIFF file formats also support multiple layers.

SAVE IN THE PHOTOSHOP FORMAT

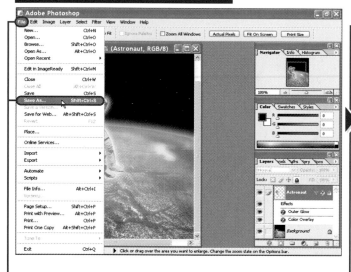

1 Click **File**.

2 Click **Save As**.

■ If you have named and saved your image previously and just want to save changes, you can click **File** and then **Save**.

■ The Save As dialog box appears.

■ To perform steps **3** and **4** on a Mac, see the Tip on the facing page.

3 In Windows, click ⌄ and click a folder in which to save the image file.

4 In Windows, click ⌄ and select the Photoshop file format.

5 Type a name for the image file.

■ Photoshop automatically assigns a .psd extension.

How do I save in Photoshop format in Mac OS X?

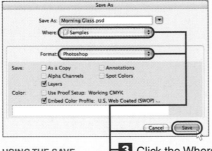

USING THE SAVE AS DIALOG BOX

1 Click **File**.

2 Click **Save As**.

■ The Save As dialog box appears.

3 Click the Where , and choose the folder.

4 Click the Format  and choose **Photoshop**; Photoshop adds the .psd extension.

5 Click **Save**.

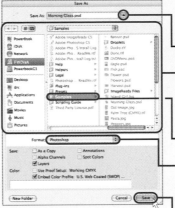

2 Click the Show More button (▼).

■ ▼ changes to ▲.

■ The Save As dialog box expands to display the File Browser and Sidebar.

3 Click the folder.

4 Click the Format ◆ and choose **Photoshop**; Photoshop adds the .psd extension.

5 Click **Save**.

USING THE FILE BROWSER

1 Repeat steps **1** and **2**.

■ The Save As dialog box appears.

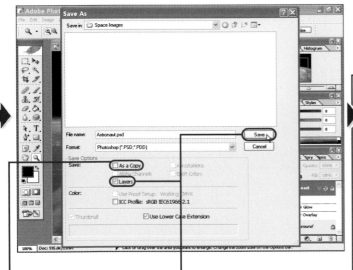

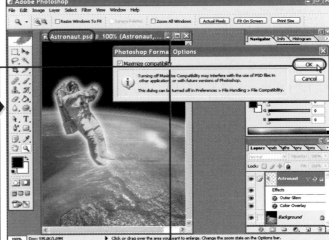

■ If you want to save a copy of the file and keep the existing file open, click **As a Copy** (☐ changes to ☑).

■ If you want to merge the multiple layers of your image into one layer, click **Layers** (☑ changes to ☐).

6 Click **Save**.

■ A Photoshop Format Options dialog box appears.

7 Click **OK** to make sure your image is compatible with other applications.

■ Photoshop saves the image file.

■ The name of the file appears in the image's title bar.

SAVE AN IMAGE FOR USE IN ANOTHER APPLICATION

You can save your image in a format that users can open and use in other imaging or page-layout applications. TIFF, Tagged Image File Format, and EPS, Encapsulated PostScript, are standard printing formats that many applications on both Windows and Macintosh platforms support.

BMP — bitmap — is a popular Windows image format, and PICT is a Macintosh image format.

Please note that most image formats — with the exception of the Photoshop PSD, Photoshop PDF, and TIFF formats — do not support layers.

SAVE AN IMAGE FOR USE IN ANOTHER APPLICATION

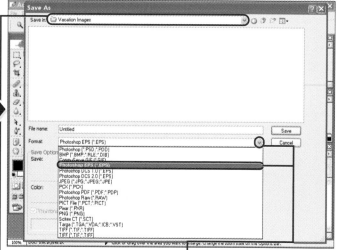

1 Click **File**.

2 Click **Save As**.

■ The Save As dialog box appears.

■ To perform steps **3** and **4** on a Mac, see the Tip in the section "Save in the Photoshop Format."

3 In Windows, click ⮟ and choose a folder in which to save the image file.

4 In Windows, click ⮟ and select a file format.

282

How do I choose a file format for my image?

You should choose the format based on how you want to use the image. If it is a multilayered image and you want to preserve the layers, save it as a Photoshop file. If you want to use it in word processing or page layout applications, save it as a TIFF or EPS file. If you want to use it on the Web, save it as a JPEG or GIF file. For more information on file formats, see the rest of this chapter as well as Photoshop's documentation.

What are some popular page-layout programs with which I might use images?

Adobe InDesign, and QuarkXPress are two popular page-layout programs. You can use them to combine text and images to create brochures, magazines, and other printed media. You can import TIFF and EPS files saved in Photoshop into both programs.

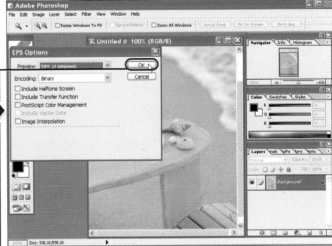

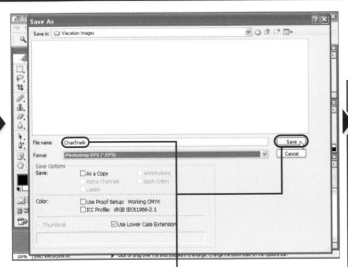

■ If you are saving a multilayer image and select a file format that does not support layers, an alert icon appears. Photoshop saves a flattened copy of the image.

Note: See the section "Save in the Photoshop Format" to save a multilayer image. For more about flattening, see Chapter 9.

5 Type a filename.

■ Photoshop automatically assigns an appropriate extension for the file format, such as .tif for TIFF or .eps for EPS.

6 Click **Save**.

■ When saving in the EPS format, as in this example, Photoshop displays a dialog box allowing you to specify optional settings. Click **OK**.

■ Photoshop saves the image.

■ If a flattened copy was saved, the original multilayer version remains in the image window.

SAVE A JPEG FOR THE WEB

You can save a file in the JPEG — Joint Photographic Experts Group — format and publish it on the Web. JPEG is the preferred file format for saving photographic images.

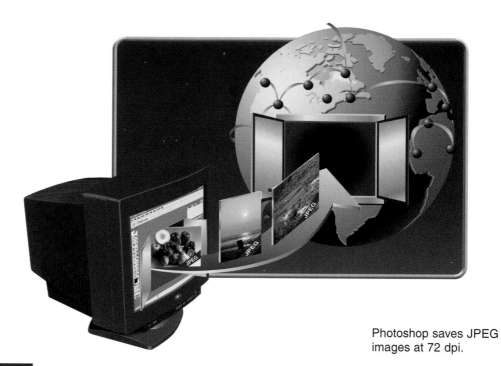

Photoshop saves JPEG images at 72 dpi.

SAVE A JPEG FOR THE WEB

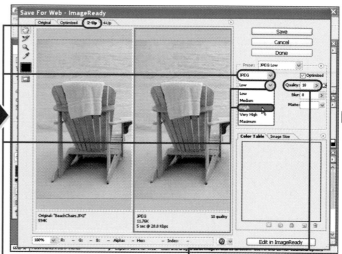

1 Click **File**.

2 Click **Save for Web**.

■ The Save For Web dialog box appears.

3 Click the **2-Up** tab.

4 Click ☑ (◆) and select **JPEG**.

5 Click ☑ (◆) and select a quality setting.

■ Alternatively, you can select a numeric quality setting from 0, low quality, to 100, high quality.

■ The higher the quality, the larger the resulting file size.

What is image compression?

Image compression involves using mathematical techniques to reduce the amount of information required to describe an image. This results in smaller file sizes, which is important when transmitting information on the Web. Some compression schemes, such as JPEG, involve some loss in quality due to the compression, but the loss is usually negligible compared to the file size savings.

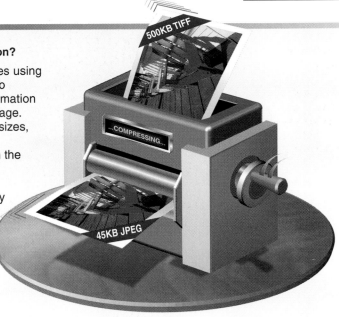

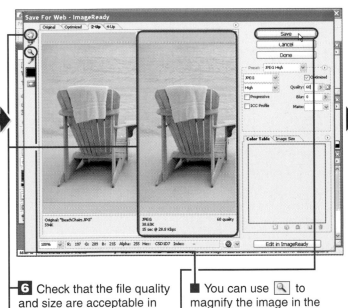

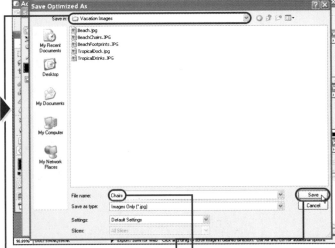

6 Check that the file quality and size are acceptable in the preview window.

■ You can use 🖐 to move the image in the preview window.

■ You can use 🔍 to magnify the image in the preview.

7 Click **Save**.

8 In Windows, click ☑ and select a folder in which to save the file.

■ Mac users should refer to the Tip in the section "Save in the Photoshop Format" to select a folder.

9 Type a filename. Photoshop automatically assigns a .jpg extension.

10 Click **Save**.

■ The original image file remains open in Photoshop.

SAVE A GIF FOR THE WEB

You can save a file as a *GIF* — Graphics Interchange Format — and publish it on the Web. The GIF format is good for saving illustrations that have a lot of solid color. The format supports a maximum of 256 colors.

Photoshop saves GIF images at 72 dpi.

SAVE A GIF FOR THE WEB

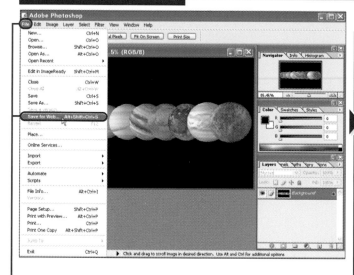

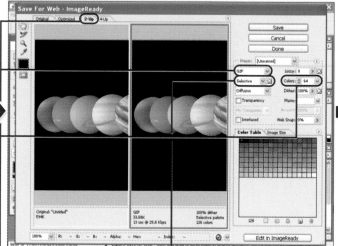

1 Click **File**.

2 Click **Save for Web**.

■ The Save For Web dialog box appears.

3 Click the **2-Up** tab.

4 Click ⌄ ( ) and select **GIF**.

5 Click ⌄ and select the number of colors to include in the image.

■ GIF allows a maximum of 256 colors.

■ You can click ⌄ ( ) to choose the algorithm that Photoshop uses to select the GIF colors.

How do I minimize the file sizes of my GIF images?

The most important factor in creating small GIFs is limiting the number of colors in the final image. GIF files are limited to 256 colors or fewer. In images that have just a few solid colors, you can often reduce the total number of colors to 16 or 8 without any noticeable reduction in quality. See step **5** below for setting the number of colors in your GIF images.

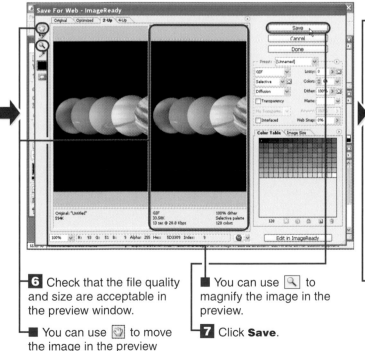

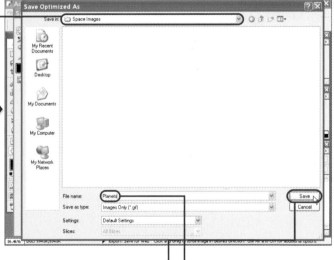

6 Check that the file quality and size are acceptable in the preview window.

■ You can use 🖐 to move the image in the preview window.

■ You can use 🔍 to magnify the image in the preview.

7 Click **Save**.

8 In Windows, click ⌄ and select a folder in which to save the file.

■ Mac users should use the Where popup menu or the File Browser to select a folder.

9 Type a filename. Photoshop automatically assigns a `.gif` extension.

10 Click **Save**.

■ The original image file remains open in Photoshop.

SAVE A GIF WITH TRANSPARENCY

You can include transparency in files saved in the GIF file format. The transparent pixels do not show up on Web pages.

Because Photoshop Background layers cannot contain transparent pixels, you need to work with layers other than the Background layer to create transparent GIFs. See Chapter 9 for more about layers.

SAVE A GIF WITH TRANSPARENCY

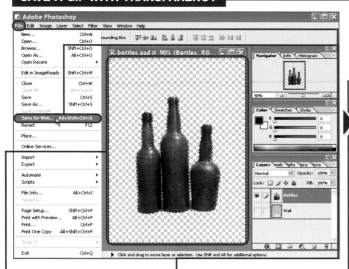

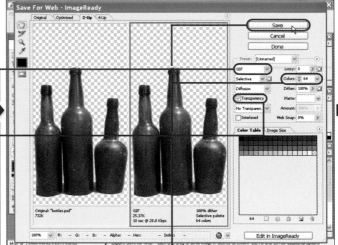

1 Select the area that you want to make transparent with a selection tool.

Note: See Chapter 4 for more about using the selection tools.

2 Press Delete to delete the pixels.

■ Photoshop replaces the deleted pixels with a checkerboard pattern.

3 Click **File**.

4 Click **Save for Web**.

5 Click ⌄ (🔹) and select GIF.

6 Click **Transparency** to retain transparency in the saved file (☐ changes to ☑).

7 Click ⌄ and select the number of colors to include in the image.

■ GIF allows a maximum of 256 colors.

8 Click **Save**.

Does the JPEG format support transparency?

No. JPEG, the other popular image format for the Web, does not support transparency. However, you can simulate transparency in a JPEG image by surrounding elements in the image with a color that matches the intended background.

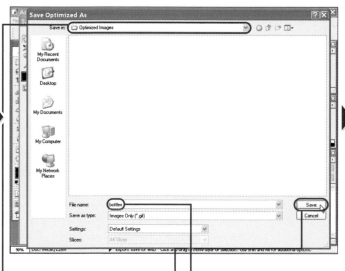

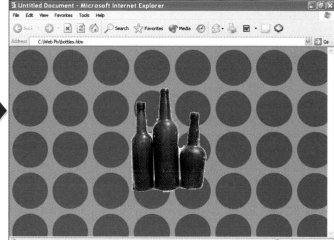

9 In Windows, click and select a folder in which to save the file.

■ Mac users should use the Where popup menu or the File Browser to select a folder.

10 Type a name for the file.

■ Photoshop automatically assigns a .gif extension.

11 Click **Save**.

■ In this example, the image has been added to a Web page and opened in a Web browser.

■ The transparency causes the Web page background to show through around the edges of the object.

SAVE A GIF WITH WEB-SAFE COLORS

You can save your GIF images using only Web-safe colors. This ensures that the images appear the way you expect in browsers running on 256-color monitors.

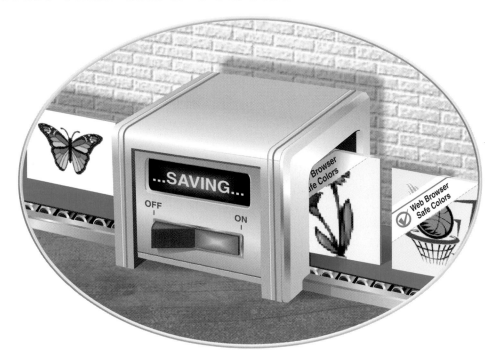

You can create Web-safe images only in the GIF format.

SAVE A GIF WITH WEB-SAFE COLORS

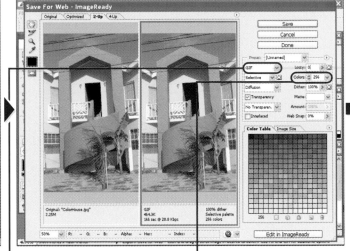

1 Click **File**.

2 Click **Save for Web**.

■ The Save For Web dialog box appears.

3 Click ⌄ (🔄) and select **GIF**.

4 Click ⌄ and select the number of colors to include in the image.

Should I save all my Web images with Web-safe colors?

Not necessarily. Nowadays, most people surf the Web on monitors set to thousands of colors or more, which makes Web safety less relevant. Also, it is better to save photographic Web images as non-Web-safe JPEGs because the GIF file format offers poor compression and quality when it comes to photos.

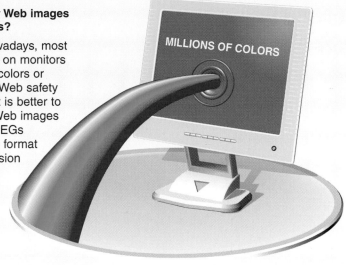

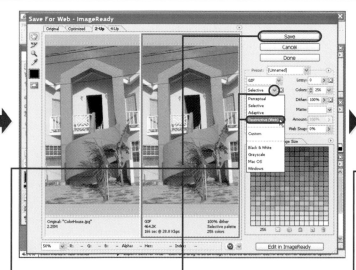

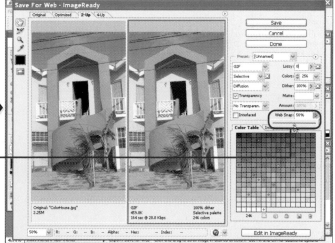

5 Click ▼ (🔼) and select **Restrictive (Web)** as the color palette type.

Note: When you do not specify Web-safe colors, Photoshop saves the image by choosing from all the colors available in the spectrum.

■ Photoshop now uses only colors from the 216-color palette available to browsers running on 256-color monitors.

6 Click **Save** to save the image.

MAKE A GIF PARTIALLY WEB SAFE

■ You can specify a degree of Web safety from 1% to 100% using the Web Snap menu.

Note: The Web Snap menu lets you find a compromise between creating a totally Web-safe image — which may display poorly — and an image that has colors from the entire spectrum.

COMPARE FILE SIZES

You can compare the results of different compression schemes on your Web images. This helps you choose which scheme is most efficient and generates the best-looking image at a reasonable file size. You can then save the image using that scheme.

You can also compare estimated download times at popular modem speeds.

COMPARE FILE SIZES

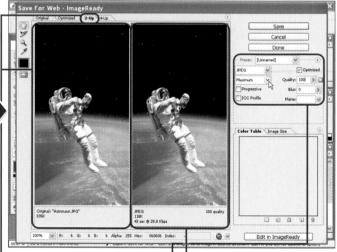

1 Click **File**.

2 Click **Save for Web**.

■ The Save For Web dialog box appears.

3 Click **2-Up**.

■ Photoshop displays the original image on the left side.

■ Photoshop displays the image with the optimized settings applied on the right side.

4 To select different settings, click either image and change the settings in the right side of the dialog box.

What file size should I make my Web images?

If a large portion of your audience uses dialup modems to view your Web pages, keep your images small enough so that total page size — which includes all the images on the page plus the HTML file — is below 50K. You can check the file size and the download speed of an image at the bottom of the Save For Web preview pane. To change an image's file size and download speed, you can adjust the quality and color settings in the Save For Web dialog box. See the sections "Save a JPEG for the Web" and "Save a GIF for the Web" for details.

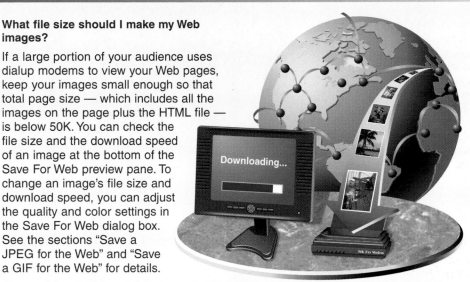

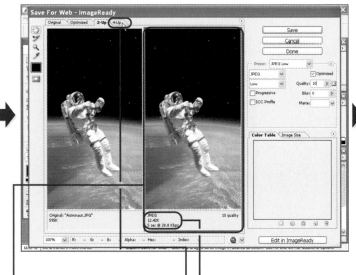

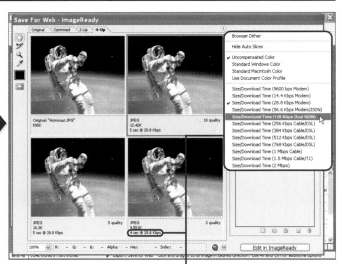

■ Photoshop displays the image with the new settings applied.

■ The new file size and download time is displayed.

5 Click **4-Up** to compare four versions of the image at a time.

■ Photoshop displays four versions of the image.

■ You can change the speed that Photoshop uses to estimate the download time by clicking the top menu (▶) and selecting an option.

ADD DESCRIPTIVE AND COPYRIGHT INFORMATION

You can store title, author, caption, and copyright information with your saved image. You may find this useful if you plan on publishing the images online.

Paradise Bay   copyright © John Wiley

Some image editing applications — such as Photoshop — can detect copyright information from an image and display it to a user who opens it.

ADD DESCRIPTIVE AND COPYRIGHT INFORMATION

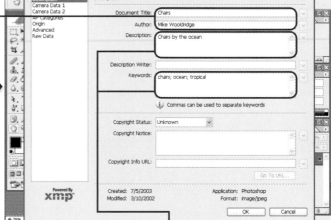

1 Click **File**.

2 Click **File Info**.

■ The File Info dialog box appears.

3 Type title and author information for the image.

4 Type a description for the image.

5 Type keywords for the image.

**How do I view information about a
photo taken with a digital
camera?**

Information about photos taken
with a digital camera can be
accessed in the File Info dialog
box. You can view it by clicking the
Camera Data 1 or **Camera Data 2**
categories in the dialog box. The
information includes the model of
the camera, the date and time the
photo was shot, and the image
dimensions.

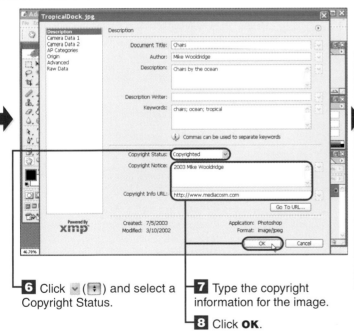

6 Click ☑ (⬍) and select a
Copyright Status.

7 Type the copyright
information for the image.

8 Click **OK**.

■ If you marked the image
as copyrighted, Photoshop
places a copyright symbol in
the title bar.

■ To save the copyrighted
image, see the other tasks in
this chapter.

SAVE A SLICED IMAGE

You can save an
image that has been
sliced with the Slice
tool. Photoshop saves
the slices as different
images and also saves
an HTML file that
organizes the slices
into a Web page.
Slices enable you to
save some parts of an
image as GIF and
others as JPEG. This
can result in an
overall image that has
a smaller file size.

For more
information
about using the
Slice tool, see
Chapter 4.

SAVE A SLICED IMAGE

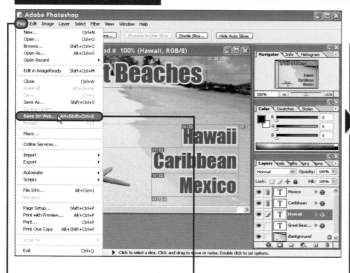

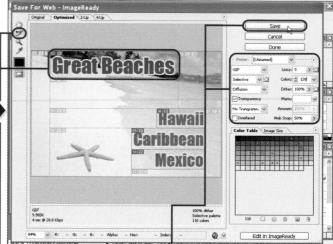

1 Open your sliced image.

2 Click **File**.

3 Click **Save for Web**.

■ The Save For Web dialog
box appears.

4 Click the Slice Select
tool ( ).

5 Click one of the image
slices to select it.

6 Specify the optimization
settings for the slice.

7 Repeat steps **5** and **6** for
each of the slices.

8 Click **Save**.

How do I publish my Web page online?

After you have created a Web page by saving your sliced Photoshop image, you can make the page available online by transferring the HTML and image files to a Web server using an FTP program. Most people arrange for Web server access through an Internet service provider, or ISP. Mac OS X users have an Apache Web server built into their computers.

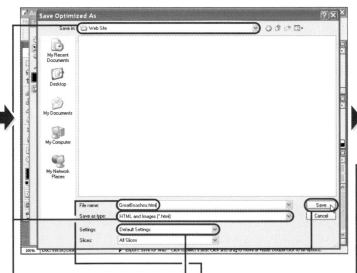

9 Choose a folder in which to save the files. In Windows, click ⌄. On a Mac, use the Where popup menu or the File Browser.

10 Select HTML and Images as the file type. In Windows, click ⌄. On a Mac, click the Format ⬚.

11 Name the HTML file that will organize the slices.

■ Photoshop saves the images by appending slice numbers to the original image name. To change the naming scheme, you can click the Settings ⌄ (⬚) and click **Other**.

12 Click **Save**.

■ You can access the HTML and image files in the folder that you specified in step **9**.

■ The image files are saved in a separate images subfolder.

13 To view the Web page, double-click the HTML file.

297

PREVIEW

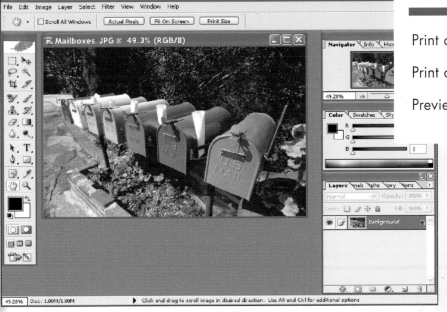

CHAPTER 16

Printing Images

Printing enables you to save the digital imagery you create in Photoshop in hard-copy form. Photoshop can print to black-and-white or color printers.

Print on a PC 300

Print on a Macintosh.........................302

Preview a Printout............................304

You can print your
Photoshop image in
color or black-and-white
on a PC using an ink-jet,
laser, or other type of
printer.

PRINT ON A PC

1 Make sure that the layers you want to print are visible.

Note: An 👁 means that a layer is visible. For more about layers, see Chapter 9.

2 Click **File**.

3 Click **Print**.

■ If your image is larger than your printer paper, a warning appears. Click **Proceed**.

■ The Print dialog box appears.

4 Click 🔽 and select a printer.

5 Click ↕ to select the number of copies.

6 Click **Properties**.

Is there a shortcut for quickly printing one copy of an image?

To print your image on the currently selected printer using the current print settings, click **File** and then **Print One Copy**. This skips the Print and Document Properties dialog boxes.

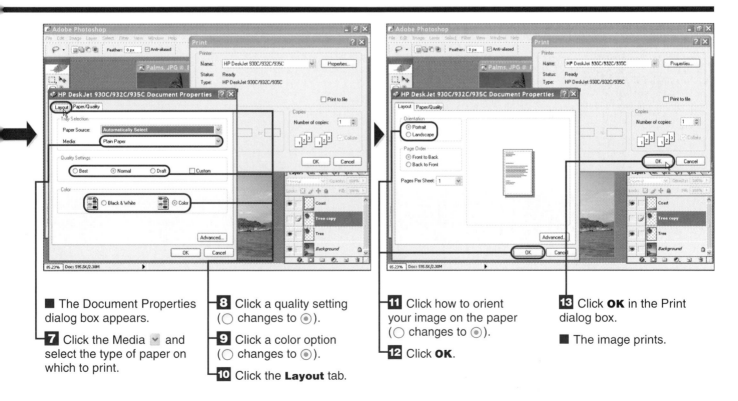

■ The Document Properties dialog box appears.

7 Click the Media ⌄ and select the type of paper on which to print.

8 Click a quality setting (○ changes to ⊙).

9 Click a color option (○ changes to ⊙).

10 Click the **Layout** tab.

11 Click how to orient your image on the paper (○ changes to ⊙).

12 Click **OK**.

13 Click **OK** in the Print dialog box.

■ The image prints.

You can print your
Photoshop image in
color or black-and-white
on a Macintosh using an
ink-jet, laser, or other
type of printer.

PRINT ON A MACINTOSH

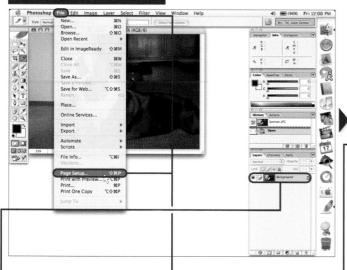

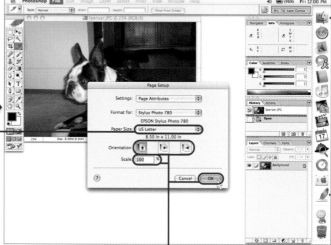

SET UP THE PAGE

1 Make sure that the layers
you want to print are visible.

*Note: An 👁 means that a layer is
visible. For more about layers, see
Chapter 9.*

2 Click **File**.

3 Click **Page Setup**.

■ The Page Setup dialog
box appears.

4 Click 🔽 and select a
paper size.

5 Click an orientation
button, 🔳, 🔳, or 🔳.

■ You can type a value to
increase or decrease the
printed size on the page.

6 Click **OK**.

What is halftoning?

In grayscale printing, halftoning is the process by which a printer creates the appearance of different shades of gray using only black ink. If you look closely at a grayscale image printed on most black-and-white laser printers, you see that the image consists of tiny, differently sized dot patterns. Larger dots produce the darker gray areas of the image while smaller dots produce the lighter gray areas.

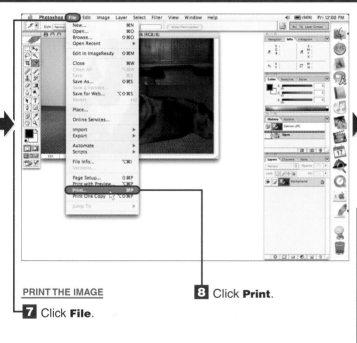

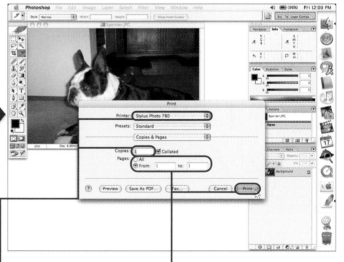

PRINT THE IMAGE

7 Click **File**.

8 Click **Print**.

■ The Print dialog box appears.

9 Click ▣ and select a printer.

10 Type the number of copies to print.

11 Click the range of pages you want to print (◯ changes to ◉) and type a range, if necessary.

12 Click **Print**.

■ The image prints.

PREVIEW A PRINTOUT

You can preview your printout, as well as adjust the size and positioning of your printed image, in a special dialog box in Photoshop. Previewing lets you check and adjust your work before putting ink on paper.

PREVIEW

Color   RT170

PREVIEW A PRINTOUT

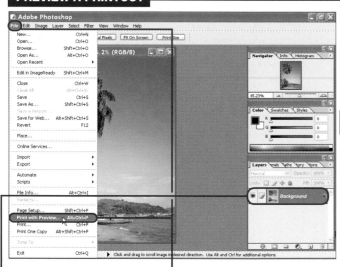

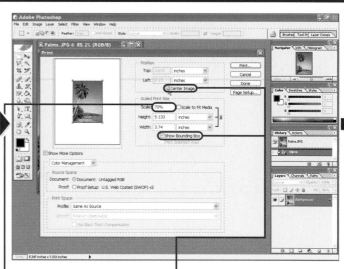

1 Make sure that the layers you want to print are visible.

Note: An 👁 means that a layer is visible. For more about layers, see Chapter 9.

2 Click **File**.

3 Click **Print with Preview**.

■ The Print dialog box appears.

4 Type a percentage in the Scale box to shrink or enlarge the image.

5 To reposition and resize the image, click **Show Bounding Box** (☐ changes to ☑).

6 Click **Center Image** to allow for the repositioning of the image (☑ changes to ☐).

How can I maximize the size of my image on the printed page?

In the Print Preview dialog box, you can click **Scale to Fit Media** (☐ changes to ☑) to scale the image to the maximum size given the current printing settings.

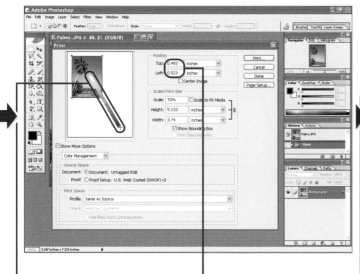

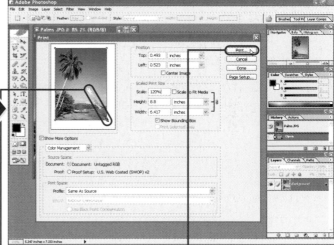

7 Click and drag in the image window to reposition the image on the page.

■ You can position your image precisely by typing values in the Top and Left fields.

8 Click and drag the handles on the image corners to scale the image by hand.

9 To print the image, click **Print**.

INDEX

A

Action Options dialog box, 265
actions
    assign key command to, 265
    batch process, 266–267
    list commands, 265
    mistakes while recording, 263
    names, 262
    play, 264–265
    play commands, 265
    predefined, 264
    record, 262–263
    stop recording, 263
    undo, 264
Actions palette
    Action Options option, 265
    Create New Action button, 262
    Play button, 264
    play actions, 264
    predefined actions, 264
    Record Again button, 263
Add Anchor Point tool, 243
Add Noise filter, 214–215
add to image type, 246–247
adjustment layers, 161, 182
    apply to part of image, 183
    blend, 189
    edit, 184
    merge with regular layers, 185
Adobe InDesign, 283
Adobe Photoshop CS folder, 9
Adobe Photoshop CS icon, 9
Airbrush tool, 7, 107
align type, 247
anchor points
    add, 243
    frequency of, 57
    Magnetic Lasso tool, 56
    move, 242
    shapes, 240
antialias images and type, 253
Append button, 108
append shapes, 236
Applications menu, 9
arrowheads, 238
art, scan, 11
Art History brush, 131
Auto Erase function, 113
automatic wrap type, 249
auto-slices, 70, 71

B

background
    delete for feathered selections, 85
    extract objects, 86–87
    move selected object, 74
background color
    canvas, 49
    Eraser tool, 100
    reset, 101
    select, 100–101
Background Color box, 102
Background Eraser tool, 133
Background layer, 74, 163
    delete selections, 78
    erase, 101
    erase elements, 132
Bas Relief filter, 255
batch process, 266–267
bend straight segment, 243
bevel layers, 196–197
bitmap images, 96–97
black-and-white images, convert color images to, 149
blank canvas, 11
blank images, 20
blend layers, 188–189
blending modes, 188–189
Bloat tool, 227
Blur filters, 208
blur images, 142–143, 208–209
Blur tool, 142–143
BMP (bitmap) format, 282
borders, feather, 84–85
bounding box, 79, 248–249
brightness, 138–141
    adjust, 144–145
    control, 154
    increase and decrease, 153
Brightness/Contrast command, 138–139
Brightness/Contrast dialog box, 138
Bring Forward command, 169
Bring to Front command, 169
Browse For Folder dialog box, 266, 268–269, 273
browse for images, 18–19
Brush menu, 108, 109, 111
brush strokes, 106–107
brushes
    add to set of, 108
    apply scattered dots with, 109
    change styles, 108–109
    custom, 108–111
    modify amount of color applied by, 107
    replace, 108
    size, 106
    types, 106, 108
Brushes palette, 109–111
burn, 140
Burn tool, 7, 140–141

C

Cancel button, 79
Cancel (Esc or ⌘+.) keyboard shortcut, 44, 79
canvas
    background color, 49
    resize, 44, 48–49
Canvas Size dialog box, 48–49
cast, remove, 150–151

channels, 91
Channels palette, 90–91
Character palette, 251
Charcoal dialog box, 218–219
Charcoal filter, 218–219
Charcoal Sketch filter, 228
charcoal sketches, 218–219
clean up flaws, 122–123
clip art collection, 11
Clone Stamp tool, 122–123, 225
Close Toolboxes and Palettes (Tab) keyboard shortcut, 29
CMYK mode, 91
Color Balance dialog box, 150–151
color cast, remove, 150–151
color images, 90–91
    convert to
        black-and-white images, 149
        grayscale, 92–93
Color mode, 189
Color Picker dialog box, 94, 101–102, 177, 253
Color Range dialog box, 60–61
Color Replacement tool, 134–135
color separations, 91
Color Swatch Name dialog box, 105
color wheel, 147
colors
    add
        custom to Swatches palette, 105
        to images with Paintbrush tool, 106–107
    adjust
        balance, 150–151
        hue, 146–147
        intensity, 148–149
        opacity, 117
        saturation, 146–149
    adjustments, 152–153
    amount replaced, 154
    brighten, 7
    change, 7
    constrain, 117
    custom shapes, 237
    darken, 7
    dialog boxes appear when selecting, 12
    erase similar, 133
    fill images with solid, 116–117
    GIF (Graphics Interchange Format) files, 286, 288
    gradients, 179
    hard-edged lines of, 112–113
    hex-code value, 102
    information about, 161
    invert bright and dark, 141
    lines, 239
    match
        between images, 154–155
        from only selected part of image, 155
    multiple selections, 135
    pixels, 7
    replace, 134–135
    select
        with Eyedropper tool, 103
        range of, 60–61
        for replacement, 135
        with Swatches palette, 104

shapes, 234, 240
strokes, 120
type, 246, 252–253
undo adjustments, 153
Web-safe, 102
commands
    feathered selections, 85
    layers, 160
    undo and redo, 34
compare file sizes, 292–293
compression, 285
constrain
    object movement, 75
    type, 248–249
Contact Sheet II dialog box, 268
contact sheets, 268–269
contrast
    automatically adjust, 139
    increase and decrease, 138–141
Contrast Selection dialog box, 67
convert color images to grayscale, 92–93
Copy (Ctrl+C or ⌘+C) keyboard shortcut, 62
copy
    pixels, 126–127
    selections between windows, 77
copy and paste selections, 76–77
copyright information, 294–295
Crop tool, 44, 45, 48, 49
crop
    adjust boundary, 44
    exit, 44
    images, 44–46
    resize canvas, 44, 48–49
    rotate image while, 45
    while straightening, 46
Crystallize dialog box, 216–217
Crystallize filter, 216–217
curved lines, edit, 243
custom
    brushes, 108–111
    colors
        shapes, 237
        on Swatches palette, 105
    patterns, 125
    shapes, 236–237
    styles, 203
Custom Colors dialog box, 95
Custom Shape tool, 236–237
customize
    Marquee tools, 53
    tools, 10

D

darken
    images, 138–141
    pixels, 215
Decrease Magnification (Alt or Option) keyboard shortcut, 25
Default icon, 101
defaults, reset tools to, 117
defects, 128–129

INDEX

delete
- feathered selection backgrounds, 85
- images, 62
- layers, 167
- selections, 78
- slices, 71
- user-slice, 71

Delete key, 78
descriptive information, 294–295
deselect selections, 52, 53, 55
destination image, 154
details, zoom, 25
Difference mode, 188
digital cameras, 11
digital collages, 5
digital images, 11
digital photographs, 4, 11
Direct Selection tool, 242
Display or Hide Menu Bar (Shift+F) keyboard shortcut, 28
Distort filters, 212

distort
- images, 212–213
- selections, 82–83
- undo, 83

Document Properties dialog box, 301
document window, 10
Documents or Pictures folder, 19
dodge, 140
Dodge tool, 7, 140–141, 148

draw
- custom shapes, 236–237
- shapes, 234–241
- straight lines, 113, 238–239

drop shadows, 7, 192–193
Dry Brush dialog box, 206
Dry Brush filter, 206–207, 220, 228
Duotone Options dialog box, 95
duotones, 94–95

duplicate
- layers, 166
- selections, 76

E

Edge Highlighter tool, 86

edges
- feather, 84–85
- glow, 220–221
- soften, 84–85

Edit (Photoshop), Preferences, File Browser command, 19
Edit, Copy command, 77, 163
Edit, Define Pattern command, 118, 125
Edit, Fill command, 118, 119
Edit, Paste command, 77, 163
Edit, Preferences, Guides, Grid & Slices command, 32
Edit, Stroke command, 120
Edit, Transform, Distort command, 83
Edit, Transform, Rotate command, 79
Edit, Transform, Scale command, 80
Edit, Transform, Skew command, 82
Edit, Transform command, 175
Edit, Undo command, 83
Edit, Undo Paintbrush command, 106
Edit, Undo Revert command, 35
Edit Preferences, General command, 12

edit
- adjustment layers, 184
- curved lines, 243
- layer effects, 200
- photographs, 4
- shapes, 242–243
- type, 251

effects, 7
- blending modes, 189
- combinations of, 257
- type, 256–257

elements
- erase, 122–123, 132–133
- inner glow, 195
- permanently combine, 173
- rearrange, 74
- repeat, 124–125

Elliptical Marquee tool, 53
elliptical selections, 53
Emboss filters, 213
emboss layers, 196–197
EPS (Encapsulated PostScript), 282
.eps extension, 283
Eraser tool, 100–101, 132–133

erase
- Background layer, 101
- elements, 122–123, 132–133
- with Pencil tool, 113
- similar colors, 133

exit Photoshop, 21
Expand Selection dialog box, 66
expand or contract selections, 66–67
Extract dialog box, 86–87
extract objects from background, 86–87
extractions, smooth edges of, 87
Eyedropper tool to select color, 103

F

Feather Selection dialog box, 84
feather, 84–85
feedback for Web Photo Gallery, 273
Fetch, 272
File, Automate, Batch command, 266
File, Automate, Conditional Mode Change command, 267
File, Automate, Contact Sheet II command, 268
File, Automate, Crop and Straighten Photos command, 46
File, Automate, Photomerge command, 274
File, Automate, Picture Package command, 270
File, Automate, Web Photo Gallery command, 272
File, Browse command, 18
File, Exit command, 21
File, File Info command, 294
File, New command, 20
File, Open command, 16
File, Open Recent command, 17
File, Page Setup command, 302
File, Print command, 300, 303
File, Print One Copy command, 301
File, Print with Preview command, 41, 304

File, Revert command, 35
File, Save As command, 280, 281, 282
File, Save command, 280
File, Save for Web command, 284, 286, 288, 290, 292, 296
File Browser, 18–19, 281, 297
File dialog box, 118
File Info dialog box, 294
files, compare sizes, 292–293
Fill command, 118
Fill dialog box, 119
fill layers, convert type, 179
Fill tool, 87
fills, 7, 118–119
Filter, Artistic, Dry Brush command, 206
Filter, Artistic, Sponge command, 207
Filter, Blur, Gaussian Blur command, 208
Filter, Blur, Motion Blur command, 209
Filter, Distort, Spherize command, 212
Filter, Distort command, 213
Filter, Extract command, 86
Filter, Filter Gallery command, 228
Filter, Liquify command, 226
Filter, Noise, Add Noise command, 214
Filter, Other, Offset command, 224
Filter, Pattern Maker command, 230
Filter, Pixelate, Crystallize command, 216
Filter, Pixelate, Mosaic command, 217
Filter, Render, Lens Flare command, 223
Filter, Sharpen, Unsharp Mask command, 210
Filter, Sketch, Bas Relief command, 255
Filter, Sketch, Charcoal command, 218
Filter, Sketch, Photocopy command, 219
Filter, Stylize, Find Edges command, 221
Filter, Stylize, Glowing Edges command, 220
Filter, Texture, Stained Glass command, 217
Filter, Texture, Texturizer command, 222
Filter Gallery, 206, 228–229
Filter Stylize command, 213
filters, 7
        Add Noise filter, 214–215
        apply multiple, 228–229
        Bas Relief filter, 255
        Charcoal filter, 218–219
        Crystallize filter, 216–217
        Dry Brush filter, 206–207, 220
        Emboss filters, 213
        Find Edges filter, 221
        fine-tune, 206
        Gaussian Blur filter, 208–209
        Glowing Edges filter, 220–221
        hidden, 229
        Liquify filter, 226–227
        Mosaic filter, 217
        Motion Blur filter, 209
        Offset filter, 224–225
        one-step, 221
        Photocopy filter, 219
        Pinch filter, 213
        preview, 206
        select, 206
        Solarize filters, 213
        Spherize filter, 212

Sponge filter, 207
Stained Glass filter, 217
Texturizer filter, 222–223
turn images into painting, 206–207
type, 254–255
Unsharp Mask filter, 210–211
Find Edges filter, 221
flatten layers, 161, 172–173
flaws, clean up, 122–123
folders to store images, 19
fonts, 251
foreground color, 100–101, 106
Foreground Color box, 100, 102, 106, 112, 116
format text in bounding box, 249
format type, 250–251
Forward Warp tool, 227
frame borders, 7
freeform
        lines, 241
        selections, 54–57
Freeform Pen tool, 241
full screen mode, 29
Full Screen Mode button, 28
Full Screen Mode with Menu Bar button, 28
full screen with menu bar mode, 28

G

Gaussian Blur dialog box, 208
Gaussian Blur filter, 208–209
ghosted white layer, 119
.gif extension, 287, 289
GIF (Graphics Interchange Format) files
        color, 286, 288
        minimize file size, 287
        partially Web safe, 291
        save, 286–287
                with transparency, 288–289
                with Web-safe colors, 290–291
Glowing Edges dialog box, 220–221
Glowing Edges filter, 220–221, 228
Gradient Editor, 114–115
Gradient Fill dialog box, 179
gradient fill layers, 178–179
Gradient tool, 114
gradients, 114–115, 179
grayscale images
        bitmap images, 96–97
        channels, 93
        convert color images to, 92–93
        duotone, 94–95
        make part of image, 93
grids, 30, 32
grow selections, 69
guides, 31

H

halftone, 303
Hand tool, 26–27
hard-edged lines of color, 112–113
Healing Brush tool, 126–128
help, 14–15
Help, Photoshop Help command, 14

INDEX

Help, System Info command, 15
Help interface, 14–15
Help (⌘+/) keyboard shortcut, 14
Help (F1) keyboard shortcut, 14
hidden filters, 229
hide
    layers, 164
    selections, 63
highlight objects, 120–121
highlights,
    adjust, 144–145
    correct, 156–157
    darken, 157
History brush, 130–131
History palette
    History slider, 34
    list recently executed commands, 34
    New Snapshot button, 130, 131
    number of states, 12
    undo
        commands, 34
        multiple commands in action, 264
horizontal guide, 30
horizontal lines, 239
hue, adjust, 146–147
Hue/Saturation command, 146
Hue/Saturation dialog box, 146–147

I

Image, Adjust, Desaturate command, 93
Image, Adjust, Threshold command, 97
Image, Adjustments, Auto Contrast command, 139, 262
Image, Adjustments, Auto Levels command, 145
Image, Adjustments, Brightness/Contrast command, 138
Image, Adjustments, Color Balance command, 150
Image, Adjustments, Desaturate command, 149
Image, Adjustments, Hue/Saturation command, 146
Image, Adjustments, Invert command, 141
Image, Adjustments, Levels command, 144
Image, Adjustments, Match Color command, 154
Image, Adjustments, Shadow/Highlight command, 156
Image, Adjustments, Variations command, 152
Image, Canvas Size command, 48
Image, Image Size command, 38, 40, 42, 263
Image, Mode, Bitmap command, 96
Image, Mode, CMYK Color command, 91
Image, Mode, Duotone command, 94
Image, Mode, Grayscale command, 92
Image, Mode, RGB Color command, 90
Image, Trim command, 47
image compression, 285
Image Size dialog box
    change resolution units, 42
    Constrain Proportions check box, 39, 41
    percent option, 38
    Resample Image check box, 38, 43
    restore default settings, 39, 41, 43
    unit of measurement, 40
Image Transform Shape command, 235
image window, 10, 20, 30
    blank canvas, 11
    move images within, 26–27

image-edit tools, 10
ImageReady, 70–71
images
    access, 5
    accurately place objects, 30–32
    add
        color with Paintbrush tool, 106–107
        noise, 214–215
        or remove graininess, 214–215
        repeat elements, 124–125
        texture, 222–223
        type, 246–247
    adjust highlights, midtones, or shadows, 144–145
    antialias, 253
    areas of solid-color shapes, 217
    Background layer, 163
    blank, 20
    blur, 142–143, 208–209
    brightness, 138–141
    browse for, 18–19
    change
        canvas size, 48–49
        number of pixels in, 39, 41
        resolution, 42–43
    charcoal sketches, 218–219
    choose file format, 283
    clip art collection, 11
    color adjustments, 152–153
    colored border, 121
    contrast, 138–141
    cool cast, 150
    copy information in, 122–123
    copyright information, 294–295
    correct defects, 126–127
    creation of, 20
    crop, 44–46
    darken, 138–141
    delete, 62
        selections, 78
    descriptive information, 294–295
    directional blur, 209
    distort, 212–213
    erase elements, 122–123, 132–133
    feather, 84
    fill areas with solid color, 116–117
    ghosted white layer, 119
    glowing edges, 220–221
    grayscale, 92–93
    hard-copy record, 268–269
    highlight objects, 120–121
    increase area with Crop tool, 45
    information about, 10
    JPEG format, 11
    keywords, 294
    labels, 7
    lens flare, 223
    lighten, 138–141
    limit area affected by Color Range command, 61
    liquify, 226–227
    made up of pixels, 96
    magnify to largest size on-screen, 27
    match colors, 154–155
    maximize on printed page, 305

move within windows, 26–27
name, 20
obtain, 11
offset, 224–225
on-screen size, 39
open, 16–17
organize, 5
panoramic, 274–277
photocopied, 219
pixelate, 216–217
pixels, 6
precisely resize, 49
preview, 5
previous state, 130–131
print size, 39, 40–41
print, 300–303
rearrange elements, 74
reduce detail, 207
replace colors, 134–135
resample, 38
resize on-screen, 38–39
return to original state, 153
revert to previously saved state, 35
RGB mode, 90–91
save
    in native Photoshop format, 280–281
    for use in another application, 282–283
    for Web, 5
scanned, 11
from scratch, 11
scroll, 26–27
seamless tiles, 225
select, 52–62
    all pixels, 62
    and drag defects, 128–129
set of solid-color squares, 217
sharpen, 142–143, 210–211
slices, 70–71
smear, 143
TIFF format, 11
title and author information, 294
titles, 7
trim, 47
turn into painting, 206–207
warm cast, 150
where to store, 19
white pixels between edges, 221
information about photos taken with digital camera, 295
inner glow, 195
inner shadow, 193
intensity, adjust, 148–149
interface options, 12
invert
    bright and dark colors, 141
    selections, 68

J

JPEG (Joint Photographic Experts Group) files, 11
    non-Web-safe, 291
    save, 284–285
    transparency, 289
.jpg extension, 285

K

keyboard, copy and paste objects, 76
keywords for images, 294

L

label picture package, 271
labels, 7
Lasso tool, 85
    Add to Selection button, 64
    fix imprecise selections, 55
    polygonal effect, 55
    select images, 54–57
Lasso tool (L) keyboard shortcut, 33
Layer, Arrange command, 169
Layer, Change Layer Content command, 179
Layer, Delete Layer command, 167
Layer, Duplicate Layer command, 166
Layer, Flatten Image command, 173
Layer, Layer Properties command, 174
Layer, Layer Style, Bevel and Emboss command, 196
Layer, Layer Style, Drop Shadow command, 192
Layer, Layer Style, Inner Glow command, 195
Layer, Layer Style, Inner Shadow command, 193
Layer, Layer Style, Outer Glow command, 194
Layer, Layer Style command, 198, 200, 256
Layer, Merge Down command, 172, 185
Layer, New, Layer command, 162
Layer, New Adjustment Layer command, 182
Layer, New Fill Layer, Gradient command, 178
Layer, New Fill Layer, Pattern command, 180
Layer, New Fill Layer, Solid Color command, 176
Layer, Rasterize, Type command, 254
Layer Backward (Ctrl+[or ⌘+[) keyboard shortcut, 169
layer effects, edit, 200
Layer Forward (Ctrl+] or ⌘+]) keyboard shortcut, 169
Layer Properties dialog box, 174
Layer Style dialog box, 196–198, 200–201, 256–257
layers, 5
    add
        objects to, 162–163
        solid color to part of, 177
    adjustment, 182–185
    apply multiple effects, 198–199
    bevel, 196–197
    blend, 188–189
    brightness, 138
    change opacity, 170–171
    commands, 160
    contrast, 138
    creation of, 162–163
    delete, 167
    display, 164
    drop shadow, 192–193
    duplicate, 166
    emboss, 196–197
    erase elements, 133
    flatten, 161, 172–173
    gradient fill, 178–179
    hide, 164
    independence, 160

inner shadow, 193
link, 186–187
lock, 187, 201
manipulate, 161
merge, 172–173, 281
move, 165
    selected object, 75
multiple, 280
name, 176
outer glow effect, 194–195
pattern fill, 180–181
rename, 174
reorder, 168–169
save, 161
select type, 250
semitransparent, 171
solid fill, 176–177
styles, 202–203
transform, 175
transparency, 161
turn off effects, 199
type, 247
Layers, Layers command, 162
Layers palette, 75, 162, 200, 250
    Add a layer style button, 192
    add effects, 199
    adjustment layer icon, 184
    Angle value, 192
    Background layer, 74, 132
    Bevel and Emboss option, 196
    blend mode, 188, 189
    Color swatch, 252
    Create new fill or adjustment layer button, 176, 178, 180, 182
    Create Warped Text button, 258
    Distance value, 193
    Drop Shadow option, 192
    Eye icon, 164
    Fill setting, 171
    Gradient option, 178
    Lock icon, 187, 201
    New Layer button, 162
    New Style option, 203
    Noise value, 194
    Opacity field, 170, 192
    Outer Glow option, 194
    Pattern option, 180
    reorder layers, 168
    shapes, 234
    Size value, 193
    Solid Color option, 176
    Spread value, 193
    Styles tab, 202
lens flare, 223
Levels command, 144–145
Levels dialog box, 144–145
lighten
    images, 138–141
    pixels, 215
line break, 247
linear gradient, 114

lines
    arrowheads, 238
    color, 112–113, 239
    freeform, 241
    horizontal, 239
    straight, 238, 241
    style, 239
    vertical, 239
    weight, 239
link layers, 186–187
links, creation of, 186
Liquify dialog box, 226–227
Liquify filter, 226–227
Liquify tools, 226–227
liquify images, 226–227
lock layers, 187, 201
Luminosity mode, 189

M

Mac OS X
    batch process with action, 267
    File Browser, 281
    open images, 17
    Save As dialog box, 281
    save in native Photoshop format, 281
    set preferences, 12
Mac OS X Jaguar, 17
Mac OS X Panther, 17
Macintosh
    Documents or Pictures folder, 19
    exit Photoshop, 21
    Fetch, 272
    File Browser, 297
    full screen with menu bar mode, 28
    print, 302–303
    set
        preferences, 12
        up page, 302
    start Photoshop, 9
    status bar, 10, 28
    Where popup menu, 297
Magic Eraser tool, 133
Magic Wand tool
    select similarly colored pixels, 58–59
    Tolerance setting, 69
Magnetic Lasso tool, 56–57
magnification, 24–25, 27
Marquee tool (M) keyboard shortcut, 33
Marquee tools, 52–53, 85
Match Color dialog box, 154–155
match colors, 154–155
measurement units, 13
memory, save by merging layers, 173
menu bar, 10
menus, 10
merge
    adjustment layers with layers, 185
    layers, 172–173, 281
    photos successfully, 275
midtones, adjust, 144–145
Mirror tool, 227

modes, change during batch process, 267
Mosaic filter, 217
Motion Blur filter, 209
mouse, copy and paste objects, 76
Move tool, 31, 165, 235, 247
Move tool (V) keyboard shortcut, 33
Move View tool, 276
move
    linked layers, 187
    selections, 74–75
multilayered images, save, 161
multiple layers, 280
Multiply mode, 189
My Pictures folder, 19

N

native Photoshop format, 280–281
Navigator palette, 27
New Action dialog box, 262
New dialog box, 20
New Layer dialog box, 178, 182
noise, 214–215

O

objects
    accurately place, 30–32
    add extra shadows, 141
    bounding box, 79
    extract from background, 86–87
    highlight, 120–121
    snap
        to grid, 32
        to guides, 31
    trace, 241
Offset dialog box, 224–225
Offset filter, 224–225
offset images, 224–225
one-step filters, 221
on-screen size and resolution, 43
Open dialog box, 16–17, 267, 274
open images, 16–17, 19
Open-style dialog box, 267
Options bar, 10, 253
    Actual Pixels button, 25
    Add to Selection button, 59
    Add to Shape Area option, 235
    Airbrush button, 107
    Auto Erase check box, 113
    Change Orientation button, 247
    Custom Shape button, 236
    customize Marquee tools, 53
    Edge Contrast option, 57
    Exclude Overlapping Shape Areas option, 235
    Feather text field, 85
    Feather value, 53
    Fit On Screen button, 27
    Frequency option, 57
    geometries in, 114
    gradient swatch, 114
    Height box, 53
    Intersect Shape Areas option, 235
    Magnetic option, 241
    shapes, 234

    Style, 53
    Subtract from Shape Area option, 235
    Tolerance value, 133
    Width box, 53, 57
Other submenu, 224
outer glow effect, 194–195
overlap shapes, 235
Overlay mode, 189

P

Page Setup dialog box, 302
page-layout programs, 283
Paint Bucket tool, 116–117
paintbrush, convert to airbrush, 107
Paintbrush tool, 7
    add color to images, 106–107
    B keyboard shortcut, 33
paint, 7, 130–131
paint tools
    cursor type, 13
    foreground color, 100
palettes, 10, 28
panoramic images, 274–277
Paragraph palette, 249
paragraphs, format text in bounding box, 249
Paste (Ctrl+V or ⌘+V) keyboard shortcut, 62
Patch tool, 128–129
patch defects, 128–129
Pattern Fill dialog box, 181
pattern fill layers, 180–181
Pattern Stamp tool, 124–125
patterns
    add to Pattern menu, 125
    border around, 231
    change, 181
    as contiguous tiles, 124
    custom, 125
    detail, 231
    generate, 230–231
    name, 125
    opacity, 125
    predefined, 127
    repeat, 181
    select, 124
    smoothness, 231
Pen tool, 240–241
Pencil tool, 7, 112–113
photo gallery Web site, 272–273
photocopied images, 219
Photocopy filter, 219
photographs
    access, 5
    edit, 4
    information about digital, 295
    merge successfully, 275
    preview, 5
    scan, 11
    washed-out areas, 148
Photomerge dialog box, 274, 276–277
Photoshop
    exit, 21
    information about, 15
    start, 8–9

INDEX

Photoshop, Preferences, Guides, Grid & Slices command, 32
Photoshop, Preferences command, 12
Photoshop, Quit Photoshop command, 21
Photoshop Format Options dialog box, 281
PICT format, 282
picture package, 270–271
Picture Package dialog box, 270–271
Pinch filter, 213
Pixelate filters, 216
pixelate images, 216–217
pixels, 6
    colors, 7
    copy, 126–127
    darken, 215
    expand or contract selections with, 66–67
    lighten, 215
    noncontiguous, 69
    select, 6
        all, 62
        similarly colored, 58–59, 69
    transparent, 133
play actions, 264–265
Polygonal lasso, 55
polygonal selections, 55
predefined actions, 264
predefined patterns, 127
preferences, set, 12–13
Preferences dialog box, 12–13
preset gradients, 114
preview
    filters, 206
    printed size, 41
    printout, 304–305
print, 5
    images, 300–303
    Macintosh, 302–303
    one-copy command, 301
    Windows, 300–303
Print dialog box, 300, 303–304
Print Preview dialog box, 305
print size, 40–41
printed images, 41–42
printout, preview, 304–305
projects with blank images, 20
properties for contact sheets, 269
proportionally scale, 81
.psd extension, 280, 281
publish Web pages, 297
Pucker tool, 227
Push Left tool, 227

Q

QuarkXPress, 283

R

rainbow gradients, 115
rearrange elements, 74
recently accessed images, open, 17
Reconstruct tool, 227
record actions, 262–263
Rectangular Marquee tool, 52, 65, 118, 230

rectangular selections, 52
redo commands, 34
reorder layers, 168–169
repeat elements, 124–125
replace colors, 134–135
reposition type, 247
resample images, 38
resize
    canvas, 48–49
    images
        on-screen, 38–39
        precisely, 49
    slices, 71
    user-slice, 71
resolution, 42–43
revert images to previously saved state, 35
RGB (Red, Green, Blue), 90
RGB images, color components, 90
RGB mode, 90–91
Rotate Image tool, 277
rotate
    image while crop, 45
    selections, 79
ruler options, 13

S

saturation
    adjust, 146–149
    control, 154
    increase and decrease, 148
save
    GIF (Graphic Interchange Format) files, 286–287
        with transparency, 288–289
        with Web-safe colors, 290–291
    images
        in native Photoshop format, 280–281
        for use in another application, 282–283
        for Web, 5
    JPEG (Joint Photographic Experts Group) file, 284–285
    layers, 161
    multilayered images, 161
    sliced images, 296–297
Save As dialog box, 281–282
Save For Web dialog box, 293
    2-Up tab, 284, 286–287, 292
    4-Up tab, 293
    GIF option, 286–287, 288, 290
    JPEG option, 284
    preview pane, 293
    Restrictive (Web) option, 291
    Slice Select tool, 296–297
    Transparency option, 288
scale selections, 80–81
scan art, 11
scanned images, 11, 211
scanners, 11
Screen mode, 189
screen modes, 28–29
scroll bars, 26–27
scroll images, 26–27
seamless tiles, 225

select
    all pixels, 62
    background color, 100–101
    color
        with Eyedropper tool, 103
        with Swatches palette, 104
    filters, 206
    foreground color, 100–101
    images with Marquee tools, 52–53
    patterns, 124
    pixels, 6
    range of colors within image, 60–61
    similarly colored pixels, 58–59
    type, 250
Select, All command, 62
Select, Color Range command, 60, 61
Select, Deselect command, 52, 53, 55
Select, Feather command, 84
Select, Grow command, 69
Select, Inverse command, 68, 85
Select, Modify, Contract command, 67
Select, Modify, Expand command, 66
Select, Modify, Smooth command, 67
Select, Similar command, 69
Select All (Ctrl+A or ⌘+A) keyboard shortcut, 62
Select an Image File dialog box, 270
Select Image tool, 276
selection border, move, 63
selection tools, 6
selections
    add to, 59, 64–65
    copy and paste, 76–77
    copy between windows, 77
    delete, 78
    delete pixels, 59
    deselect, 52, 53, 55
    determine defects, 129
    distort, 82–83
    duplicate, 76
    elliptical, 53
    expand or contract, 66–67
    feather border, 84–85
    fill, 118–119
    fix imprecise, 55
    free form, 54–57
    grow, 69
    hide, 63
    invert, 68
    move, 74–75
    polygonal, 55
    rectangular, 52
    rotate, 79
    scale, 80–81
    similarly colored, neighboring pixels, 69
    skew, 82–83
    smooth edges of, 67
    soften edges, 53
    straight-line move, 75
    strokes, 120–121
    subtract from, 64–65
semitransparent type, 255
Send Backward command, 169

Send to Back command, 169
Shadow/Highlight command, 156–157
Shadow/Highlight dialog box, 156–157
shadows, 144–145, 156–157
Shape tool, 235
shapes
    anchor points, 240
    append, 236
    bend straight segment, 243
    color, 234, 240
    custom, 236–237
    draw, 234–241
        with Pen tool, 240–241
    edit, 242–243
    freeform lines, 241
    initial anchor point, 240
    move, 235
        anchor points, 242
    overlap, 235
    resize, 235
    solid, 234
    straight lines, 238–239, 241
    stylized, 235
    trace, 241
Sharpen filters, 210
Sharpen tool, 142–143
sharpen images, 142–143, 210–211
shortcuts to select tools, 33
similar colors, erase, 133
Sketch filters, 218
skew selections, 82–83
Slice Select tool, 71
Slice tool, 70
slices, 70–71, 296–297
smear images, 143
smooth edges of selections, 67
Smooth Selection dialog box, 67
Smudge tool, 143
snap objects, 31–32
soften edges, 84–85
Solarize filters, 213
solid color, fill images with, 116–117
solid fill layers, 176–177
solid shapes, 234
source image, 154
Spherize dialog box, 212–213
Spherize filter, 212
Sponge filter, 207
Sponge tool, 148–149
Stained Glass filter, 217
Start, All Programs, Photoshop CS command, 8
status bar, 10
    current magnification, 24–25
    Macintosh, 28
store images, 19
straight lines, 113, 241
straight segments, bend, 243
straighten images and crop, 46
Stroke dialog box, 120
strokes, 120–121
styles, 202–203, 257
Styles palette, 202, 203

INDEX

Stylize filter, 220
Stylize menu, 213
stylized shapes, 235
Swatches palette, 104–105
switch screen modes, 28–29

T

text. *See* type
Texture filters, 222
texture in images, 222–223
Texturizer dialog box, 222–223
Texturizer filter, 222–223, 228
three-dimensional buttons, 197
Threshold adjustment layer, 189
thumbnail images, enlarge on contact sheet, 269
.tif extension, 283
TIFF (Tagged Image File Format) files, 11, 282
title bar, current magnification, 24–25
titles, 7
tones, information about, 161
toolboxes, 10, 28
tools, 6, 10
    reset to default, 117
    shortcuts to select, 33
trace objects, 241
transform layers, 175
transparency, 161, 288–289
Trim dialog box, 47
trim images, 47
Turbulence tool, 227
Twirl Clockwise tool, 227
type, 7
    add to image, 246–247
    align, 247
    antialias, 253
    automatically wrap, 249
    bounding box, 248–249
    color, 246, 252–253
    constrain, 248–249
    default units, 13
    edit, 251
    effects, 256–257
    filters, 254–255
    fonts, 246, 251
    format, 250–251
    layers, 247
    line break, 247
    rasterize, 254
    reposition, 247
    select, 250
    semitransparent, 255
    size, 246, 251
    style, 246, 251
    unwarp, 259
    vertical, 247
    warp, 258–259
Type tool, 246
Type tool (T) keyboard shortcut, 33
Type tools, 7

U

undo
    actions, 264
    color adjustments, 153
    commands, 34
    distort, 83
    revert to previous state, 35
    skew, 83
Unsharp Mask dialog box, 210–211
Unsharp Mask filter, 210–211
unwarp type, 259
user-slices, 70–71

V

Vanishing Point tool, 277
Variations command, 152
Variations dialog box, 152–153
vertical guide, 30
vertical lines, 239
vertical type, 247
Vertical Type tool, 247
View, Actual Pixels command, 25
View, Fit on screen command, 27
View, Rulers command, 30
View, Selection Edges command, 63
View, Show, Grid command, 32
View, Snap To, Grid command, 32
View, Snap To, Guides command, 31
views, adjust, 26–27

W

Warp Text dialog box, 258–259
warp type, 258–259
Web, save
    GIF (Graphics Interchange Format) files, 286–287
    images for, 5
    JPEG (Joint Photographic Experts Group) files, 284
Web browsers, 14
Web images, 291, 293
Web pages, publish, 297
Web Photo Gallery, 5, 272–273
Web Photo Gallery dialog box, 273
Web Snap menu, 291
Web-safe colors, 102, 290–291
Welcome Screen window, 8–9
Window, Actions command, 262
Window, Brushes command, 109
Window, Channels command, 90, 93
Window, Character command, 251
Window, History command, 34, 130
Window, Paragraph command, 249
Windows
    exit Photoshop, 21
    native Photoshop format, 280
    print, 300–303
    set preferences, 12
    start Photoshop, 8
    WS FTP, 272

windows
        copy selections between, 77
        move images within, 26–27
        ruler options, 13
        scroll bars, 26–27
workspace elements, 10
WS FTP, 272

Z

Zoom In button, 25
Zoom Out button, 25
Zoom tool, 6, 24, 33
zoom, 6, 24–25, 275

 **Visual**

Read Less – Learn More™

with these full-color Visual™ guides

May 03

The Fast and Easy Way to Learn

Discover how to use what you learn with "Teach Yourself" tips

Title	ISBN	Price
Teach Yourself FrontPage 2000 VISUALLY	0-7645-3451-3	$29.99
Teach Yourself HTML VISUALLY	0-7645-3423-8	$29.99
Teach Yourself the Internet and World Wide Web VISUALLY, 2nd Ed.	0-7645-3410-6	$29.99
Teach Yourself Microsoft Access 2000 VISUALLY	0-7645-6059-X	$29.99
Teach Yourself Microsoft Excel 2000 VISUALLY	0-7645-6056-5	$29.99
Teach Yourself Microsoft Office 2000 VISUALLY	0-7645-6051-4	$29.99
Teach Yourself VISUALLY Access 2002	0-7645-3691-9	$29.99
Teach Yourself VISUALLY Adobe Acrobat 5 PDF	0-7645-3667-2	$29.99
Teach Yourself VISUALLY Adobe Premiere 6	0-7645-3664-8	$29.99
Teach Yourself VISUALLY Computers, 3rd Ed.	0-7645-3525-0	$29.99
Teach Yourself VISUALLY Digital Photography	0-7645-3565-X	$29.99
Teach Yourself VISUALLY Digital Video	0-7645-3688-5	$29.99
Teach Yourself VISUALLY Dreamweaver MX	0-7645-3694-7	$29.99
Teach Yourself VISUALLY E-commerce with FrontPage	0-7645-3579-X	$29.99
Teach Yourself VISUALLY Excel 2002	0-7645-3594-3	$29.99
Teach Yourself VISUALLY Fireworks 4	0-7645-3566-8	$29.99
Teach Yourself VISUALLY Flash MX	0-7645-3661-3	$29.99
Teach Yourself VISUALLY Flash 5	0-7645-3540-4	$29.99
Teach Yourself VISUALLY FrontPage 2002	0-7645-3590-0	$29.99
Teach Yourself VISUALLY Illustrator 10	0-7645-3654-0	$29.99
Teach Yourself VISUALLY iMac	0-7645-3453-X	$29.99
Teach Yourself VISUALLY Investing Online	0-7645-3459-9	$29.99
Teach Yourself VISUALLY Mac OS X v. 10.2 Jaguar	0-7645-1802-X	$29.99
Teach Yourself VISUALLY Macromedia Web Collection	0-7645-3648-6	$39.99
Teach Yourself VISUALLY More Windows XP	0-7645-3698-2	$29.99
Teach Yourself VISUALLY Networking, 2nd Ed.	0-7645-3534-X	$29.99
Teach Yourself VISUALLY Office XP	0-7645-0854-7	$29.99
Teach Yourself VISUALLY Photoshop 6	0-7645-3513-7	$29.99
Teach Yourself VISUALLY Photoshop 7	0-7645-3682-6	$29.99
Teach Yourself VISUALLY Photoshop Elements 2	0-7645-2515-8	$29.99
Teach Yourself VISUALLY PowerPoint 2002	0-7645-3660-5	$29.99
Teach Yourself VISUALLY Restoration and Retouching with Photoshop Elements 2	0-7645-2610-4	$29.99
Teach Yourself VISUALLY Windows 2000 Server	0-7645-3428-9	$29.99
Teach Yourself VISUALLY Windows Me Millennium Edition	0-7645-3495-5	$29.99
Teach Yourself VISUALLY Windows XP	0-7645-3619-2	$29.99
Teach Yourself VISUALLY Word 2002	0-7645-3587-0	$29.99
Teach Yourself Windows 95 VISUALLY	0-7645-6001-8	$29.99
Teach Yourself Windows 98 VISUALLY	0-7645-6025-5	$29.99
Teach Yourself Windows 2000 Professional VISUALLY	0-7645-6040-9	$29.99